OSTER DIGITAL COUNTERTOP CONVECTION OVEN

COOKBOOK

600 Easy and Quick Delicious Air Fryer Oven Recipes Tailored For your New Oster Digital Convection Oven| Bake, Fry, and Roast Crisp Recipes for Your Whole Family

CAROL J. WRIGHT

Copyright ©2021 By Carol J. Wright All rights reserved.

No part of this guide may be reproduced in any form without permission in writing from the publisher except in the case of brief quotations embodied in critical articles or reviews.

Legal & Disclaimer

The information contained in this book and its contents is not designed to replace or take the place of any form of medical or professional advice; and is not meant to replace the need for independent medical, financial, legal or other professional advice or services, as may be required. The content and information in this book has been provided for educational and entertainment purposes only.

The content and information contained in this book has been compiled from sources deemed reliable, and it is accurate to the best of the Author's knowledge, information and belief. However, the Author cannot guarantee its accuracy and validity and cannot be held liable for any errors and/or omissions. Further, changes are periodically made to this book as and when needed. Where appropriate and/or necessary, you must consult a professional (including but not limited to your doctor, attorney, financial advisor or such other professional advisor) before using any of the suggested remedies, techniques, or information in this book.

Table of Contents

INTRODUCTION ... 1

Chapter 1
Understanding Oster Digital Countertop Convection Oven ... 2
How to Start Cooking in an Oster Digital Countertop convection Oven? ... 3
Benefits of Convection Oven ... 3
Pros and Cons of Digital Countertop Convection Oven ... 4
Frequently Asked Questions on Oster Digital Countertop Convection Oven Cook book ... 4

Chapter 2
Breakfasts ... 5
Oat Porridge with Chia Seeds ... 6
Parmesan Ranch Onion Risotto ... 6
Parmesan Egg and Sausage Muffins ... 6
Mozzarella Pepperoni Pizza ... 6
Bacon-Cheese Muffin Sandwiches ... 6
Ricotta Spinach Omelet with Parsley ... 6
Brown Rice Porridge with Coconut and Dates ... 7
Buttermilk Biscuits ... 7
Spinach Scrambled Eggs with Basil ... 7
Blueberry Muffins ... 7
Seed and Nut Muffins with Carrots ... 8
Vanilla Cinnamon Toasts ... 8
Vanilla Bourbon French Toast ... 8
Maple Blueberry Granola Cobbler ... 8
Cheddar Ham and Tomato Sandwiches ... 9
Chicken Sausage and Tater Tot Casserole ... 9
Parmesan Bacon-Ham Cups ... 9
Vanilla Soufflé ... 9
Gouda Egg-Bacon Bread Cups ... 10
Cheddar Onion Omelet ... 10
Cheddar Ham Hash Brown Cups ... 10
Cheddar Veggie Bacon-Egg Casserole ... 10
Cheddar Onion Hash Brown Casserole ... 11
Yellow Cornmeal Pancake ... 11
Cheddar Baked Eggs ... 11
Havarti Asparagus Strata ... 11
Halloumi Pepper and Spinach Omelet ... 12
Egg in a Hole with Cheddar and Ham ... 12
Delicious Butter Muffins ... 12
Maple Milky Toast ... 13
Pepper Spiced Broccoli Pastry ... 13
Sugar Sprinkled Citrus Scones ... 14
Bacon Whole Grain Tortilla Bar ... 14
Cheesy Egg Bread Toast ... 14
Sweet and Yummy Milk Pancake ... 15
Cinnamon Applesauce Oatmeal ... 15
Sweet and Sour Tomato Egg Skillet ... 16
Vanilla flavored Milky Butter Cake ... 16
Vanilla flavored Peanut Bar ... 17
Enticing Virginia Ham Pizza ... 17

Chapter 3
Lunch ... 18
Moms Special Garlic Knots ... 19
Double Pepper Zucchini Bake ... 19
Milky Pumpkin Pie ... 20
Sweet Almond Butter Cookies ... 20
Pecan Walnut Sweet Pie ... 20
Cheesy Spinach Pinwheels ... 21
Golden Pepper Twists ... 21
Garlic Cheese Crust ... 22
Elegant Cheesy Pasta ... 22
Egg- Tomato Cheese Bread ... 23
Chicken Balls in Pasta Sauce ... 23
Homemade Honeyed Butter Biscuits ... 24
Spicy Cake with Whipped Cream ... 24
Spicy Cheesy Pasta Chicken ... 25
Spinach stuffed Chicken Bake ... 25
Toasted Cereal Fish Mix ... 25

Chapter 4
Dinner ... 26
Beef Mixture Topped Potato Fries ... 27
Cheesy Tomato Skewers with Pasta ... 27
Coconut Chicken Fingers ... 28
Homemade Cheese Puffs ... 28
Lettuce and Tomato Topped Cheeseburger ... 29
Chocolate Sprinkles Rolled Butter Cookies ... 29
Squash Bowls with Meatballs ... 30
Sugar Dusted Blueberry Tart ... 30
Chicken Fingers with Marinara Sauce ... 31
Golden Crisp Chicken Tortilla ... 31
Half-and-half Broccoli Soup ... 32
Mayo Lettuce Pork Burger ... 32
The Best French Egg Dish ... 33
The Best Ever Dark Chocolate Cake ... 33

Chapter 5
Meats ... 34
Dill-Thyme Beef Steak ... 35
Dijon-Lemon Pork Tenderloin ... 35
Taco Pork Chops with Oregano ... 35
Dijon Mustard Pork Tenderloin ... 35
BBQ Sausage with Pineapple and Bell Peppers ... 36
Balsamic Ribeye Steaks with Rosemary ... 36
Chipotle Flank Steak with Oregano ... 36
Beef, Kale and Tomato Omelet ... 36
Beef and Mushroom Meatloaf ... 37
Beef Meatloaf with Tomato Sauce ... 37
Beef Stroganoff with Mushrooms ... 37
Miso-Sake Marinated Flank Steak ... 37
Beef Kofta with Cinnamon ... 38
Pork Ribs with Honey-Soy Sauce ... 38
Lemongrass Pork Chops with Fish Sauce ... 38
Lamb Kofta with Mint ... 38
Beef and Carrot Meatballs ... 39
Pork and Mushroom Rolls with Teriyaki ... 39
Beef and Spaghetti Squash Lasagna ... 39
Paprika Lamb Chops with Sage ... 39
Cheddar Prosciutto and Potato Salad ... 40
Crispy Baked Venison ... 40
Panko Breaded Wasabi Spam ... 40
Smoky Beef with Jalapeño Peppers ... 40

Orange Pork Ribs with Garlic — 41

Chapter 6
Poultry — 42
Chicken Cordon Bleu with Swiss Cheese — 43
Curried Chicken with Orange and Honey — 43
Chicken and Bell Pepper Fajitas — 43
Curried Cinnamon Chicken — 43
Chicken Lettuce Tacos with Peanut Sauce — 44
Curried Cranberry and Apple Chicken — 44
Chicken Nuggets with Almond Crust — 44
Chili-Garlic Chicken Tenders — 44
Chicken Manchurian with Ketchup Sauce — 45
Cilantro Chicken with Lime — 45
Havarti Chicken and Ham Burgers — 45
Pineapple and Peach Chicken Breasts — 45
BBQ Chicken Breast with Creamy Coleslaw — 46
Smoked Paprika Chicken Wings — 46
Dill Chicken Strips with Italian Dressing — 46
Fajita Chicken Strips with Bell Peppers — 46
Garlic Chicken Thighs with Scallions — 47
Ginger Chicken Thighs with Cilantro — 47
Turkey, Cauliflower and Onion Meatloaf — 47
Garlic Whole Chicken Bake — 47
Garlic Baked Chicken Wings — 48
Pineapple Chicken Thighs with Ginger — 48
Panko Breaded Chicken Nuggets — 48
Buttermilk-Marinated Chicken Breast — 48
Spice-Marinated Chicken Drumsticks — 49

Chapter 7
Fish and Seafood — 50
Honey-Glazed Cod with Sesame Seeds — 51
Almond-Coconut Flounder Fillets — 51
Lemon-Caper Salmon Burgers — 51
Almond-Lemon Crusted Fish — 52
Italian-Style Salmon Patties — 52
Old Bay Salmon Patty Bites — 52
Garlic-Lemon Shrimp — 52
Trout Amandine with Lemon Butter Sauce — 53
Parmesan Sriracha Tuna Patty Sliders — 53
Paprika Tilapia with Garlic Aioli — 53
Breaded Calamari Rings with Lemon — 53
Baked Bacon-Wrapped Scallops — 54
Breaded Fresh Scallops — 54
Cajun Cod with Lemon Pepper — 54
Cayenne Prawns with Cumin — 54
Tuna Casserole with Peppers — 55
Tomato Chili Fish Curry — 55
Crab Ratatouille with Tomatoes and Eggplant — 55
Crab and Fish Cakes with Celery — 55
Salmon and Carrot Spring Rolls — 56
Swordfish Steaks with Jalapeño — 56
White Fish, Carrot and Cabbage Tacos — 56
Mustard-Lemon Sole Fillets — 56
Salmon and Scallion Patties — 57
Smoked Paprika Salmon in White Wine — 57
Shrimp and Artichoke Paella — 57

Chapter 8
Wraps and Sandwiches — 58
BBQ Bacon and Bell Pepper Sandwich — 59
Mozzarella Chicken and Cabbage Sandwich — 59
Swiss Greens Sandwich — 59
Beef Sloppy Joes — 59
Colby Shrimp Sandwich with Mayo — 60
Chicken and Lettuce Pita Sandwich — 60
Parmesan Eggplant Hoagies — 60
Tilapia Tacos with Mayo — 60
Turkey Sliders with Chive Mayo — 60
Turkey and Pepper Hamburger — 61

Chapter 9
Desserts — 62
Graham Cracker Chocolate Cheesecake — 63
Honey-Glazed Pears with Walnuts — 63
Brown Sugar-Lemon Applesauce — 63
Blueberry Chocolate Cupcakes — 63
Lemon Blackberry and Granola Crisp — 64
Apple Cinnamon Fritters — 64
Raisin Oatmeal Bars — 64
Orange Cornmeal Cake — 64
Apple and Pear Crisp with Walnuts — 65
Carrot, Cherry and Oatmeal Cups — 65
Chocolate Pineapple Cake — 65
Ginger Pumpkin Pudding — 65
Vanilla Chocolate Cookie — 66
Vanilla Pound Cake — 66
Vanilla Chocolate Brownies — 66
Vanilla-Rum Pineapple Galette — 66
Vanilla Peaches with Fresh Blueberries — 67
Lemon Poppy Seed Cake — 67
Ginger Cinnamon Cookies — 67
Chocolate Cake with Fresh Blackberries — 67
Peach Blackberry Cobbler with Oats — 68
Coconut Chia Pudding — 68
Coconut Chocolate Cake — 68
Chocolate Pie with Pecans — 68
Pumpkin Apple Turnovers — 69
Peppermint Chocolate Cheesecake — 69
Coffee Coconut Chocolate Cake — 69
Candied Cinnamon Apples — 69
Cinnamon S'mores — 70
Mixed Berry Crisp with Coconut Chips — 70

Chapter 10
Appetizers and Snacks — 71
Almond-Stuffed Dates with Turkey Bacon — 72
Paprika-Mustard Pork Spareribs — 72
Baked Bacon-Wrapped Dates — 72
Balsamic Mango and Beef Skewers — 72
Beef Cubes with Cheese Pasta Sauce — 72
Mozzarella Bruschetta with Basil Pesto — 72
Cayenne Mixed Nuts with Sesame Seeds — 73
Cheesy Salsa Stuffed Mushrooms — 73
Mozzarella Hash Brown Bruschetta — 73
Broccoli, Spinach and Bell Pepper Dip — 73
Apple Chips — 73
Ricotta Phyllo Artichoke Triangles — 74
Prosciutto-Wrapped Asparagus Spears — 74
Chili Kale Chips with Sesame Seeds — 74
Garlic-Paprika Potato Chips — 74
Paprika Deviled Eggs with Dill Pickle — 74
Parmesan Cauliflower with Turmeric — 74

Spanish Mango Pastry	75
Sweet Butter Puffs	75
Cinnamon Nut Mix	75
Golden Choux Pastry	76
Chocolate Drizzled Cocoa Puffs	76
Meringue Dessert with Whipped Cream	77
Cinnamon Pumpkin Bread	77
Butter Choco Soufflé	78
Basil Egg Frittata	78
Butter Loaf with Dried Currants	78
Cinnamon Oats Granola	79
Creamy Choco Cookies	79
Rich Blackberry Cupcake	80
Vanilla flavored Choco sweets	80
Rich Vanilla Butter Cake	81
Cocoa Butter Brownies	81
Cheesy Garlic Bake	82
Cheese and Herb mixed Breadsticks	82
Moms Special Apple Crisp	82
Grandma's Best Ever Chocolate Cake	83
Easy Vanilla Square Cakes	83
Enticing Blueberry Crumble Pie	84
Healthy Banana Bread	84
Easy Buttermilk Bread	84
Homemade Coconut Tart	85
Milky Bread and Honeyed Butter	85
Mini Apple Muffins	85
Milk Chocolate Cookies	86
Sweet and Citrus Pastry	86
Sweet Butter Cookies	87
Simple Bread Dessert	87
Orange Almond Cookies	88
The Best Orange Choco Cake	88
Vanilla Butter Biscuits	88

Chapter 11
Custards and Puddings 89

Custard Dessert with Caramelized Sugar	90
Sweet Savory Pastry with Figs	90
Cheese Glazed Sweet Rolls	91
Cream and Chocolate filled Pies	91
Pistachios Topped Rice Pudding	92
Cinnamon Peach Dessert	92
Sweet Strawberry Pastry	93
Sweet Bread Roll	93
Cheesy Turkey filled Pies	94
Cherry Tomato topped Pizza	94
Homemade Simple Bread	94
Homemade Butter Biscuits	95
Olive Oil Dressed Tomato salad	95
Citrusy Anchovies Salad	95
Citrusy Brussels sprouts Shallots Roast	95
Delicious delicata rings	96
Rosemary Herbed Carrots	96
Citrusy Cauliflower with Crème Fraîche Sauce	96

Chapter 12
Casseroles, Frittatas, and Quiches 97

Asparagus Frittata with Goat Cheese	98
Asparagus and Grits Casserole	98
Shrimp and Cauliflower Casserole	98
Pumpkin-Cauliflower Casserole with Pecans	98
Parmesan Shrimp Quiche	99
Prosciutto Casserole with Pepper Jack	99
Pork Gratin with Ricotta Cheese	99
Parmesan Green Bean Casserole	99
Tomato, Carrot and Broccoli Quiche	100
Mushroom and Beef Casserole	100
Swiss Chicken and Ham Casserole	100
Spinach and Mushroom Frittata	100
Cheddar Broccoli Casserole	100
Broccoli and Chicken Sausage Casserole	101
Feta-Cheddar Vegetable Frittata	101
Feta Chorizo and Potato Frittata	101
Corn Casserole with Bell Pepper	101

Chapter 13
Fast and Easy Everyday Favorites 102

Buttery Egg and Broccoli Bake	103
Baked Chicken Wings	103
Baked Peanuts with Hot Pepper Sauce	103
Beef Hot Dog with Bacon	103
Cheddar Jalapeño Poppers with Bacon	103
Cheese Capicola Sandwich with Mayo	103
Potato Patties with Colby Cheese	104
Manchego Frico with Cumin Seeds	104
Cherry Tomato Bake with Basil	104
Halloumi Cheese Bake with Greek Salsa	104
Chile Toast with Mozzarella Cheese	104
Cheddar Sausage Balls	104
Old Bay Shrimp with Cayenne	105
Green Beans and Bacon Bake	105
Green Beans Bake with Lemon Pepper	105
Chicken Wings with Hot Sauce	105
Carrot Chips with Parsley	105
Okra Chips	105
Shrimp, Sausage and Potato Bake	106
Panko-Chorizo Scotch Eggs	106

Chapter 14
Holiday Specials 107

Breaded Olives with Thyme	108
Monkey Bread with Peacans	108
Eggnog Bread with Pecans and Fruit	108
Maple Vanilla Pecan Tart	108
Asiago Cheese Bread	109
Pigs in a Blanket with Sesame Seeds	109
Risotto Croquettes with Tomato Sauce	109

Appendix 1 Measurement Conversion Chart	110
Appendix 2 The Dirty Dozen and Clean Fifteen	111
Appendix 3 Index	112

INTRODUCTION

Are you a busy home chef or a person running out of time in the kitchen especially in the hectic mornings! Then the Oster Digital countertop convection oven can be a true life saviour for you as it delivers healthy meals to you and your family in no time. Using this oven you can bake and roast nicely, grill perfectly and can prepare crispy food quickly. Dual fans inside the oven will provide even air circulation for consistent baking results. Since every time you cook with the convection oven, it works by heating the air and circulating it around the food and cooks it evenly. It does have six diverse cooking modes so that you can select the apt cooking temperature and cooking time for your favourite meals. Likewise, it is designed in such a way that you can clean it easily after preparing your much-loved meals.

The 'Oster brand' has a reputation for high quality advanced range of small appliances like coffee maker, toaster, blender and many more that are trustworthy and reasonable as well. Since you can definitely go for the 'Oster brand' as they offer the efficient and compact ovens available in the market. This edition entirely talks about Oster countertop convection oven and the tempting recipes from it. You can explore diverse palates from breakfast muffins to holiday special cakes. So just dive in to the different flavours. Happy cooking!

Chapter 1: Understanding Oster Digital Countertop Convection Oven

How to Start Cooking in an Oster Digital Countertop convection Oven?

The Oster counter top convection oven appears like a regular toaster oven, but has some of the advantages of a larger convection oven, like interior light, a broiler and an adjustable rack. Let us see how to start cooking in an Oster Digital Countertop convection Oven.

1.	You can select a function from the Oven keypad	There are multiple options and Choose between them (for baking, convection baking and broiling), Toast, Pizza, Dehydrate and Defrost. The up or down arrows can be used to adjust baking time, temperature and toast shade. You can switch from time to temperature by selecting Timer/Temp. There are other options like Clock, Lamp, Stop/Cancel and Start which are easy to follow.
2.	You can Preheat the oven by pressing the "Oven" button one time.	Select the desired temperature using the up and down arrows. Wait to count down displayed to zero before placing the food in the oven. You can move the rack to the preferred height before turning on the oven.
3.	Now, open the oven door and place the food items on the rack	Once the food is placed, press the "Oven" button and use the up and down arrows to adjust your baking temperature and then press the "Timer/Temp" button to select the required baking time, and press "Start." Once the baking cycle has completed and the timer sounds, you can take your food out.
4.	You can use 'convection function' to cook food faster and comprehensively.	Repeat Step 3 but press the "Oven" button twice. "Fan Bake" will show on the display.
5.	You can use 'Toast function' to toast bread, waffles or pastries.	Place the rack at the required height. Press the "Toast" button, use the up and down arrows to select the preferred shade as well. Press "Start." Once the toasting cycle has completed, you can remove your bread items from the oven.
6.	You can use Pizza, Defrost and Dehydrate functions by pressing the corresponding buttons.	Press the up and down arrow keys to select the preferred time, and then press the "Start" button. You can remove your items from the oven once the function has completed its cycle.

Benefits of Convection Oven

Here are the benefits of Oster Digital Countertop Oven offers:
- It is a widely accepted fact that the food that comes out from the convection oven would be crispier comparing to other ovens.
- It would be delicious as well as tender comparing to other ovens.
- Temperature in the oven is said to be just right unlike some other ovens having too hot temperature settings.
- You can undoubtedly go for Oster Digital counter top convection oven as it works much faster than the traditional ovens.
- It can cook food two times faster than normal ones so that you can prepare your meals in no time that too for a large family or preparing bulk meals.
- You get a lot of cooking options in this oven and the easy-to-use digital controls make it simple to switch functions and set temperatures.
- You can switch to the convection mode if you need your baked food to be crispy on the outside and juicy inside, as it manages to circulate hot air around every part of the dish accordingly.

Pros and Cons of Digital Countertop Convection Oven

Pros
- It can be used as a slow cooker, air fryer, and also used for dehydrating your food.
- It has got an LCD display to watch the cooking time, temperature, and functioning preset. It will notify when a cooking preset is ended.
- The interior light will facilitate you to monitor your cooking.
- It comes with extra-large capacity, which will help you to cook food in bulk.
- It does have IQ system and precision heating, which will help you choose the sections of the interior chamber you want the most heat and the one you want the least heat.
- It carries 4 racks at a time so that so you can cook four different meals at a time.
- It guarantees faster and even cooking of food items as the smart oven uses super convection technology to circulate the air around the chamber.
- It is also attached with some useful accessories like two oven racks, a 13-inch pizza pan, enamel roasting pan, a 9 x 13" broil rack, and a mesh basket for dehydrating and air frying.

Cons
- There are occasional grievances of the glass door shattering.
- There were some complaints of the oven not working eventually.

Frequently Asked Questions on Oster Digital Countertop Convection Oven Cook book

1.	What is the use and importance of Oster countertop oven?	❖ It is more useful for busy people. ❖ It will save your valuable kitchen counter space as it takes only one-third of the cooking area ❖ You can cook separate items at one time by storing them in the smaller microwave compartment while preheating for another one.
2.	What is a countertop convection oven best at?	A convection oven is best for baking as it circulates hot air around the food in different directions to create a better crust and gives you great flavoured food with best textures. It bakes foods much faster than regular ovens so they really do save a lot of time.
3.	Can I choose Oster brand appliances confidently?	Oster is a popular brand providing quality products at affordable costs are durable and last long. They produce an extensive range of small appliances and variety of kitchen appliances such as blenders, food processor, toasters and many more. They provide a range of professional-quality equipment for restaurants and laboratories as well.
4.	Which is better for cooking --convection oven cooking or toaster oven cooking?	A toaster oven works on electricity but you can run convection ovens on electricity and gas. Convection ovens, cooks food more compared to toaster ovens. Time of cooking would be comparatively same for both ovens. Since Convection is excellent for cooking.

Chapter 2
Breakfasts

Oat Porridge with Chia Seeds
Prep time: 10 minutes | Cook time: 5 minutes | Serves 4

2 tablespoons peanut butter
4 tablespoons honey
1 tablespoon butter, melted
4 cups milk
2 cups oats
1 cup chia seeds

1. Preheat the Oster to 390°F (199°C).
2. Put the peanut butter, honey, butter, and milk in a bowl and stir to mix. Add the oats and chia seeds and stir.
3. Transfer the mixture to a bowl and bake in the Oster for 5 minutes. Give another stir before serving.

Parmesan Ranch Onion Risotto
Prep time: 10 minutes | Cook time: 30 minutes | Serves 2

1 tablespoon olive oil
1 clove garlic, minced
1 tablespoon unsalted butter
1 onion, diced
¾ cup Arborio rice
2 cups chicken stock, boiling
½ cup Parmesan cheese, grated

1. Preheat the Oster to 390°F (199°C).
2. Grease a round baking tin with olive oil and stir in the garlic, butter, and onion.
3. Transfer the tin to the Oster and bake for 4 minutes. Add the rice and bake for 4 more minutes.
4. Turn the Oster to 320°F (160°C) and pour in the chicken stock. Cover and bake for 22 minutes.
5. Scatter with cheese and serve.

Parmesan Egg and Sausage Muffins
Prep time: 5 minutes | Cook time: 20 minutes | Serves 4

6 ounces (170 g) Italian sausage, sliced
6 eggs
⅛ cup heavy cream
Salt and ground black pepper, to taste
3 ounces (85 g) Parmesan cheese, grated

1. Preheat the Oster to 350°F (177°C). Grease a muffin pan.
2. Put the sliced sausage in the muffin pan.
3. Beat the eggs with the cream in a bowl and season with salt and pepper.
4. Pour half of the mixture over the sausages in the pan.
5. Sprinkle with cheese and the remaining egg mixture.
6. Bake in the preheated Oster for 20 minutes or until set.
7. Serve immediately.

Mozzarella Pepperoni Pizza
Prep time: 10 minutes | Cook time: 6 minutes | Serves 1

1 teaspoon olive oil
1 tablespoon pizza sauce
1 pita bread
6 pepperoni slices
¼ cup grated Mozzarella cheese
¼ teaspoon garlic powder
¼ teaspoon dried oregano

1. Preheat the Oster to 350°F (177°C). Grease the baking pan with olive oil.
2. Spread the pizza sauce on top of the pita bread. Put the pepperoni slices over the sauce, followed by the Mozzarella cheese.
3. Season with garlic powder and oregano.
4. Put the pita pizza inside the Oster and place a trivet on top.
5. Bake in the preheated Oster for 6 minutes and serve.

Bacon-Cheese Muffin Sandwiches
Prep time: 5 minutes | Cook time: 8 minutes | Serves 4

4 English muffins, split
8 slices Canadian bacon
4 slices cheese
Cooking spray

1. Preheat the Oster to 370°F (188°C).
2. Make the sandwiches: Top each of 4 muffin halves with 2 slices of Canadian bacon, 1 slice of cheese, and finish with the remaining muffin half.
3. Put the sandwiches in the baking pan and spritz the tops with cooking spray.
4. Bake for 4 minutes. Flip the sandwiches and bake for another 4 minutes.
5. Divide the sandwiches among four plates and serve warm.

Ricotta Spinach Omelet with Parsley
Prep time: 10 minutes | Cook time: 10 minutes | Serves 1

1 teaspoon olive oil
3 eggs
Salt and ground black pepper, to taste
1 tablespoon ricotta cheese
¼ cup chopped spinach
1 tablespoon chopped parsley

1. Grease the baking pan with olive oil. Preheat the Oster to 330°F (166°C).
2. In a bowl, beat the eggs with a fork and sprinkle salt and pepper.
3. Add the ricotta, spinach, and parsley and then transfer to the pan. Bake for 10 minutes or until the egg is set.
4. Serve warm.

Brown Rice Porridge with Coconut and Dates
Prep time: 5 minutes | Cook time: 23 minutes | Serves 1 or 2

½ cup cooked brown rice
1 cup canned coconut milk
¼ cup unsweetened shredded coconut
¼ cup packed dark brown sugar
4 large Medjool dates, pitted and roughly chopped
½ teaspoon kosher salt
¼ teaspoon ground cardamom
Heavy cream, for serving (optional)

1. Preheat the Oster to 375°F (191°C).
2. Place all the ingredients except the heavy cream in a baking pan and stir until blended.
3. Transfer the pan to the Oster and bake for about 23 minutes until the porridge is thick and creamy. Stir the porridge halfway through the cooking time.
4. Remove from the Oster and ladle the porridge into bowls.
5. Serve hot with a drizzle of the cream, if desired.

Buttermilk Biscuits
Prep time: 5 minutes | Cook time: 18 minutes | Makes 16 biscuits

2½ cups all-purpose flour
1 tablespoon baking powder
1 teaspoon kosher salt
8 tablespoons (1 stick) unsalted butter, at room temperature
1 cup buttermilk, chilled

1. Stir together the flour, baking powder, salt, sugar, and baking powder in a large bowl.
2. Add the butter and stir to mix well. Pour in the buttermilk and stir with a rubber spatula just until incorporated.
3. Place the dough onto a lightly floured surface and roll the dough out to a disk, ½ inch thick. Cut out the biscuits with a 2-inch round cutter and re-roll any scraps until you have 16 biscuits.
4. Preheat the Oster to 325°F (163°C).
5. Working in batches, arrange the biscuits in the baking pan in a single layer. Bake for about 18 minutes until the biscuits are golden brown.
6. Remove from the pan to a plate and repeat with the remaining biscuits.
7. Serve hot.

Spinach Scrambled Eggs with Basil
Prep time: 10 minutes | Cook time: 10 minutes | Serves 2

2 tablespoons olive oil
4 eggs, whisked
5 ounces (142 g) fresh spinach, chopped
1 medium tomato, chopped
1 teaspoon fresh lemon juice
½ teaspoon coarse salt
½ teaspoon ground black pepper
½ cup of fresh basil, roughly chopped

1. Grease a baking pan with the oil, tilting it to spread the oil around. Preheat the Oster to 280°F (138°C).
2. Mix the remaining ingredients, apart from the basil leaves, whisking well until everything is completely combined.
3. Bake in the Oster for 10 minutes.
4. Top with fresh basil leaves before serving.

Blueberry Muffins
Prep time: 10 minutes | Cook time: 12 minutes | Makes 8 muffins

1⅓ cups flour
½ cup sugar
2 teaspoons baking powder
¼ teaspoon salt
⅓ cup canola oil
1 egg
½ cup milk
⅔ cup blueberries, fresh or frozen and thawed

1. Preheat the Oster to 330°F (166°C).
2. In a medium bowl, stir together flour, sugar, baking powder, and salt.
3. In a separate bowl, combine oil, egg, and milk and mix well.
4. Add egg mixture to dry ingredients and stir just until moistened.
5. Gently stir in the blueberries.
6. Spoon batter evenly into parchment paper-lined muffin cups.
7. Put 4 muffin cups in the baking pan and bake for 12 minutes or until tops spring back when touched lightly.
8. Repeat previous step to bake remaining muffins.
9. Serve immediately.

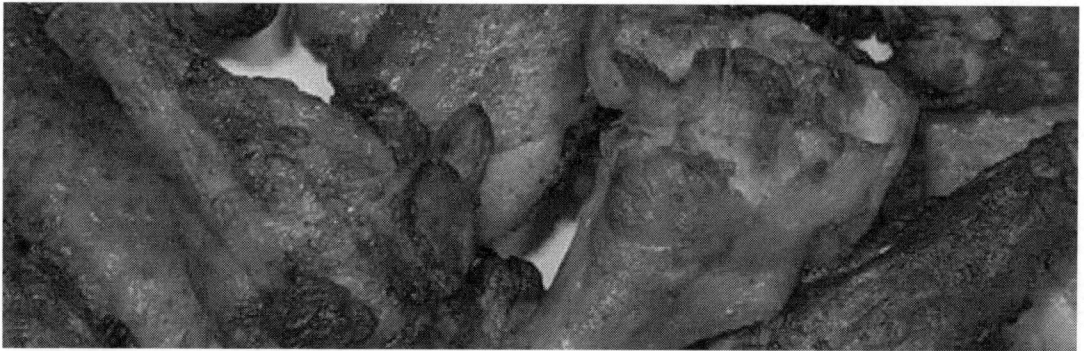

7 | Oster Digital Countertop Convection Oven Cookbook

Seed and Nut Muffins with Carrots
Prep time: 15 minutes | Cook time: 10 minutes | Makes 8 muffins

½ cup whole-wheat flour, plus 2 tablespoons
¼ cup oat bran
2 tablespoons flaxseed meal
¼ cup brown sugar
½ teaspoon baking soda
½ teaspoon baking powder
¼ teaspoon salt
½ teaspoon cinnamon
½ cup buttermilk
2 tablespoons melted butter
1 egg
½ teaspoon pure vanilla extract
½ cup grated carrots
¼ cup chopped pecans
¼ cup chopped walnuts
1 tablespoon pumpkin seeds
1 tablespoon sunflower seeds
Cooking spray

SPECIAL EQUIPMENT:
16 foil muffin cups, paper liners removed

1. Preheat the Oster to 330°F (166°C).
2. In a large bowl, stir together the flour, bran, flaxseed meal, sugar, baking soda, baking powder, salt, and cinnamon.
3. In a medium bowl, beat together the buttermilk, butter, egg, and vanilla. Pour into flour mixture and stir just until dry ingredients moisten. Do not beat.
4. Gently stir in carrots, nuts, and seeds.
5. Double up the foil cups so you have 8 total and spritz with cooking spray.
6. Put 4 foil cups in the baking pan and divide half the batter among them.
7. Bake for 10 minutes or until a toothpick inserted in center comes out clean.
8. Repeat step 7 to bake remaining 4 muffins.
9. Serve warm.

Vanilla Cinnamon Toasts
Prep time: 5 minutes | Cook time: 4 minutes | Serves 4

1 tablespoon salted butter
2 teaspoons ground cinnamon
4 tablespoons sugar
½ teaspoon vanilla extract
10 bread slices

1. Preheat the Oster to 380°F (193°C).
2. In a bowl, combine the butter, cinnamon, sugar, and vanilla extract. Spread onto the slices of bread.
3. Put the bread inside the Oster and bake for 4 minutes or until golden brown.
4. Serve warm.

Vanilla Bourbon French Toast
Prep time: 15 minutes | Cook time: 6 minutes | Serves 4

2 large eggs
2 tablespoons water
⅔ cup whole or 2% milk
1 tablespoon butter, melted
2 tablespoons bourbon
1 teaspoon vanilla extract
8 (1-inch-thick) French bread slices
Cooking spray

1. Preheat the Oster to 320°F (160°C). Line the baking pan with parchment paper and spray it with cooking spray.
2. Beat the eggs with the water in a shallow bowl until combined. Add the milk, melted butter, bourbon, and vanilla and stir to mix well.
3. Dredge 4 slices of bread in the batter, turning to coat both sides evenly. Transfer the bread slices onto the parchment paper.
4. Bake for 6 minutes until nicely browned. Flip the slices halfway through the cooking time.
5. Remove from the pan to a plate and repeat with the remaining 4 slices of bread.
6. Serve warm.

Maple Blueberry Granola Cobbler
Prep time: 5 minutes | Cook time: 15 minutes | Serves 4

¾ teaspoon baking powder
⅓ cup whole-wheat pastry flour
Dash sea salt
⅓ cup unsweetened nondairy milk
2 tablespoons maple syrup
½ teaspoon vanilla
Cooking spray
½ cup blueberries
¼ cup granola
Nondairy yogurt, for topping (optional)

1. Preheat the fryer to 347°F (175°C). Spritz a baking pan with cooking spray.
2. Mix together the baking powder, flour, and salt in a medium bowl. Add the milk, maple syrup, and vanilla and whisk to combine.
3. Scrape the mixture into the prepared pan. Scatter the blueberries and granola on top.
4. Transfer the pan to the Oster and bake for 15 minutes, or until the top begins to brown and a knife inserted in the center comes out clean.
5. Let the cobbler cool for 5 minutes and serve with a drizzle of nondairy yogurt.

Cheddar Ham and Tomato Sandwiches
Prep time: 5 minutes | Cook time: 8 minutes | Serves 2

1 teaspoon butter, softened
4 slices bread
4 slices smoked country ham
4 slices Cheddar cheese
4 thick slices tomato

1. Preheat the Oster to 370°F (188°C).
2. Spoon ½ teaspoon of butter onto one side of 2 slices of bread and spread it all over.
3. Assemble the sandwiches: Top each of 2 slices of unbuttered bread with 2 slices of ham, 2 slices of cheese, and 2 slices of tomato. Place the remaining 2 slices of bread on top, butter-side up.
4. Arrange the sandwiches in the baking pan, buttered side down.
5. Bake for 8 minutes until the sandwiches are golden brown on both sides and the cheese has melted, flipping the sandwiches halfway through.
6. Allow to cool for 5 minutes before slicing to serve.

Chicken Sausage and Tater Tot Casserole
Prep time: 5 minutes | Cook time: 17 to 19 minutes | Serves 4

4 eggs
1 cup milk
Salt and pepper, to taste
12 ounces (340 g) ground chicken sausage
1 pound (454 g) frozen tater tots, thawed
¾ cup grated Cheddar cheese
Cooking spray

1. Whisk together the eggs and milk in a medium bowl. Season with salt and pepper to taste and stir until mixed. Set aside.
2. Place a skillet over medium-high heat and spritz with cooking spray. Place the ground sausage in the skillet and break it into smaller pieces with a spatula or spoon. Cook for 3 to 4 minutes until the sausage starts to brown, stirring occasionally. Remove from heat and set aside.
3. Preheat the Oster to 400°F (204°C). Coat a baking pan with cooking spray.
4. Arrange the tater tots in the baking pan. Bake in the preheated Oster for 6 minutes. Stir in the egg mixture and cooked sausage. Bake for another 6 minutes.
5. Scatter the cheese on top of the tater tots. Continue to bake for 2 to 3 minutes more until the cheese is bubbly and melted.
6. Let the mixture cool for 5 minutes and serve warm.

Parmesan Bacon-Ham Cups
Prep time: 5 minutes | Cook time: 20 minutes | Serves 2

3 slices bacon, cooked, sliced in half
2 slices ham
1 slice tomato
2 eggs
2 teaspoons grated Parmesan cheese
Salt and ground black pepper, to taste

1. Preheat the Oster to 375°F (191°C). Line 2 greased muffin tins with 3 half-strips of bacon
2. Put one slice of ham and half slice of tomato in each muffin tin on top of the bacon
3. Crack one egg on top of the tomato in each muffin tin and sprinkle each with half a teaspoon of grated Parmesan cheese. Sprinkle with salt and ground black pepper, if desired.
4. Bake in the preheated Oster for 20 minutes. Remove from the Oster and let cool.
5. Serve warm.

Vanilla Soufflé
Prep time: 10 minutes | Cook time: 22 minutes | Serves 4

⅓ cup butter, melted
¼ cup flour
1 cup milk
1 ounce (28 g) sugar
4 egg yolks
1 teaspoon vanilla extract
6 egg whites
1 teaspoon cream of tartar
Cooking spray

1. In a bowl, mix the butter and flour until a smooth consistency is achieved.
2. Pour the milk into a saucepan over medium-low heat. Add the sugar and allow to dissolve before raising the heat to boil the milk.
3. Pour in the flour and butter mixture and stir rigorously for 7 minutes to eliminate any lumps. Make sure the mixture thickens. Take off the heat and allow to cool for 15 minutes.
4. Preheat the Oster to 320°F (160°C). Spritz 6 soufflé dishes with cooking spray.
5. Put the egg yolks and vanilla extract in a separate bowl and beat them together with a fork. Pour in the milk and combine well to incorporate everything.
6. In a smaller bowl mix the egg whites and cream of tartar with a fork. Fold into the egg yolks-milk mixture before adding in the flour mixture. Transfer equal amounts to the 6 soufflé dishes.
7. Put the dishes in the Oster and bake for 15 minutes.
8. Serve warm.

Gouda Egg-Bacon Bread Cups

Prep time: 10 minutes | Cook time: 8 to 12 minutes | Serves 4

4 (3-by-4-inch) crusty rolls
4 thin slices Gouda or Swiss cheese mini wedges
5 eggs
2 tablespoons heavy cream
3 strips precooked bacon, chopped
½ teaspoon dried thyme
Pinch salt
Freshly ground black pepper, to taste

1. Preheat the Oster to 330°F (166°C).
2. On a clean work surface, cut the tops off the rolls. Using your fingers, remove the insides of the rolls to make bread cups, leaving a ½-inch shell. Place a slice of cheese onto each roll bottom.
3. Whisk together the eggs and heavy cream in a medium bowl until well combined. Fold in the bacon, thyme, salt, and pepper and stir well.
4. Scrape the egg mixture into the prepared bread cups.
5. Transfer the bread cups to the Oster and bake for 8 to 12 minutes, or until the eggs are cooked to your preference.
6. Serve warm.

Cheddar Onion Omelet

Prep time: 10 minutes | Cook time: 12 minutes | Serves 2

3 eggs
Salt and ground black pepper, to taste
½ teaspoons soy sauce
1 large onion, chopped
2 tablespoons grated Cheddar cheese
Cooking spray

1. Preheat the Oster to 355°F (179°C).
2. In a bowl, whisk together the eggs, salt, pepper, and soy sauce.
3. Spritz the baking pan with cooking spray. Spread the chopped onion across the bottom of the pan, then transfer the pan to the Oster.
4. Bake in the preheated Oster for 6 minutes or until the onion is translucent.
5. Add the egg mixture on top of the onions to coat well. Add the cheese on top, then continue baking for another 6 minutes.
6. Allow to cool before serving.

Cheddar Ham Hash Brown Cups

Prep time: 10 minutes | Cook time: 8 to 10 minutes | Serves 6

4 eggs, beaten
2¼ cups frozen hash browns, thawed
1 cup diced ham
½ cup shredded Cheddar cheese
½ teaspoon Cajun seasoning
Cooking spray

1. Preheat the Oster to 350°F (177°C). Lightly spritz a 12-cup muffin tin with cooking spray.
2. Combine the beaten eggs, hash browns, diced ham, cheese, and Cajun seasoning in a medium bowl and stir until well blended.
3. Spoon a heaping 1½ tablespoons of egg mixture into each muffin cup.
4. Bake in the preheated Oster for 8 to 10 minutes until the top is golden brown.
5. Allow to cool for 5 to 10 minutes on a wire rack and serve warm.

Cheddar Veggie Bacon-Egg Casserole

Prep time: 10 minutes | Cook time: 14 minutes | Serves 4

6 slices bacon
6 eggs
Salt and pepper, to taste
Cooking spray
½ cup chopped green bell pepper
½ cup chopped onion
¾ cup shredded Cheddar cheese

1. Place the bacon in a skillet over medium-high heat and cook each side for about 4 minutes until evenly crisp. Remove from the heat to a paper towel-lined plate to drain. Crumble it into small pieces and set aside.
2. Whisk the eggs with the salt and pepper in a medium bowl.
3. Preheat the Oster to 400°F (204°C). Spritz a baking pan with cooking spray.
4. Place the whisked eggs, crumbled bacon, green bell pepper, and onion in the prepared pan. Bake in the preheated Oster for 6 minutes.
5. Scatter the Cheddar cheese all over and bake for 2 minutes more.
6. Allow to sit for 5 minutes and serve on plates.

Cheddar Onion Hash Brown Casserole

Prep time: 15 minutes | Cook time: 30 minutes | Serves 4

3½ cups frozen hash browns, thawed
1 teaspoon salt
1 teaspoon freshly ground black pepper
3 tablespoons butter, melted
1 (10.5-ounce / 298-g) can cream of chicken soup
½ cup sour cream
1 cup minced onion
½ cup shredded sharp Cheddar cheese
Cooking spray

1. Put the hash browns in a large bowl and season with salt and black pepper. Add the melted butter, cream of chicken soup, and sour cream and stir until well incorporated. Mix in the minced onion and cheese and stir well.
2. Preheat the Oster to 325°F (163°C). Spray a baking pan with cooking spray.
3. Spread the hash brown mixture evenly into the baking pan.
4. Place the pan in the Oster and bake for 30 minutes until browned.
5. Cool for 5 minutes before serving.

Yellow Cornmeal Pancake

Prep time: 10 minutes | Cook time: 10 to 12 minutes | Serves 4

1½ cups yellow cornmeal
½ cup all-purpose flour
2 tablespoons sugar
1 teaspoon salt
1 teaspoon baking powder
1 cup whole or 2% milk
1 large egg, lightly beaten
1 tablespoon butter, melted
Cooking spray

1. Preheat the Oster to 350°F (177°C). Line the baking pan with parchment paper.
2. Stir together the cornmeal, flour, sugar, salt, and baking powder in a large bowl. Mix in the milk, egg, and melted butter and whisk to combine.
3. Working in batches, drop tablespoonfuls of the batter onto the parchment paper for each pancake.
4. Spray the pancakes with cooking spray and bake for 3 minutes. Flip the pancakes, spray with cooking spray again, and bake for an additional 2 to 3 minutes.
5. Remove from the pan to a plate and repeat with the remaining batter.
6. Cool for 5 minutes and serve immediately.

Cheddar Baked Eggs

Prep time: 5 minutes | Cook time: 6 minutes | Serves 2

2 large eggs
2 tablespoons half-and-half
2 teaspoons shredded Cheddar cheese
Salt and freshly ground black pepper, to taste
Cooking spray

1. Preheat the Oster to 330°F (166°C).
2. Spritz 2 ramekins lightly with cooking spray. Crack an egg into each ramekin.
3. Top each egg with 1 tablespoon of half-and-half and 1 teaspoon of Cheddar cheese. Sprinkle with salt and black pepper. Stir the egg mixture with a fork until well combined.
4. Place the ramekins in the Oster and bake for 6 minutes until set. Check for doneness and cook for 1 minute as needed.
5. Allow to cool for 5 minutes in the Oster before removing and serving.

Havarti Asparagus Strata

Prep time: 10 minutes | Cook time: 14 to 19 minutes | Serves 4

6 asparagus spears, cut into 2-inch pieces
1 tablespoon water
2 slices whole-wheat bread, cut into ½-inch cubes
4 eggs
3 tablespoons whole milk
2 tablespoons chopped flat-leaf parsley
½ cup grated Havarti or Swiss cheese
Pinch salt
Freshly ground black pepper, to taste
Cooking spray

1. Preheat the Oster to 330°F (166°C).
2. Add the asparagus spears and 1 tablespoon of water in a baking pan. Bake for 3 to 5 minutes until crisp-tender. Remove the asparagus from the pan and drain on paper towels. Spritz the pan with cooking spray.
3. Place the bread and asparagus in the pan.
4. Whisk together the eggs and milk in a medium mixing bowl until creamy. Fold in the parsley, cheese, salt, and pepper and stir to combine. Pour this mixture into the baking pan.
5. Bake for 11 to 14 minutes or until the eggs are set and the top is lightly browned.
6. Let cool for 5 minutes before slicing and serving.

Halloumi Pepper and Spinach Omelet

Prep time: 10 minutes | Cook time: 13 minutes | Serves 2

2 teaspoons canola oil
4 eggs, whisked
3 tablespoons plain milk
1 teaspoon melted butter
1 red bell pepper, seeded and chopped
1 green bell pepper, seeded and chopped
1 white onion, finely chopped
½ cup baby spinach leaves, roughly chopped
½ cup Halloumi cheese, shaved
Kosher salt and freshly ground black pepper, to taste

1. Preheat the Oster to 350°F (177°C).
2. Grease a baking pan with canola oil.
3. Put the remaining ingredients in the baking pan and stir well.
4. Transfer to the Oster and bake for 13 minutes.
5. Serve warm.

Egg in a Hole with Cheddar and Ham

Prep time: 5 minutes | Cook time: 5 minutes | Serves 1

1 slice bread
1 teaspoon butter, softened
1 egg
Salt and pepper, to taste
1 tablespoon shredded Cheddar cheese
2 teaspoons diced ham

1. Preheat the Oster to 330°F (166°C). Place a baking dish in the Oster.
2. On a flat work surface, cut a hole in the center of the bread slice with a 2½-inch-diameter biscuit cutter.
3. Spread the butter evenly on each side of the bread slice and transfer to the baking dish.
4. Crack the egg into the hole and season as desired with salt and pepper. Scatter the shredded cheese and diced ham on top.
5. Bake in the preheated Oster for 5 minutes until the bread is lightly browned and the egg is cooked to your preference.
6. Remove from the Oster and serve hot.

Delicious Butter Muffins

Prep time: 10 minutes | Cook time: 10 minutes | serves 6

FOR THE MUFFINS
Nonstick cooking spray
1¾ cups flour
1½ teaspoons baking powder
1½ teaspoons pumpkin pie spice
¼ to ½ cup butter, melted
½ teaspoon salt
1 cup pumpkin purée (not pumpkin pie filling)
¾ cup sugar
⅓ cup vegetable oil
1 large egg
FOR THE COATING
⅓ cup sugar
1 tablespoon pumpkin pie spice
¼ to ½ cup butter, melted
TOOLS/EQUIPMENT
Mini muffin pan
1 medium bowl, 1 large bowl, and 2 small bowls
Mixing spoon
Toothpick
Parchment paper
Wire rack (optional)

1. Preheat the Oster. Preheat the Oster to 350°F(177°C), and spray a mini muffin pan with cooking spray.
2. Mix the dry ingredients. In a medium bowl, mix together the flour, baking powder, pumpkin pie spice, and salt. Set aside.
3. Mix the wet ingredients. In a large bowl, combine the pumpkin purée, sugar, oil, and egg. Add the dry ingredients to the wet ingredients, and stir until combined.
4. Bake the muffins. Fill the muffin cups three-quarters full with batter. Bake for 8 to 9 minutes, or until a toothpick inserted into the center of a muffin comes out clean.
5. Prepare the coating. In a small bowl, mix the sugar and pumpkin pie spice. Set this bowl next to your bowl of melted butter.
6. Coat and serve. Transfer the muffins onto parchment paper. While still hot, dip them one by one into the melted butter, then immediately roll in the sugar mixture, coating the muffin entirely. Enjoy hot or place on a wire rack to cool.

Maple Milky Toast

Prep time: 10 minutes | Cook time: 40 minutes | Makes 12 cups

6 large eggs
¾ cup milk
¼ cup granulated sugar
¼ teaspoon ground cinnamon
Pinch of ground nutmeg
Pinch of salt
12 slices potato bread or country white bread
4 tablespoons unsalted butter
Confectioners' sugar, for topping
Pure maple syrup, for dipping

1. Preheat the Oster to 375°F (191°C). Line a baking sheet with parchment paper. Put the sausages on the baking sheet and bake until lightly browned and cooked through, about 10 minutes.
2. Remove the pan from the Oster with Oster mitts and let cool slightly.
3. Meanwhile, combine the eggs, milk, granulated sugar, cinnamon, nutmeg and salt in a large bowl and whisk to combine. Cut each slice of bread into a 2-by-4-inch rectangle with a chef's knife, cutting off the crusts, then press the bread gently with your fingertips to flatten slightly.
4. Starting at a short end, roll each piece of bread around a sausage link, pressing firmly with your fingers to seal the seam. Add the bread-wrapped sausages to the bowl with the egg mixture and let soak for 5 minutes.
5. Melt 2 tablespoons butter in a large nonstick skillet over medium heat. Remove 6 of the bread-wrapped sausages from the egg mixture, letting the excess egg drip back into the bowl, then add to the skillet. Cook, turning occasionally with a spatula, until golden brown, about 5 minutes.
6. Carefully remove the pigs in a blanket to paper towels using the spatula. Bunch up a paper towel and hold it with tongs to wipe out the skillet.
7. Add the remaining 2 tablespoons butter to the skillet and repeat with the other 6 bread-wrapped sausages.
8. Sprinkle the confectioners' sugar over the wrapped pigs in a blanket. Serve with maple syrup for dipping.

Pick a Filling

9. Place ½ cup of one of the following ingredients in a medium bowl.
10. Softened cream cheese   Mashed banana
    Ricotta cheese   Marshmallow cream

Add Mix-Ins

11. Stir in ¼ cup total of the following ingredients (choose 1 or 2).
12. Stuff the Bread
13. Carefully cut four 1½-inch-thick slices from a loaf of challah bread with a serrated knife. With the bread slices flat on a cutting board, carefully cut a 2- to 3-inch-wide slit into the bottom edge of each bread slice with a paring knife to create a deep pocket. Put the filling in a resealable plastic bag and snip a corner. Pipe some filling into each pocket.

Make the Custard

14. Combine 2 eggs, 1 cup half-and-half, 1 tablespoon granulated sugar, 1 teaspoon vanilla, ½ teaspoon ground cinnamon, ¼ teaspoon ground nutmeg and a pinch of salt in a shallow bowl and whisk until combined.

Cook the French Toast

15. Preheat the Oster to 250°. Dip a stuffed bread slice in the custard and soak 20 seconds per side; let the excess drip off and place on a plate. Repeat with the remaining bread slices.
16. Heat a large nonstick skillet over medium heat. Melt 1 tablespoon butter in the skillet, then add 2 stuffed bread slices and cook until browned, 4 to 5 minutes per side.
17. Place on a baking sheet and keep warm in the Oster. Bunch up a paper towel and hold it with tongs to wipe out the skillet.

Pepper Spiced Broccoli Pastry

Prep time: 10 minutes | Cook time: 50 minutes | serves 6

1 frozen deep-dish piecrust
1½ cups whole milk
3 large eggs
1 tablespoon flour
1 tablespoon melted butter
Dash salt
Dash freshly ground black pepper
½ cup diced broccoli (frozen and thawed works best)
6 ounces (170 g) shredded Cheddar cheese
TOOLS/EQUIPMENT
Grater
Deep-dish pie pan (if needed)
Rimmed baking sheet
Large bowl
Whisk
Mixing spoon
Knife

1. Preheat the Oster. Preheat the Oster to 375°F(191°C).
2. Prepare the crust. If your pie dough is not already in a disposable pie tin, press it into a deep-dish pie pan. Place the dough-filled pie pan on a rimmed baking sheet.
3. Mix the ingredients. In a large bowl, whisk together the milk, eggs, flour, butter, salt, and pepper until combined. Stir in the broccoli and cheese.
4. Pour, bake, and serve. Pour the mixture into the pie pan, being careful not to overfill past three-quarters full.
5. Place the pie on the rimmed baking sheet in the Oster, and bake for 45 to 50 minutes, or until the quiche is puffed up and golden brown on top. Once removed from the Oster, allow the quiche to set for at least 10 minutes before slicing and serving.

Sugar Sprinkled Citrus Scones
Prep time: 10 minutes | Cook time: 20 minutes | serves 6

1½ cups all-purpose flour, plus more for scattering
¼ cup sugar, plus more for sprinkling
½ tablespoon baking powder
⅛ teaspoon salt
6 tablespoons cold butter, cut into 12 pieces
½ cup dried blueberries
½ cup buttermilk, plus more for brushing the dough
½ tablespoon lemon zest
TOOLS/EQUIPMENT
Cutting board
Knife
Microplane or zester
Baking sheet
Parchment paper or silicone baking mat
Large bowl
Whisk
Mixing spoon
Pastry cutter (optional)
Chef's knife
Pastry brush
Toothpick

1. Preheat the Oster. Preheat the Oster to 400°F(204°C). Line a baking sheet with parchment paper or a silicone baking mat
2. Mix the ingredients. In a large bowl, combine the flour, sugar, baking powder, and salt, and whisk together. Using a pastry cutter or your clean fingertips, work the butter into the flour mixture until it resembles pea-size balls.
3. Add the blueberries, stirring to combine. Add the buttermilk and lemon peel, and mix until a dough forms.
4. Prepare the dough. Scatter some flour onto a clean countertop. Transfer the dough to the floured counter, and use your hands to work it until all the flour is mixed in.
5. Shape the dough into a round disk. Break the dough into two pieces and shape into two 1-inch-high disks. Transfer the disks to the prepared baking sheet. Using a chef's knife, cut each disk into 4 to 6 wedges. Space the wedges slightly apart.
6. Bake the scones. Brush the tops of the dough with a bit of buttermilk, and sprinkle with sugar and lemon zest.
7. Bake for 15 to 20 minutes, or until a toothpick inserted into the thickest part comes out mostly clean, and serve.

Bacon Whole Grain Tortilla Bar
Prep time: 10 minutes | Cook time: 12 minutes | serves 12

4 to 8 whole-grain (8- or 10-inch) tortillas
6 to 8 eggs, scrambled
2 cups canned black beans, drained and rinsed
3 strips cooked bacon, crumbled
1 cup Greek yogurt or sour cream
1 cup bite-size cilantro sprigs
1½ cups Salsa Fresca
½ cup orange, red, or green bell peppers, diced
1½ cups shredded sharp Cheddar or Monterey Jack cheese
1½ cups diced avocado or No-Nonsense Guacamole
Sriracha or Cholula hot sauce, for garnish
TOOLS / EQUIPMENT
Different-size
Festive bowls
Dish towel
Box grater
Colander
Sauté pan
Aluminum foil

1. Preheat the Oster to 375°F(191°C). Warm the tortillas.
2. Wrap a stack of 4 tortillas in aluminum foil and warm for 5 to 10 minutes. If you are preparing 8 tortillas, make 2 wrapped bundles. Wrap the warmed foil bundles in a dish towel to keep them toasty.
3. Serve the fillings and toppings in festive, colorful bowls.
4. Arrange them together on the table or counter, along with the towel-wrapped tortillas, and allow your guests to assemble their own burrito creations.

Cheesy Egg Bread Toast
Prep time: 10 minutes | Cook time: 20 minutes | serves 4

1 loaf ciabatta bread or French bread
4 to 6 large eggs
2 to 3 tablespoons heavy or light cream, divided
1 tablespoon chopped fresh parsley
1 tablespoon chopped scallion
Salt and Freshly ground black pepper, to taste
2 to 3 tablespoons shredded Parmesan or Cheddar cheese
TOOLS/EQUIPMENT
Cutting board
Knife
Baking sheet

1. Preheat the Oster. Preheat the Oster to 350°F(177°C). Assemble the loaf.
2. Set the bread on a baking sheet. Depending on the size of your bread loaf, cut 4 to 6 circles in the top ½ inch or so apart and about 2 inches in diameter. Scoop out the bread from the circles about an inch deep to form holes.
3. Fill the holes. Crack an egg into each hole, top each with ½ tablespoon of cream and some parsley, scallions, salt, and pepper. Sprinkle with the cheese.
4. Bake and serve. Bake for 20 minutes, or until the eggs are done to your liking. Cut into equal size pieces and serve.

Sweet and Yummy Milk Pancake

Prep time: 5 minutes | Cook time: 15 minutes | serves 4

¾ cup all-purpose flour
¾ cup whole milk
4 eggs, lightly beaten
2 tablespoons cane sugar
Pinch freshly grated nutmeg
¼ teaspoon sea salt
4 tablespoons butter, divided into 4 pats
Confectioners' sugar, for dusting
Lemon wedges, for serving
Delicious additions
Jam
Cinnamon sugar
Fresh berries
Stewed apples
Whipped cream or crème fraîche
TOOLS / EQUIPMENT
Small, shallow ramekins
Baking sheet
Blender

1. Preheat the Oster to 425°F(218°C). Prep the ramekins.
2. Arrange the ramekins on a rimmed baking sheet, and place in the Oster to heat.

Blend the ingredients.

3. In a blender, mix the flour, milk, eggs, sugar, nutmeg, and salt until frothy.
4. Butter the ramekins. When the ramekins are hot, add a pat of butter to each and, using pot holders for protection, swirl to coat. Butter should foam. Replace in Oster until fully melted.
5. Bake the Dutch Babies. Remove baking sheet from the Oster. Divide the batter evenly among the ramekins, and bake until the Dutch Babies are puffed and golden brown, 10 to 15 minutes.
6. Serve.

Cinnamon Applesauce Oatmeal

Prep time: 10 minutes | Cook time: 30 minutes | serves 6

2 cups old-fashioned oats
2 teaspoons ground cinnamon or apple pie spice
Pinch salt
1 heaping cup peeled, diced Granny Smith apples
¾ cup Cinnamon Applesauce
¼ cup whole milk
¼ cup grape seed or olive oil
2 large eggs
3 tablespoons maple syrup, plus more for drizzling
TOOLS/EQUIPMENT
Cutting board
Knife
Peeler
8-by-8-inch baking dish
Large bowl
Mixing spoon
Nonstick cooking spray

1. Preheat the Oster. Preheat the Oster to 350°F(177°C). Spray an 8-by-8-inch baking dish with cooking spray, and set aside.
2. Mix the ingredients. In a large bowl, combine all the ingredients and stir until fully blended.
3. Bake the oatmeal and serve. Scrape the batter into the prepared baking dish and spread evenly. Bake for 30 minutes, or until golden brown on top.
4. Allow to sit for 5 minutes before serving. Drizzle with additional maple syrup if desired.

Sweet and Sour Tomato Egg Skillet
Prep time: 10 minutes | Cook time: 20 minutes | serves 4

1 onion, chopped
2 tablespoons olive oil
2 garlic cloves, chopped
1 (28-ounce) can tomatoes
1 tablespoon za'atar
2 teaspoons cumin seeds, toasted and ground in a mortar and pestle
Kosher salt and freshly ground black pepper, to taste
4 eggs
¼ cup fresh cilantro leaves, for garnish
⅔ cup Greek yogurt or sour cream
Crusty bread, torn, for serving
Delicious additions
Chickpeas
Artichoke hearts
Feta
TOOLS / EQUIPMENT
Toaster Oster
Mortar and pestle
Large
Enameled skillet
Wooden spoon

1. Preheat the Oster to 375°F(191°C). Cook the onion and garlic.
2. In a large enameled skillet over medium heat, sauté the onion in olive oil for 3 to 5 minutes. Add the chopped garlic, and cook for another minute.
3. Add the tomatoes and aromatics. Add the tomatoes, and bring to a simmer. Add the za'atar and cumin, season with salt and pepper, and simmer uncovered for a few minutes, until the sauce thickens.
4. Break the tomatoes into chunks using the edge of a wooden spoon. Taste and adjust seasoning as needed.
5. Add the eggs. Use the wooden spoon to make four nests in the sauce and crack an egg into each. Season the eggs with salt and pepper, and transfer the skillet to the Oster, cooking for 7 to 10 minutes, or until the eggs are just set.
6. Serve from the skillet on a trivet at the table. Season with salt and pepper to taste, and garnish with fresh cilantro and a few dollops of yogurt. Serve with the bread to mop up the sauce and yolks.

Vanilla flavored Milky Butter Cake
Prep time: 10 minutes | Cook time: 50 minutes | serves 6

FOR THE CAKE
Nonstick cooking spray
2 cups all-purpose flour
2½ tablespoons baking powder
½ teaspoon salt
3 overripe bananas
2 cups granulated sugar
1 cup whole milk
½ cup melted and cooled butter
2 large eggs
1 teaspoon vanilla extract
FOR THE CRUMB TOPPING
1½ cups brown sugar
1½ cups all-purpose flour
6 tablespoons cold butter, cut into 12 pieces
TOOLS/EQUIPMENT
Cutting board
Knife
13-by-9-inch baking dish
1 small, 1 large, and 1 medium bowl
Whisk
Potato masher
Pastry cutter (optional)
Toothpick
Preheat the Oster.

1. Preheat the Oster to 350°F(177°C). Spray a 13-by-9-inch baking dish with cooking spray. Set aside. Mix the dry ingredients.
2. In a small bowl, whisk together the flour, baking powder, and salt. Set aside. Mix the batter.
3. In a large bowl, mash the bananas with a potato masher until mushy. Add the granulated sugar, milk, butter, eggs, and vanilla, and stir until fully combined. Add the flour mixture, and mix until fully combined. Scrape the batter into the prepared baking dish.
4. Add the topping. In a medium bowl, combine the brown sugar, flour, and butter. Using a pastry cutter or your fingertips, blend until the mixture resembles crumbs. Sprinkle the topping over the batter.
5. Bake the cake and serve. Bake for 45 to 50 minutes, or until a toothpick inserted into the middle comes out dry. Allow the cake to cool, then cut into squares and serve.

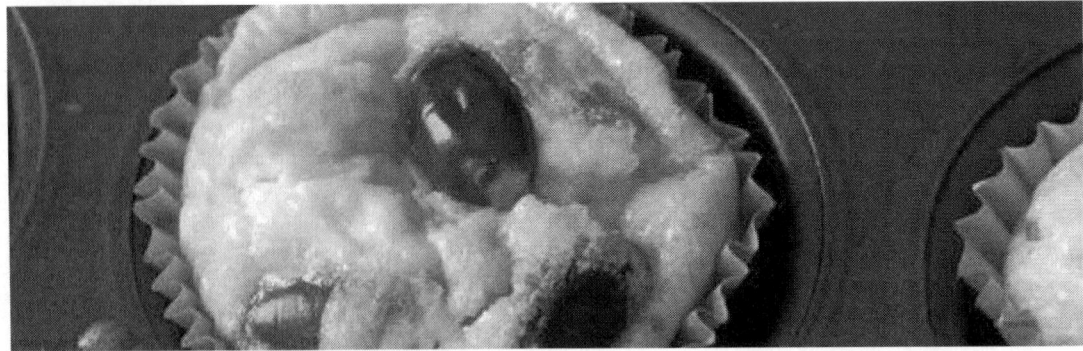

Vanilla flavored Peanut Bar

Prep time: 10 minutes | Cook time: 25 minutes | makes 16 bars

Butter, for greasing
1¼ cups white and/or black sesame seeds
¾ cup unsweetened shredded coconut
½ cup dried apricots, chopped
¼ teaspoon sea salt
¼ cup honey
⅓ cup crunchy peanut butter
¼ teaspoon pure vanilla extract
TOOLS / EQUIPMENT
8-inch-square
glass baking dish
Parchment paper
Large bowl
Small bowl
Rubber spatula
Wire cooling rack

1. Preheat the Oster to 350°F(177°C). Prep the baking dish.
2. Butter an 8-inch-square glass baking dish, and line it with parchment paper long enough so that it extends beyond the dish by at least 2 inches on all sides. Cut slits at the corners so the parchment lays flat.
3. Mix the ingredients. In a large bowl, mix together the sesame seeds, coconut, apricots, and salt. In a small bowl, stir the honey, peanut butter, and vanilla extract. Add the honey mixture to the seed-and-fruit mixture, and stir well to combine.
4. Transfer the ingredients and bake.
5. Use a rubber spatula to scrape the mixture into the prepared baking dish, using the broad side of the spatula to press everything into an even layer. Bake until golden around the edges, 20 to 25 minutes. Transfer the baking dish to a wire cooling rack and let cool until firm, about 30 minutes.
6. Serve. Use the parchment tabs to lift the seeded block out of the baking dish—if it starts to crumble, let it cool longer. Using a sharp knife, cut 16 bars. Eat the fruit-seed-nut bars at room temperature. Store any leftovers in a sealed container at room temperature for up to 5 days.

Enticing Virginia Ham Pizza

Prep time: 10 minutes | Cook time: 15 minutes | serves 4

Flour, for dusting the pan
1 disk fresh pizza dough, store-bought or from a pizza shop
Olive oil
Salt and Freshly ground black pepper, to taste
15 asparagus spears, woody ends trimmed
10 slices Virginia ham, torn into pieces
1 cup shredded Monterey Jack cheese
½ cup shredded mozzarella
4 large eggs, each cracked into a separate small bowl or ramekin
TOOLS/EQUIPMENT
Grater
4 small bowls or ramekins
Pizza stone or baking sheet
Basting brush (or paper towel)
Large bowl
Pizza cutter or knife

1. Prepare the Oster. Position an Oster rack in the middle of the Oster. Prepare a pizza stone or baking sheet by scattering flour lightly onto the surface. Preheat the Oster to 450°F(232°C).
2. Prepare the dough. Shape the pizza dough into either a rustic rectangle or a traditional round, depending on the shape of your pan. Brush the dough lightly with oil, and season with salt and pepper.
3. Add the asparagus. Place a small amount of oil in your clean hands. In a large bowl, toss the asparagus spears with your hands, lightly coating them. Season the asparagus with salt and pepper, then arrange the asparagus in a sunburst pattern, with the tips pointing outward.
4. Bake the pizza and eggs and serve. Place in the Oster and bake for 5 minutes. Remove from the Oster, place ham all over the pizza, top with the cheeses, and slide each egg onto a separate quarter of the pizza.
5. Sprinkle the eggs with salt and pepper, and quickly return the pizza to the Oster.
6. Bake for an additional 10 minutes, or until the crust is golden and the eggs are set to your liking. Cool slightly, slice into 4 wedges, and serve.

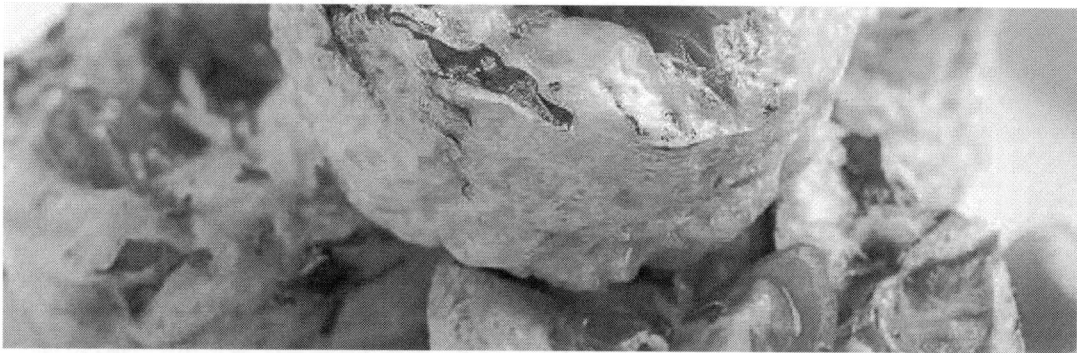

Chapter 3
Lunch

Moms Special Garlic Knots
Prep time: 10 minutes | Cook time: 20 minutes | makes 12 garlic knots

GARLIC BUTTER
8 tablespoons (1 stick/4 ounces (113 g) unsalted butter, divided
8 large garlic cloves, minced
DOUGH
2 cups all-purpose flour, plus more for shaping
1½ teaspoons instant (Rapid Rise) yeast
1 teaspoon garlic powder
1 tablespoon extra-virgin olive oil, plus more for the bowl
FOR SERVING
2 tablespoons minced fresh flat-leaf parsley
2 tablespoons finely grated Parmesan cheese, plus more as needed
½ teaspoon kosher salt
Extra-virgin olive oil, as needed
cup marinara sauce, warmed

1. Make the garlic butter: In a small saucepan, melt 2 tablespoons of the butter over medium heat. Stir in the garlic; reduce the heat to low, and cook, stirring often, until the garlic is soft and fragrant but not browned, about 3 minutes.
2. Add the remaining 6 tablespoons butter and swirl the pan until the butter has melted, about 1 minute. Strain the garlic butter through a fine-mesh sieve into a large bowl. Reserve the garlic solids in a small bowl. Set both bowls aside.
3. Make the dough: In the bowl of a stand mixer, whisk together the flour, yeast, and garlic powder. In a small bowl, whisk together the oil, reserved garlic solids, and ¾ cup warm water.
4. Attach the dough hook to the stand mixer and, with the mixer on medium-low speed, drizzle the oil-garlic mixture into the flour mixture and knead, scraping down the sides of the bowl as needed, until a sticky dough starts to come together, about 3 minutes. Increase the speed to medium-high and knead until the dough is smooth and shiny and pulling away from the side of the bowl, about 6 minutes more.
5. Transfer the dough to a lightly floured work surface and knead it once or twice. Turn the dough over, push, and shape it into a ball. Lightly grease a large bowl with oil, then place the dough in the bowl, seam-side down.
6. Cover the bowl with plastic wrap and transfer it to a warm spot to rest until the dough is doubled in size, about 1½ hours.
7. Transfer the dough to a lightly floured work surface. Using your hands, lightly stretch it into a 7 × 12-inch rectangle. With a long side facing you, use a sharp knife or a pizza cutter to cut the dough crosswise into 12 (1-inch-wide) strips. Cover the strips lightly with plastic wrap.
8. Line a baking sheet with parchment paper. Working with one at a time, place a dough strip on a lightly floured work surface and roll it into a 12-inch rope. Tie the rope into a loose overhand knot, tucking the ends underneath.
9. Transfer the knot to the prepared baking sheet and repeat with the remaining dough, leaving 2 inches of space between the knots. Lightly cover the baking sheet with plastic wrap or a kitchen towel and transfer it to a warm spot to rest until the knots have nearly doubled in size, about 1½ hours.
10. Preheat the Oster to 475°F(246°C). Measure out 2 tablespoons of the reserved garlic butter and brush it over the knots. Bake until deeply golden, about 12 minutes.
11. Meanwhile, whisk the parsley, Parmesan, and salt into the garlic butter remaining in the large bowl to combine, While the knots are still warm, add them to the bowl with the garlic butter mixture and toss them until well coated (if the mixture looks a little dry, drizzle in a bit of oil). Serve immediately, with the marinara sauce on the side for dipping.

Double Pepper Zucchini Bake
Prep time: 15 minutes | Cook time: 30 minutes | serves 4

2 large zucchini
Salt and Freshly ground black pepper, to taste
Homemade Breakfast Sausage or 1 (12-ounce/340 g) package breakfast sausage patties or links
⅓ cup chopped Vidalia (sweet) onion
1 cup chopped pepper (green, red, or poblano work well)
⅓ cup chopped grape tomatoes
2 cups shredded mozzarella cheese, divided
TOOLS/EQUIPMENT
Cutting board
Chef's knife
Grater
Teaspoon
Large, rimmed baking sheet
Large nonstick skillet

1. Preheat the Oster. Preheat the Oster to 375°F(191°C).
2. Prepare the zucchini. Halve the zucchini lengthwise, and using a teaspoon, scrape out half to three-quarters of the insides, scraping out all of the seeds. Place the zucchini, flat-side down, on a large, rimmed baking sheet.
3. Bake the zucchini. Bake for 15 minutes. Remove from the Oster, flip the zucchini over, and season the insides with salt and pepper.
4. Cook the sausage. Meanwhile, cut each sausage piece into quarters. In a large nonstick skillet over medium-high heat, cook the sausage for 3 minutes, turning occasionally. Add 3 tablespoons of water and the onion and pepper to the pan.
5. Cook the veggies. Continue to simmer until the sausage is cooked through and the pepper and onion are soft, about 7 minutes.
6. Add the tomatoes, and cook for another minute. Remove from the heat, add ½ cup of cheese, and stir until incorporated.
7. Fill the zucchini. Fill the zucchini with the vegetable mixture, and top with the remaining 1½ cups of cheese. Bake for 3 minutes, or until the cheese is melted, cool slightly, and serve.

Milky Pumpkin Pie
Prep time: 10 minutes | Cook time: 1 hour 30 minutes | serves 12

1 refrigerated ready-to-use piecrust (for a 9-inch pie), softened as label directs
3 large eggs
¼ cup packed light brown sugar
1 (15-ounce) can pure pumpkin
½ cup whole milk
1 teaspoon vanilla extract
¾ teaspoon ground cinnamon
¾ teaspoon ground ginger
½ cup plus 6 tablespoons pure maple syrup
1 cup heavy cream
¼ teaspoon kosher salt

1. Heat Oster to 350°F(177°C). Line 9-inch pie plate with piecrust. Gently press dough against bottom and up side of pie plate without stretching it. Tuck overhang under and crimp to form raised edge. Refrigerate until ready to fill.
2. In large bowl with wire whisk, beat eggs, brown sugar, pumpkin, milk, vanilla, cinnamon, ginger, ½ cup maple syrup, ¼ cup cream, and salt until combined.
3. Pour pumpkin mixture into prepared pie shell. Bake for 60 to 65 minutes or until edge of filling is just set but center still jiggles slightly and crust is golden brown. Cool pie on wire rack to room temperature.
4. About 10 minutes before serving, in large bowl with mixer on medium-high speed, beat remaining ¾ cup cream and remaining 6 tablespoons maple syrup until soft peaks form. Serve with pie.

Sweet Almond Butter Cookies
Prep time: 10 minutes | Cook time: 1 hour 10 minutes | makes 3 dozen cookies

3 cups all-purpose flour
¾ teaspoon baking powder
½ teaspoon salt
1 cup (2 sticks) butter, softened
1 cup sugar
1 large egg
2 teaspoons vanilla extract
1 teaspoon almond extract

1. Preheat Oster to 375°F(191°C). In large bowl with wire whisk, mix flour, baking powder, and salt. In another large bowl with mixer on medium-high speed, beat butter and sugar until smooth.
2. Beat in egg, then extracts, occasionally scraping bowl with rubber spatula. Reduce speed to low; gradually beat in flour mixture just until blended.
3. Divide dough into 4 equal pieces; flatten each into a disk.
4. Wrap each disk tightly in plastic wrap and refrigerate for 30 minutes or until dough is firm but not hard.
5. For cutouts: Remove 1 disk of dough from refrigerator. On one half of lightly floured large sheet parchment paper, with floured rolling pin, roll dough ⅛ inch thick.
6. With floured cookie cutter, cut out shapes. With paring knife or small metal spatula, remove dough between cutouts. On other half of parchment, reroll the scraps of dough and cut out more shapes.
7. Slide parchment onto large cookie sheet. Bake for 10 to 12 minutes or until edges are golden. With spatula, transfer cookies to wire racks to cool completely. Repeat with remaining dough.

Pecan Walnut Sweet Pie
Prep time: 10 minutes | Cook time: 1 hour | serves 12

1 refrigerated ready-to-use piecrust (for a 9-inch pie), softened as label directs
4 cups mixed unsalted pecans, walnuts, and hazelnuts, toasted
1½ cups sugar
3 tablespoons light corn syrup
6 tablespoons unsalted butter, cut into small pieces
½ teaspoon kosher salt
1 cup heavy cream
Flaked sea salt, optional

1. Heat Oster to 375°F(191°C). Line 9-inch pie plate with piecrust. Gently press dough against bottom and up side of plate without stretching it. Tuck overhang under and crimp to form raised edge.
2. Line crust with nonstick foil; fill with pie weights or dried beans. Bake for 15 minutes. Remove parchment and weights.
3. Bake for 5 to 10 minutes longer or until pastry just starts to turn golden. Transfer crust to wire rack; spread nuts in crust.
4. Reduce Oster temperature to 350°F(177°C). In heavy-bottomed medium saucepan, place sugar, ½ cup water, and corn syrup. Without stirring, cook over medium-high heat for about 1 minute or until bubbles begin to form at edges, swirling pan occasionally.
5. Bring to a simmer, then increase heat to high and boil for 6 to 10 minutes or until mixture is a rich caramel color, swirling pan occasionally. Immediately remove pan from heat, add butter and kosher salt, and swirl pan until butter melts.
6. Return pan to medium heat, add cream (it will bubble up), and whisk for about 1 minute or until smooth, slightly thickened, and a deep amber color. Pour caramel over nuts; place pie in Oster. Bake for 10 to 15 minutes or until filling is gently bubbling.
7. Cool pie completely on wire rack. Sprinkle with flaked sea salt, if using.

Cheesy Spinach Pinwheels

Prep time: 10 minutes | Cook time: 20 minutes | makes 24 pinwheels

10 ounces frozen chopped spinach, thawed and drained
8 ounces (227 g) crumbled feta cheese, at room temperature
¼ cup sour cream
2 tablespoons chopped fresh dill
2 teaspoons crushed red pepper flakes
½ teaspoon garlic powder
½ teaspoon kosher salt
2 tablespoons all-purpose flour
2 sheets frozen puff pastry, thawed (from one 16-ounce /454 g package)
1 large egg, beaten

1. Sandwich the spinach between two layers of paper towels and press out any excess water.
2. In a medium bowl, combine the spinach, feta, sour cream, dill, red pepper flakes, garlic powder, and salt and mix to combine.
3. Dust a work surface with the flour and place the thawed puff pastry sheets on it. Divide the feta mixture in half and spoon it evenly over each pastry sheet, leaving a ½-inch border on all sides.
4. Starting with a long side, roll each puff pastry sheet into a log. Wrap the logs tightly with plastic wrap and set them seam-side down on a baking sheet. Freeze until firm, about 30 minutes. (To store longer, transfer the logs to an airtight freezer bag and freeze; they will keep for up to 2 months.)
5. Preheat the Oster to 400°F(204°C). Line two baking sheets with parchment paper.
6. Remove the pastry logs from the freezer, unwrap, and place them seam-side down on your work surface. Slice each log crosswise into twelve ¾-inch-thick rounds.
7. Arrange the slices cut-side down on the prepared baking sheets. In a small bowl, mix the beaten egg with 1 tablespoon water to make an egg wash and brush it over the top and sides of each slice.
8. Bake until the pinwheels are puffed and golden brown, 15 to 20 minutes. Serve warm or at room temperature.

Golden Pepper Twists

Prep time: 10 minutes | Cook time: 20 minutes | makes about 44 twists

1 cup finely grated Parmesan cheese (about 4 ounces (113 g)
1⅓ cups shredded sharp cheddar cheese (about 4 ounces (113 g)
4 tablespoons (½ stick) unsalted butter, at room temperature
1¾ cups all-purpose flour, plus more for rolling
1½ teaspoons kosher salt
½ teaspoon freshly ground black pepper
1 jalapeño pepper, halved, seeded, and minced
¼ cup plus 1 tablespoon heavy cream

1. Line two baking sheets with parchment paper. In a food processor, combine the Parmesan, cheddar, butter, flour, salt, black pepper, and jalapeño and pulse in 5-second bursts until the mixture is sandy, with a few pea-size pieces of butter still visible, about 45 seconds.
2. Drizzle in the cream and process until the dough forms a ball, about 15 seconds.
3. On a lightly floured work surface, use a rolling pin to roll the dough into a 14-inch square about ⅛ inch thick. Halve the dough into two 7 × 14-inch rectangles, and then cut each rectangle crosswise into strips ½ inch wide. In the end you will have about 50 (7 × ½-inch) strips. Working with one at a time, gently twist each strip into a spiral.
4. Transfer the strips to the prepared baking sheets, leaving ½ inch between them. Gently press the ends of the strips against the baking sheets so that the spirals hold their shape.
5. Transfer the baking sheets to the refrigerator to chill the twists for at least 20 minutes or cover with plastic wrap and refrigerate for up to 3 days.
6. Preheat the Oster to 400°F(204°C).
7. Bake until the twists are firm and golden, about 15 minutes. Let the twists rest on the baking sheets for 5 minutes, then transfer to a wire rack to cool completely. The twists will keep in an airtight container at room temperature for up to 1 week.

Garlic Cheese Crust

Prep time: 10 minutes | Cook time: 20 minutes | serves 4

CRUST

1½ cups all-purpose flour, plus more for dusting
1 stick (4 ounces (113 g) unsalted butter, cubed and frozen
½ teaspoon kosher salt
1 large egg, beaten
2 tablespoons ice water, plus more if needed

"EVERYTHING BAGEL" SEASONING

2 tablespoons poppy seeds
2 tablespoons toasted sesame seeds
2 tablespoons dried garlic
2 tablespoons dried onion
4 teaspoons kosher salt

FILLING

6 ounces (170 g) scallion cream cheese, at room temperature
1 large egg
¼ teaspoon kosher salt
¼ teaspoon freshly ground black pepper
2 ounces smoked salmon, finely chopped (about ¼ cup)
2 large tomatoes (about 1½ pounds), thinly sliced
1 large egg

1. Make the crust: In a food processor, combine the flour, butter, and salt and pulse until the mixture is sandy, with a few pea-size pieces of butter still visible, about 1 minute.
2. Add the egg and ice water and pulse until moistened and the dough is starting to pull away from the sides of the bowl, about 30 seconds. (If the dough is still dry, add more ice water 1 teaspoon at a time; do not over process.)
3. Shape the dough into a 1-inch-thick disc and wrap it tightly with plastic wrap.
4. Transfer to the refrigerator to chill for at least 30 minutes or up to 3 days.
5. Make the "everything bagel" seasoning: In a small jar, combine the poppy seeds, sesame seeds, dried garlic, dried onion, and salt. Seal the jar and shake until well combined. (Store for up to 3 months.)
6. Position a rack in the center of the Oster and preheat the Oster to 400°F(204°C).
7. Make the filling: In a large bowl, using an electric mixer with the whisk attachment, beat the cream cheese and egg on medium-high speed until smooth, about 1 minute. Stir in the salt and pepper.
8. Pull off a 15-inch-long piece of parchment paper and dust it lightly with flour. Remove the chilled dough from the freezer, unwrap it, and place it on the parchment.
9. Using a rolling pin, roll the dough into a 12-inch-diameter round. Using the parchment as support, transfer the dough on the parchment to a baking sheet
10. Spoon the cream cheese mixture into the center of the dough and spread it into an even layer, leaving a 2-inch border around the edges. Scatter the smoked salmon over the cream cheese.
11. Arrange the tomatoes on top, overlapping the slices slightly so the cream cheese mixture is completely covered. Fold the bare edges of the dough up and over the tomatoes.
12. In a small bowl, whisk together the egg and 2 tablespoons water to make an egg wash. Brush the egg wash onto the crust and, while still moist, sprinkle the crust with the 1½ tablespoons of "everything bagel" seasoning. (Reserve the rest of the jar for another use.)
13. Bake until the crust is deeply golden brown and the tomatoes are soft, about 40 minutes. Let the tart rest on the baking sheet for 10 minutes, and then use the parchment to transfer it to a wire rack. Let cool to room temperature, about 20 minutes, before slicing and serving.
14. Wrap any leftovers in plastic wrap and store in the refrigerator for up to 2 days.

Elegant Cheesy Pasta

Prep time: 10 minutes | Cook time: 45 minutes | serves 6

Nonstick cooking spray
2 cups pasta sauce
24 to 30 ounces frozen cheese ravioli, divided
½ cup grated Parmesan cheese
1½ cups shredded mozzarella cheese

TOOLS/EQUIPMENT

Grater
8-by-8-inch baking dish
Aluminum foil

1. Preheat the Oster. Preheat the Oster to 375°F(191°C), and spray an 8-by-8-inch baking dish with cooking spray.
2. Layer and bake. Spread a layer of pasta sauce across the bottom of the baking dish, and cover the sauce with an even layer of ravioli.
3. Top with about half each of the remaining sauce, Parmesan cheese, and mozzarella.
4. Top the cheese with a second layer of ravioli, and top with the remaining sauce and cheeses.
5. Cover with foil and bake for 35 to 45 minutes, until the pasta is tender, removing the foil during the last 10 minutes of cooking.
6. Allow to rest for 10 to 15 minutes before serving.

Egg- Tomato Cheese Bread
Prep time: 10 minutes | Cook time: 20 minutes | serves 8

4¼ cups all-purpose flour
1 tablespoon kosher salt, plus more for seasoning
2½ teaspoons instant yeast
1¾ cups warm water
5 tablespoons extra-virgin olive oil, divided, plus more for the bowl
2 pints multicolored cherry tomatoes, halved (about 3½ cups)
8 large eggs
1 cup finely grated Parmesan cheese
Freshly ground black pepper, to taste
1 tablespoon chopped fresh chives

1. In a food processor, pulse together the flour, salt, and yeast. Add the water and 2 tablespoons of the oil and pulse until a rough ball of dough forms, about 1 minute. The dough will be sticky.
2. Using a rubber spatula, transfer the dough to a clean work surface. Shape the dough into a ball; place it in a lightly oiled large bowl, and turn to coat the dough with oil.
3. Cover the bowl with plastic wrap and let rest at room temperature until doubled in size, 1½ to 2 hours.
4. Drizzle the remaining 3 tablespoons oil onto a rimmed baking sheet. Punch down the dough and transfer it to the baking sheet, turning it to coat with oil. Stretch the dough to the edges of the baking sheet.
5. Lightly cover the baking sheet with plastic wrap and let sit at room temperature until nearly doubled in size again, 1 to 1½ hours.
6. Position a rack in the center of the Oster and preheat the Oster to 450°F(232°C).
7. Use your fingertips to press 8 evenly spaced wells across the dough (these will hold the eggs later). Scatter the tomatoes over the dough (avoiding the wells) and season with salt.
8. Bake the focaccia until the edges are lightly golden brown, 20 to 25 minutes. Remove from the Oster.
9. Crack an egg into a small bowl, then carefully add it to one of the wells. Repeat with the remaining eggs.
10. Sprinkle with Parmesan and season with pepper. Bake until the egg whites are just set and the yolks are soft, 8 to 10 minutes.
11. Garnish with the chives. Let rest for 2 minutes in the pan, then slice into squares with a pizza cutter and serve.

Chicken Balls in Pasta Sauce
Prep time: 10 minutes | Cook time: 20 minutes | serves 4

1 pound (454 g) ground chicken
1 garlic clove, minced, or 1 tablespoon garlic paste
½ cup bread crumbs
Salt and Freshly ground black pepper, to taste
1 large egg
2 tablespoons fresh basil, chopped, or 1 tablespoon dried basil
16 ounces (170 g) pasta sauce
1 cup fresh or shredded mozzarella cheese
TOOLS/EQUIPMENT
Cutting board
Knife
Rimmed baking sheet
Large bowl
Spatula
Plastic wrap
Medium casserole dish
Nonstick cooking spray or olive oil

1. Preheat the Oster. Preheat the Oster to 375°F(191°C). Spray a baking sheet with cooking spray or lightly coat with olive oil.
2. Mix the ingredients. In a large bowl, combine the chicken, garlic, bread crumbs, salt, pepper, egg, and basil. Mix with clean hands or a spatula until combined. Cover with plastic wrap and refrigerate for 30 minutes.
3. Form the meatballs and bake. Using clean hands, form the chicken mixture into meatballs. Arrange the meatballs, not touching each nother, on the prepared baking sheet. Bake for 10 to 12 minutes, until they begin to brown.
4. Assemble the dish and serve. Pour the pasta sauce into a medium casserole dish. Place the baked meatballs in the dish, turning to coat with sauce.
5. Top each meatball with a slice of mozzarella or a mound of shredded cheese.
6. Return to the Oster and cook for an additional 7 to 10 minutes, or until the sauce is bubbly and the cheese is melted. Serve hot.

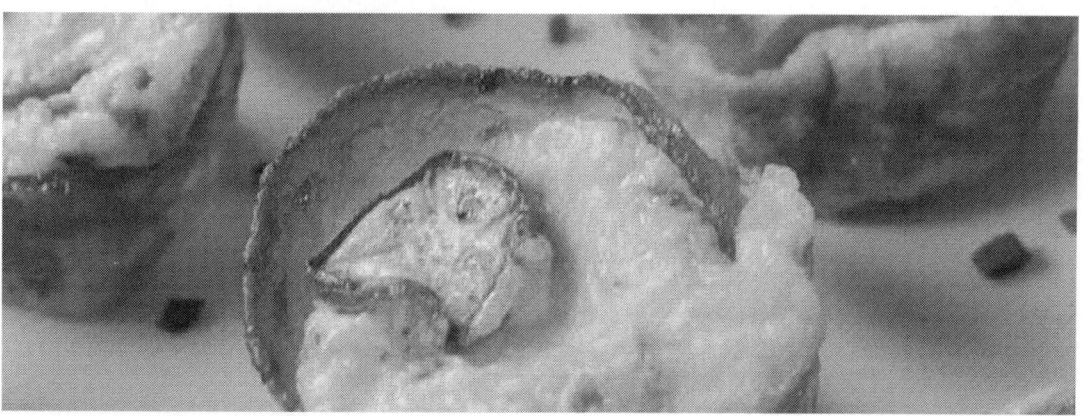

23 | Oster Digital Countertop Convection Oven Cookbook

Homemade Honeyed Butter Biscuits
Prep time: 10 minutes | Cook time: 20 minutes | makes 6 pretzels

2¼ teaspoons instant (Rapid Rise) yeast
2 tablespoons honey
2 tablespoons unsalted butter, melted, plus more for serving
1 teaspoon kosher salt
2¾ cups all-purpose flour, plus more for dusting and shaping
1 tablespoon canola oil, for the bowl
3 tablespoons baking soda
1 large egg, beaten
Coarse kosher salt, for sprinkling

1. In a stand mixer fitted with the dough hook, whisk together 1 cup warm water, the yeast, honey, melted butter, and salt. Add the flour and knead on low speed until a smooth, elastic ball of dough forms, about 6 minutes.
2. Place the dough in a lightly oiled large bowl and turn to coat the dough with oil. Cover the bowl with plastic wrap or a kitchen towel and set aside in a warm place to rise until the dough has doubled in size, 45 minutes to 1 hour.
3. Punch down the dough, cover the bowl, and let rise until nearly doubled again, 30 to 40 minutes more.
4. Line two large baking sheets with parchment paper and dust the parchment lightly with flour.
5. Divide the dough into 6 equal pieces. Starting at the center and rolling outward, use the palms of your hands to roll each piece into a 20-inch-long rope (flour your hands if the dough is sticky).
6. Form the rope into a "U" shape, twist the ends of the rope around each other, then flip the twisted section down and press the ends lightly onto the bottom of the "U." Transfer the pretzel to the prepared baking sheets and repeat with the remaining dough pieces.
7. Position racks in the upper and lower thirds of the Oster and preheat the Oster to 450°F(232°C). At the same time, in a wide saucepan or large Dutch Oster, bring 6 cups water and the baking soda to a boil.
8. Working in batches, use a spatula to carefully lower 2 pretzels into the boiling water. Cook the dough for 30 seconds, then use a spatula or tongs to flip the pretzels over and cook for 30 seconds more.
9. Use a slotted spoon to remove the pretzels from the water, letting any excess water drip off, and return them to the baking sheets. Repeat with the remaining pretzels in batches of 2.
10. Brush the pretzels with the beaten egg and sprinkle with coarse salt. Bake until the pretzels are deeply golden brown and shiny, 12 to 14 minutes, switching the pans from the top to bottom rack halfway through.
11. Brush the pretzels with melted butter and serve warm. Store leftovers at room temperature for up to 2 days or freeze in zip-top freezer bags for up to 1 month.

Spicy Cake with Whipped Cream
Prep time: 10 minutes | Cook time: 1 hour 5 minutes | serves 12

3 cups all-purpose flour
2 teaspoons ground ginger
1 teaspoon baking soda
1 teaspoon ground cinnamon
½ teaspoon ground allspice
½ teaspoon ground nutmeg
½ teaspoon salt
¼ teaspoon ground cloves
¼ teaspoon ground black pepper
¾ cup (1½ sticks) butter, softened
1½ cups granulated sugar
1 teaspoon vanilla extract
2 large eggs
1 cup light (mild) molasses
Whipped cream and confectioners' sugar, for garnish

1. Preheat Oster to 350°F(177°C). Grease and flour a 9-inch spring form pan.
2. In medium bowl with wire whisk, mix flour, ginger, baking soda, cinnamon, allspice, nutmeg, salt, cloves, and pepper.
3. In large bowl with mixer on medium-high speed, beat butter, granulated sugar, and vanilla for 3 minutes or until creamy, occasionally scraping down side of bowl with rubber spatula.
4. Reduce speed to medium; add eggs, 1 at a time, beating well after each addition.
5. In 4-cup measuring cup or medium bowl, stir molasses into 1 cup very hot water. Reduce mixer speed to low. Alternately add flour mixture and molasses, beginning and ending with flour mixture, just until blended.
6. Pour batter into prepared spring form pan; firmly tap pan against counter to release any bubbles. Bake for 45 to 55 minutes or until toothpick inserted in center of cake comes out clean. Cool cake, in pan, on wire rack for 15 minutes.
7. With small metal spatula or knife, loosen edges and remove spring form ring. Cool completely.
8. Cake can be made ahead, wrapped in double layer of plastic wrap, then foil, and frozen for up to 1 month. Thaw in refrigerator.
9. To serve, top cake with whipped cream and dust with confectioners' sugar.

Spicy Cheesy Pasta Chicken

Prep time: 10 minutes | Cook time: 20 minutes | serves 4

4 (6-ounce/170 g) skinless, boneless chicken breasts
Salt and Freshly ground black pepper, to taste
Olive oil
2 cups pasta sauce
4 (½-inch-thick) slices fresh mozzarella cheese
4 large pieces jarred or fresh roasted red peppers
Chopped fresh parsley (optional)
TOOLS/EQUIPMENT
Large nonstick skillet
Tongs or spatula
Small pot
Meat thermometer

1. Preheat the Oster. Preheat the Oster to 375°F(191°C). Season the chicken.
2. Season the chicken breasts with salt and pepper, and set aside. Cook the chicken and heat the sauce.
3. Pour enough oil into a large nonstick skillet to just cover the bottom. Heat over medium-high heat until the oil is shimmering.
4. Cook the chicken, turning once, until the outside is browned and the chicken is cooked through, 4 to 6 minutes per side depending on size, or until the internal temperature reaches 165°F(74°C) on a meat thermometer. Meanwhile, in a small pot over medium heat, heat the pasta sauce.
5. Assemble the dish. Once the chicken is done cooking, place a slice of mozzarella on each piece of chicken, followed by a slice of roasted red pepper.
6. Place the stacks in the skillet over medium-low heat for 3 to 5 minutes, until the cheese begins to melt.
7. Spoon warm pasta sauce onto individual plates, place a stack on top, add a little more sauce over top, garnish with a little chopped parsley, if desired, and serve.

Spinach stuffed Chicken Bake

Prep time: 10 minutes | Cook time: 35 minutes | serves 6

6 to 8 boneless chicken breasts
Salt and Freshly ground black pepper, to taste
1 (10-ounce/283 g) box frozen chopped spinach, thawed
1 (8-ounce/226 g block) cream cheese, room temperature
4 scallions, chopped
⅓ cup grainy Dijon mustard
TOOLS/EQUIPMENT
Cutting board
Chef's knife
Baking sheet or large baking dish
Medium bowl
Meat thermometer
Nonstick cooking spray

1. Preheat the Oster. Preheat the Oster to 350°F(177°C), and coat a baking sheet or baking dish with cooking spray.
2. Prepare the chicken. Trim any fat off of each chicken breast, and season with salt and pepper. Carefully slice a "pocket" into each breast by slicing on the diagonal through the breast, almost halving it but leaving one side and bottom and edge intact, like a flap. Set aside.
3. Mix the stuffing. In small handfuls, squeeze all the water from the spinach. In a medium bowl, combine the spinach, cream cheese, and scallions, and season with additional salt and pepper. Mix well, using clean hands if necessary.
4. Stuff and bake. Stuff each breast with plenty of the mixture. Pack it in, press it down, and pull the flap over the top. Place on the baking sheet. Spread the mustard over top of each breast.
5. Bake for 25 to 30 minutes until the meat is firm and opaque, any juices run clear, and a meat thermometer inserted in the thickest part of the breast, registers 165°F(74°C). Cook time will vary based on the thickness of the chicken breasts.

Toasted Cereal Fish Mix

Prep time: 10 minutes | Cook time: 20 minutes | makes 12 cups

3½ cups corn squares cereal (such as Corn Chex)
3½ cups wheat squares cereal (such as Wheat Chex)
2 cups pretzel fish (such as Goldfish) or other bite-size pretzels
1 cup oyster crackers
1 cup unsalted dry-roasted peanuts
1 stick (4 ounces (113 g) unsalted butter, melted
⅓ cup Worcestershire sauce
1 tablespoon plus 2 teaspoons Old Bay seasoning
½ teaspoon garlic powder
⅛ teaspoon cayenne pepper

1. Preheat the Oster to 300°F. Line a baking sheet with parchment paper.
2. In a large bowl, combine the cereals, pretzels, oyster crackers, and peanuts. In a 4-cup measuring cup, stir together the melted butter, Worcestershire sauce, Old Bay seasoning, garlic powder, and cayenne.
3. Pour the butter mixture over the cereal mixture and stir gently with a rubber spatula until well combined.
4. Spoon the mixture onto the prepared baking sheet and spread it out into an even layer.
5. Bake until the mixture looks lightly toasted and smells fragrant, about 1 hour, tossing the mixture every 15 minutes. Let the mix cool on the baking sheets, then transfer to an airtight container and store for up to 2 weeks.

Chapter 4
Dinner

Beef Mixture Topped Potato Fries

Prep time: 15 minutes | Cook time: 35 minutes | serves 4

3 large russet potatoes
3 tablespoons extra-virgin olive oil
1 teaspoon chili powder
1 pound (454 g) ground beef
1 bunch scallions, sliced (white and green parts separated)
1 clove garlic, chopped
¾ cup ketchup
2 tablespoons packed light brown sugar
2½ teaspoons Worcestershire sauce
1 cup shredded cheddar cheese
1 cup cubed mozzarella
Chopped cherry tomatoes and pickled jalapeños, for topping (optional)

1. Make the fries: Preheat the Oster to 425°. Cut the potatoes into thin wedges; toss with 1 tablespoon olive oil and ½ teaspoon chili powder on a baking sheet.
2. Spread in a single layer and bake, 15 minutes. Carefully remove from the Oster with Oster mitts and flip the potatoes with a spatula. Return to the Oster and bake until golden, about 15 more minutes.
3. Meanwhile, heat the remaining 2 tablespoons olive oil in a large skillet over medium-high heat. Add the beef and the remaining ½ teaspoon chili powder. Cook, breaking up the meat with a wooden spoon, until browned, about 5 minutes.
4. Add the scallion whites and garlic and cook until slightly softened, about 2 minutes. Add the ketchup, brown sugar, Worcestershire sauce and 1½ cups water; reduce the heat to medium and simmer until thickened slightly, about 8 minutes.
5. Divide the fries among plates. Top with the beef mixture, cheddar, mozzarella, scallion greens, tomatoes and pickled jalapeños.

Cheesy Tomato Skewers with Pasta

Prep time: 15 minutes | Cook time: 20 minutes | serves 4

Kosher salt, to taste
12 ounces (340 g) bow tie pasta
1 small head broccoli, cut into florets
1 tablespoon extra-virgin olive oil, plus more for drizzling
3 tablespoons grated parmesan cheese
1 clove garlic, grated
2 tablespoons unsalted butter
3 tablespoons all-purpose flour
1½ cups milk
½ teaspoon dijon or yellow mustard
1½ cups shredded cheddar cheese
Freshly ground pepper, to taste
8 mini mozzarella balls (bocconcini), halved
12 cherry tomatoes, halved

1. Preheat the Oster to 450°. Fill a large pot with water and season with salt. Bring to a boil over high heat.
2. Add the pasta and cook as the label directs for al dente. Carefully drain the pasta in a colander set in the sink. Reserve the pot.
3. Meanwhile, toss the broccoli on a baking sheet with 1 tablespoon olive oil, the parmesan and garlic. Carefully place in the Oster and roast until the broccoli is slightly charred and the cheese starts browning, about 12 minutes.
4. Melt the butter in the reserved pasta pot over medium heat. Sprinkle in the flour and cook, whisking, until lightly toasted, about 2 minutes.
5. Add the milk and mustard and cook, whisking occasionally, until thick and creamy, 4 to 5 minutes. Whisk in the cheddar and season with salt and pepper; continue cooking until the cheese is melted, 1 to 2 more minutes. Stir in the pasta until coated and warmed through, about 1 minute.
6. Thread the mozzarella and tomatoes onto 8 small skewers. Drizzle with olive oil and season with salt and pepper. Serve with the pasta and broccoli.

27 | Oster Digital Countertop Convection Oven Cookbook

Coconut Chicken Fingers

Prep time: 15 minutes | Cook time: 20 minutes | serves 4

FOR THE CHICKEN FINGERS
½ cup sweetened shredded coconut
1¼ cups panko
1 teaspoon paprika
3 tablespoons coconut oil, melted
2 large eggs
Kosher salt, to taste
Cooking spray
2 large skinless, boneless chicken breasts, each cut into 8 strips
FOR THE DIPPING SAUCE
⅓ cup Thai sweet chili sauce
2 tablespoons mayonnaise
Juice of ½ lime

1. Make the chicken fingers: Preheat the Oster to 425°. Spread the coconut on a baking sheet and bake, stirring occasionally with a spatula, until golden brown, about 10 minutes.
2. Carefully remove the baking sheet from the Oster with Oster mitts and spoon the toasted coconut into a shallow dish. Let cool, and then stir in the panko, paprika and coconut oil. (The mixture should look like wet sand.) Combine the eggs and ½ teaspoon salt in a separate shallow dish and whisk until smooth.
3. Put a wire rack on a baking sheet and coat the rack with cooking spray. Dip the chicken in the egg mixture, letting any excess drip off, then coat with the coconut mixture, pressing firmly so it sticks. Place the chicken on the rack and coat generously with more cooking spray.
4. Bake until cooked through and golden brown, 15 to 20 minutes.
5. Meanwhile, make the dipping sauce: Combine the sweet chili sauce, mayonnaise and lime juice in a bowl and whisk to combine. Serve with the chicken fingers.

Homemade Cheese Puffs

Prep time: 10 minutes | Cook time: 25 minutes | serves 4

½ cup water
4 tablespoons butter
Pinch salt
½ cup all-purpose flour
Pinch freshly ground black pepper
1 large egg, plus 1 large egg white
½ cup grated extra-sharp Cheddar cheese
TOOLS/EQUIPMENT
Grater
Baking sheet
Parchment paper
Medium saucepan
Wooden spoon or rubber spatula
Medium bowl

1. Preheat the Oster. Preheat the Oster to 400°F(204°C), and line a baking sheet with parchment paper.
2. Melt the butter.
3. In a medium saucepan, bring the water, butter, and salt to a simmer. When the butter has melted, remove the pan from the heat.
4. Add the flour and pepper. Mix vigorously with a wooden spoon or rubber spatula until it forms thick dough.
5. Add the eggs and cheese.
6. Transfer the dough to a medium bowl. Using the spoon or a mixer, add the egg and then the egg white, continuing to mix until fully incorporated. Allow the dough to cool to just slightly warm, then mix in the cheese.
7. Bake the puffs.
8. Spoon 1-inch pieces of dough onto the baking sheet about 1 inch apart. Bake until golden and crisp, about 25 minutes. Serve warm.

Lettuce and Tomato Topped Cheeseburger
Prep time: 15 minutes | Cook time: 20 minutes | serves 6

Kosher salt, to taste
12 ounces (340 g) spaghetti
3 stale hamburger buns
2 tablespoons extra-virgin olive oil
½ cup whole milk
1 pound (454 g) ground beef
½ cup finely chopped onion
¼ cup finely chopped dill pickle slices, plus pickle slices for serving
¼ cup ketchup
1 tablespoon yellow mustard
1 tablespoon Worcestershire sauce
Freshly ground pepper, to taste
1½ ounces sharp white cheddar cheese, cut into 24 small cubes, plus grated cheese for topping
4 cloves garlic, sliced
2 tablespoons tomato paste
Thinly sliced romaine lettuce and chopped tomato, for topping

1. Preheat the Oster to 350°. Fill a large pot with water and season with salt. Bring to a boil over high heat.
2. Add the spaghetti and cook as the label directs for al dente. Carefully remove 1 cup of the pasta cooking water with a liquid measuring cup; set aside. Carefully drain the spaghetti in a colander set in the sink.
3. Meanwhile, put 2 hamburger buns in a food processor and pulse into coarse crumbs. Heat 1 tablespoon olive oil in a large nonstick skillet over medium heat.
4. Add the breadcrumbs and cook, stirring, until toasted, about 3 minutes, then spoon into a bowl. Bunch up a paper towel and hold it with tongs to wipe out the skillet.
5. Tear up the remaining hamburger bun; put in a large bowl along with the milk and let soak 5 minutes.
6. Drain, squeezing the excess milk from the bread. Return the soaked bread to the empty bowl and add half of the toasted breadcrumbs, the ground beef, onion, chopped pickles, 2 tablespoons ketchup, the mustard, Worcestershire sauce, ½ teaspoon salt and a few grinds of pepper.
7. Mix with your hands until combined. Divide the meat mixture into 24 pieces. Press a cheese cube into the center of each and shape into meatballs around the cheese.
8. Heat the remaining 1 tablespoon olive oil in the same skillet over medium heat. Add the meatballs and cook, turning with the tongs, until browned, about 4 minutes.
9. Arrange the meatballs on a rimmed baking sheet; place in the Oster and bake until just cooked through, about 5 minutes. Reserve the skillet.
10. Add the garlic to the skillet; cook over medium heat until golden, about 30 seconds. Add the tomato paste and the remaining 2 tablespoons ketchup; cook 1 minute, then stir in the reserved pasta cooking water until smooth. Simmer until slightly thickened, about 3 minutes.
11. Add the spaghetti to the skillet and toss to coat with the tongs. Use the tongs to serve the spaghetti and top with the remaining toasted breadcrumbs, the meatballs, grated cheddar, lettuce and tomato. Serve with pickle slices.

Chocolate Sprinkles Rolled Butter Cookies
Prep time: 15 minutes | Cook time: 10 minutes | serves 6

1¾ cups all-purpose flour, divided
¼ teaspoon salt
1 teaspoon baking soda
2 sticks butter, softened
¾ cup granulated sugar
¾ cup brown sugar
2 large eggs
1 teaspoon vanilla extract
6 tablespoons cocoa powder
1 cup chocolate sprinkles
TOOLS/EQUIPMENT
Baking sheet
Parchment paper or silicone baking mat
2 medium bowls and 1 large bowl
Spatula
Cooling rack
Cookie scoop
Small metal spatula

1. Preheat the Oster. Preheat the Oster to 375°F(191°C), and line a baking sheet with parchment paper or a silicone baking mat.
2. Mix the dry ingredients. In a medium bowl, combine 1¼ cups of flour, salt, and baking soda. Set aside.
3. Mix the wet ingredients. In a large bowl, combine the butter, granulated sugar, and brown sugar, and mix until smooth. Add the eggs and vanilla, and mix until blended. Add the flour and baking soda mixture, and mix until smooth and creamy.
4. Prepare the dough.
5. Divide the dough in half, placing one half into the medium bowl you used for the flour mixture and the other half in another medium bowl.
6. Add the remaining ½ cup of flour to one batch of dough, and the cocoa powder to the other batch. Mix both doughs until smooth and creamy.
7. Scoop the light dough into balls about the size of a walnut and place on a piece of parchment paper. Repeat with the chocolate dough. Shape and bake.
8. Take one of each color ball of dough, press together and flatten so that one side is half-light and the other is half dark. Roll the edges liberally in the chocolate sprinkles. Place on the baking sheet 1 inch apart, and bake for 11 minutes. Don't let the edges brown.
9. Cool and enjoy. Let the cookies cool for a few minutes, and then, using a cookie spatula, transfer them to a cooling rack until completely cool. Store in an airtight container.

Squash Bowls with Meatballs
Prep time: 20 minutes | Cook time: 1 hour 20 minutes | serves 4

1 medium spaghetti squash (about 2 pounds)
Kosher salt, to taste
3 tablespoons extra-virgin olive oil, plus more for brushing
2 stalks celery, chopped
1 medium carrot, roughly chopped
1 medium onion, roughly chopped
6 cloves garlic
1 cup fresh parsley
1 pound (454 g) ground beef
1 pound (454 g) ground pork
2 large eggs
1 cup Italian-style breadcrumbs
1 cup plus 3 tablespoons grated parmesan cheese
2 28-ounce (794 g) cans tomato puree
2 large sprigs basil
1 teaspoon dried oregano

1. Preheat the Oster to 425°. Carefully cut the spaghetti squash in half lengthwise with a chef's knife and scoop out the seeds with a spoon. Sprinkle the cut sides with ½ teaspoon salt, and then brush both sides with olive oil.
2. Put the squash cut-side up in a baking dish and cover tightly with foil. Place in the Oster and roast 20 minutes, then carefully remove from the Oster with Oster mitts and uncover. Return to the Oster and continue roasting until the squash is tender, about 35 more minutes.
3. Meanwhile, make the meatballs: Brush a baking sheet with olive oil. Combine the celery, carrot, onion, garlic and parsley in a food processor and pulse to make a paste.
4. Spoon half of the vegetable paste into a large bowl; add the ground beef, ground pork, eggs, breadcrumbs, 1 cup parmesan and 1 teaspoon salt and mix with your hands until just combined.
5. Form into about 24 meatballs (about 2 inches each); place on the oiled baking sheet. Once the squash is done, bake the meatballs until firm but not cooked through, about 10 minutes.
6. Make the sauce: Heat 3 tablespoons olive oil in a large pot over medium-high heat. Add the remaining vegetable paste and cook, stirring occasionally with a wooden spoon, until it looks dry, about 5 minutes.
7. Stir in the tomato puree; add 1 cup water to each empty can, then add the water to the pot (you'll get any tomato puree that's stuck to the can). Stir in the basil, oregano and 1½ teaspoons salt. Bring to a simmer, then add the meatballs and simmer until the sauce thickens and the meatballs are cooked through, 15 to 20 minutes. Remove the basil.
8. Use a fork to scrape the spaghetti squash flesh into strands; put in a large bowl and add 2 tablespoons grated parmesan.
9. Season with salt and toss. Spoon the squash into bowls and top with the meatballs, sauce and the remaining 1 tablespoon parmesan.

Sugar Dusted Blueberry Tart
Prep time: 15 minutes | Cook time: 1 hour 15 minutes | serves 6

FOR THE CRUST
Nonstick cooking spray
14 tablespoons cold butter, cut into ½-inch cubes
1½ cups all-purpose flour
½ cup sugar
FOR THE CUSTARD
2½ cups fresh blueberries
3 large eggs
¾ cup granulated sugar
Juice of 2 large lemons
¼ cup all-purpose flour
¼ cup powdered sugar
TOOLS/EQUIPMENT
Knife
8- or 9-inch spring form pan
Rimmed baking sheet
Pastry cutter (optional)
2 medium bowls
Whisk
Toothpick (optional)
Mesh strainer (optional)

1. Preheat the Oster. Preheat the Oster to 400°F(204°C). Spray an 8- or 9-inch springform pan with cooking spray. Place the pan on a rimmed baking sheet.
2. Make the crust. In a medium bowl, combine the butter, flour, and sugar. Use a pastry cutter or clean fingers to cut in the butter until the mixture forms coarse crumbs.
3. Press the crust mixture into the bottom of the prepared pan. Bake for 16 to 20 minutes, or just until the crust begins to turn lightly golden in color. Remove from the Oster and reduce the temperature to 325°F(163°C).
4. Reduce the Oster temperature. Reduce the Oster temperature to 325°F(163°C).
5. Prepare the filling. Scatter the blueberries over the crust. In a medium bowl, whisk the eggs and granulated sugar until thick and frothy, about 2 minutes.
6. Add the lemon juice and flour, and whisk until blended and smooth. Pour the custard mixture over the crust with the blueberries.
7. Bake the tart. Bake until the custard is set, 35 to 45 minutes. It is done if it jiggles only slightly when the pan is shaken a bit, and the center is not wet.
8. Rest the tart. Allow the tart to rest for 15 minutes. Run a sharp knife gently around the crust, then slowly release the pan. After you see that the sides have released, close the pan back up and allow to cool for an hour at room temperature. Chill in the refrigerator until ready to serve.
9. Garnish and serve. Just before serving, use a mesh strainer to dust the tart with powdered sugar.

Chicken Fingers with Marinara Sauce
Prep time: 10 minutes | Cook time: 20 minutes | serves 4

FOR THE CHICKEN FINGERS:
½ cup sliced pepperoni
½ teaspoon Italian seasoning
¾ cup breadcrumbs
1 tablespoon extra-virgin olive oil
2 large eggs
Kosher salt, to taste
Cooking spray
2 large skinless, boneless chicken breasts, each cut into 8 strips
FOR THE DIPPING SAUCE:
1 cup marinara sauce
¼ cup shredded mozzarella cheese

1. Make the chicken fingers: Preheat the Oster to 425°. Pulse the pepperoni in a food processor until finely chopped.
2. Spoon into a shallow dish and add the Italian seasoning, breadcrumbs and olive oil; stir together. Combine the eggs and a pinch of salt in a separate shallow dish and whisk until smooth.
3. Put a wire rack on a baking sheet and coat the rack with cooking spray. Dip the chicken in the egg mixture, letting any excess drip off, then coat with the pepperoni breadcrumbs, pressing firmly so they stick.
4. Place the chicken on the prepared rack and coat generously with cooking spray. Bake until cooked through and golden brown, 15 to 20 minutes.
5. Meanwhile, make the dipping sauce: Combine the marinara sauce and mozzarella in a microwave-safe bowl. Just before serving, microwave, stirring every 30 seconds, until the sauce is hot and the cheese melts. Serve with the chicken fingers.

Golden Crisp Chicken Tortilla
Prep time: 20 minutes | Cook time: 25 minutes | serves 4

Cooking spray
4 large flour tortillas
3 tablespoons all-purpose flour
½ teaspoon ground cumin
½ teaspoon chili powder
Kosher salt and freshly ground pepper, to taste
1 pound (454 g) skinless, boneless chicken breasts, chopped
2 tablespoons extra-virgin olive oil
½ small onion, finely chopped
2 stalks celery, finely chopped
2 carrots, finely chopped
1 red bell pepper, finely chopped
14.5-ounce (411 g) can diced fire-roasted tomatoes
1 cup low-sodium chicken broth
¼ cup chopped fresh cilantro
1 cup shredded Monterey jack or pepper jack cheese

1. Preheat the Oster to 350°. Coat 4 cups of a muffin pan with cooking spray. Fold each tortilla in half, and then form into a cone, overlapping the sides.
2. Fold up the point of each cone slightly, and then press the tortillas into the prepared muffin pan to form a cup shape.
3. Coat the tortillas with cooking spray. Bake until golden and crisp, about 15 minutes. Meanwhile, combine the flour, cumin, chili powder, ½ teaspoon salt and a few grinds of pepper in a large bowl. Add the chicken and toss to coat.
4. Heat the olive oil in a large nonstick skillet over medium-high heat. Add the chicken in a single layer and cook, stirring occasionally with a wooden spoon, until lightly browned, about 2 minutes.
5. Add the onion, celery, carrots and bell pepper and cook until the vegetables begin softening, about 2 minutes. Add the tomatoes and chicken broth to the skillet and bring to a simmer.
6. Cook until the vegetables are tender and the sauce thickens slightly, about 5 minutes. Stir in the cilantro and season with salt and pepper.
7. Spoon the chicken mixture into the tortilla cups. Top with the cheese.

Half-and-half Broccoli Soup
Prep time: 10 minutes | Cook time: 20 minutes | serves 4

2 slices bacon, chopped
1 bunch scallions, chopped
1 stalk celery, chopped
3 tablespoons all-purpose flour
1 head broccoli, florets and tender stems chopped
2 cups low-sodium chicken broth
Kosher salt and freshly ground pepper, to taste
1 cup frozen shelled edamame, thawed
¾ cup half-and-half
1 cup shredded white cheddar cheese

1. Cook the bacon in a large Dutch Oster over medium-high heat, stirring occasionally with a wooden spoon, until crisp, about 10 minutes. Remove with a slotted spoon and put on paper towels; set aside to drain.
2. Add the scallions and celery to the drippings in the pot and cook, stirring with the wooden spoon, until slightly softened, about 2 minutes. Sprinkle in the flour and cook, stirring, until incorporated.
3. Add the broccoli, chicken broth, 3 cups water, 1 teaspoon salt and a few grinds of pepper. Increase the heat to high and bring to a boil.
4. Add the edamame, reduce the heat to medium low and simmer until slightly thickened, about 10 minutes.
5. Working in batches, carefully ladle the soup into a blender, filling it no more than halfway. Keeping the lid slightly open at the top (cover it with a kitchen towel to prevent splatters), puree the soup until smooth. Return the soup to the pot.
6. Stir in the half-and-half and simmer 5 minutes. Stir in the cheese and continue to cook, stirring, until the cheese melts and the soup thickens, about 5 more minutes. Season with salt and pepper. Ladle into bowls and top with the bacon.

Mayo Lettuce Pork Burger
Prep time: 15 minutes | Cook time: 10 minutes | serves 4

Cooking spray
2 tablespoons hoisin sauce
2 tablespoons plus 1 teaspoon rice vinegar (not seasoned)
12 ounces (340 g) ground pork
2 tablespoons panko
1 scallion (white and light green parts only), sliced
1 teaspoon grated peeled ginger
Kosher salt and freshly ground pepper, to taste
¼ small head green cabbage, chopped
2 small carrots, chopped
½ cup chopped pineapple
1 tablespoon mayonnaise, plus more for the buns
12 mini potato slider buns
Shredded romaine lettuce, for topping

1. Position a rack in the upper third of the Oster and preheat to 425°. Coat a rimmed baking sheet with cooking spray. Combine 1 tablespoon hoisin sauce and 1 teaspoon rice vinegar in a small bowl; set aside.
2. Combine the pork, panko, the remaining 1 tablespoon hoisin sauce, the scallion, ginger, ½ teaspoon salt and a few grinds of pepper in a medium bowl.
3. Mix with your hands until combined, then roll the mixture into twelve 1½-inch meatballs; put on the prepared baking sheet.
4. Bake until browned, 5 to 6 minutes, then carefully remove from the Oster with Oster mitts and turn the meatballs with tongs. Return to the Oster and bake until browned and cooked through, 5 to 6 more minutes. Remove from the Oster and brush with the reserved hoisin sauce mixture.
5. Meanwhile, combine the cabbage, carrots, pineapple, the remaining 2 tablespoons rice vinegar, the mayonnaise and ½ teaspoon salt in a food processor and pulse until the vegetables and pineapple are roughly chopped.
6. Spread mayonnaise on the bottom half of each bun, then fills with some shredded lettuce and a meatball. Serve with the pineapple salad.

The Best French Egg Dish
Prep time: 20 minutes | Cook time: 20 minutes | serves 6

2 tablespoons butter, softened
5 tablespoons granulated sugar, divided
3 large egg yolks, plus 5 large egg whites
1 cup milk
1 tablespoon vanilla extract
¼ cup all-purpose flour
4 tablespoons freshly squeezed lemon juice, plus 2 tablespoons lemon zest, finely grated
1 tablespoon powdered sugar, plus more for dusting
TOOLS/EQUIPMENT
Micro plane or zester
6 (8-ounce) ramekins
Baking sheet
3 small bowls
Heavy saucepan
Medium bowl
Whisk
Knife
Mesh strainer

1. Preheat the Oster. Preheat the Oster to 400°F(204°C).
2. Prepare the ramekins. Using your fingertips, coat 6 (8-ounce) ramekins with the butter. Dust the ramekins with 2 tablespoons of granulated sugar, rolling it around the sides and emptying the excess out into the next ramekin. Place the ramekins on a baking sheet in the refrigerator to chill.
3. Separate the eggs. Separate the eggs, placing the yolks in one small bowl and egg whites in another. Chill the egg whites until ready to use.
4. Heat the milk. In a heavy saucepan, bring the milk to a boil. Remove from the heat.
5. Mix the ingredients. In a medium bowl, whisk together the egg yolks, vanilla, and 1 tablespoon of granulated sugar. Whisk in the flour. Whisk ¼ cup of the hot milk into the egg yolk mixture until blended. Continue mixing the hot milk into the egg yolk mixture, ¼ cup at a time, until all the milk is incorporated.
6. Thicken the mixture. Pour the mixture back into the saucepan, and stir constantly over medium-low heat until thickened, about 2 minutes, moving the pot on and off the heat as you do so the mixture does not get too hot. If clumps begin to form, remove from the heat and whisk vigorously to smooth it out. Remove the custard from the heat.
7. Mix the lemon. In a small bowl, mix together the lemon zest, lemon juice, and powdered sugar, and then add to the custard, whisking until smooth.
8. Beat the egg whites. Beat the egg whites on high speed until they hold soft peaks. Sprinkle the remaining 2 tablespoons of granulated sugar over the egg whites, and beat until stiff and shiny.
9. Fold ¼ of the egg whites into the custard until the whites disappear. Fold in the remaining egg whites until just blended; don't over blend or you'll deflate the egg whites and the batter will turn soupy.
10. Fill the ramekins.
11. Spoon the batter into the ramekins, filling just to the top. Level the tops with a knife. Use your finger to go around the inside perimeter of each ramekin to clean the edges.
12. Bake the soufflés. Reduce the Oster temperature to 375°F(191°C), and immediately place the ramekins in the Oster on a baking sheet. Bake until puffed and the tops turn golden brown, 12 to 14 minutes. They should still be wobbly; move them slowly and carefully.
13. Garnish and serve. Use a small mesh strainer to sprinkle with powdered sugar and enjoy immediately.

The Best Ever Dark Chocolate Cake
Prep time: 15 minutes | Cook time: 45 minutes | serves 6

8 ounces (227 g) dark chocolate (60% cacao)
2 sticks butter
1 teaspoon vanilla extract
1 cup plus 2 tablespoons sugar
6 large eggs (or 5 extra-large eggs)
1 cup unsweetened cocoa powder
TOOLS/EQUIPMENT
8- or 9-inch round spring form pan or cake pan
Parchment paper or wax paper
Cutting board
Knife
Large metal bowl
Small pot
Spatula
Whisk
Toothpick
Nonstick cooking spray

1. Prepare the pan. Preheat the Oster to 375°F(191°C). Prepare an 8- or 9-inch spring form pan or round cake pan by spraying the inside of the pan with cooking spray then lining the bottom with parchment or wax paper cut into a circle to fit the bottom of the pan. Spray the paper after you place it in the pan.
2. Break the chocolate. Break the chocolate apart into small ½-inch pieces, and place in a large metal bowl. Cut the butter into ½-inch chunks and add to the same bowl.
3. Melt the chocolate. Fill a small pot halfway with water and bring to a simmer. Carefully place the metal bowl with the chocolate and butter on top of the pot, and allow the mixture to begin melting. First stir with a spatula, and then as it melts, whisk to incorporate it.
4. Whisk in the eggs, two at a time, until incorporated. Spoon in the cocoa powder, folding it in with a spatula until just combined.
5. Scrape the batter into the prepared pan, smoothing evenly. Alternatively, hold both sides of the pan and hit it flat against the counter to help the batter even out.
6. Bake and cool. Bake for 35 to 45 minutes, or until the top of the cake crisps up and a toothpick inserted comes out mostly clean.
7. Allow to cool for 15 minutes. If using a spring form pan, release the sides and invert the cake carefully onto a plate. Remove the bottom of the pan and paper lining.
8. Allow to cool. If using a cake pan, run a butter knife around the sides of the pan. Invert the pan onto a plate, carefully pull off the paper lining, and allow the cake to cool completely.

Chapter 5
Meats

Dill-Thyme Beef Steak

Prep time: 5 minutes | Cook time: 26 minutes | Serves 6

1 teaspoon dried dill
1 teaspoon dried thyme
1 teaspoon garlic powder
2 pounds (907 g) beef steak
3 tablespoons butter

1. Preheat the Oster to 385°F (196°C).
2. Combine the dill, thyme, and garlic powder in a small bowl, and massage into the steak.
3. Bake the steak in the Oster for 24 minutes, then remove, shred, and return to the Oster.
4. Add the butter and bake the shredded steak for a further 2 minutes at 365°F (185°C). Make sure the beef is coated in the butter before serving.

Dijon-Lemon Pork Tenderloin

Prep time: 10 minutes | Cook time: 30 minutes | Serves 4 to 6

¼ cup olive oil
¼ cup soy sauce
¼ cup freshly squeezed lemon juice
1 garlic clove, minced
1 tablespoon Dijon mustard
1 teaspoon salt
½ teaspoon freshly ground black pepper
2 pounds (907 g) pork tenderloin

1. In a large mixing bowl, make the marinade: Mix the olive oil, soy sauce, lemon juice, minced garlic, Dijon mustard, salt, and pepper. Reserve ¼ cup of the marinade.
2. Put the tenderloin in a large bowl and pour the remaining marinade over the meat. Cover and marinate in the refrigerator for about 1 hour.
3. Preheat the Oster to 400°F (204°C).
4. Put the marinated pork tenderloin into the baking pan. Bake for 10 minutes. Flip the pork and baste it with half of the reserved marinade. Bake for 10 minutes more.
5. Flip the pork, then baste with the remaining marinade. Bake for another 10 minutes, for a total cooking time of 30 minutes.
6. Serve immediately.

Taco Pork Chops with Oregano

Prep time: 5 minutes | Cook time: 18 minutes | Serves 2

¼ teaspoon dried oregano
1½ teaspoons taco seasoning mix
2 (4-ounce / 113-g) boneless pork chops
2 tablespoons unsalted butter, divided

1. Preheat the Oster to 425°F (218°C).
2. Combine the dried oregano and taco seasoning in a small bowl and rub the mixture into the pork chops. Brush the chops with 1 tablespoon butter.
3. In the Oster, bake the chops for 18 minutes, turning them over halfway through to bake on the other side.
4. When the chops are a brown color, check the internal temperature has reached 145°F (63°C) and remove from the Oster. Serve with a garnish of remaining butter.

Dijon Mustard Pork Tenderloin

Prep time: 5 minutes | Cook time: 12 minutes | Serves 6

2 large egg whites
1½ tablespoons Dijon mustard
2 cups crushed pretzel crumbs
1½ pounds (680 g) pork tenderloin, cut into ¼-pound (113-g) sections
Cooking spray

1. Preheat the Oster to 375°F (191°C). Spritz the baking pan with cooking spray.
2. Whisk the egg whites with Dijon mustard in a bowl until bubbly. Pour the pretzel crumbs in a separate bowl.
3. Dredge the pork tenderloin in the egg white mixture and press to coat. Shake the excess off and roll the tenderloin over the pretzel crumbs.
4. Arrange the well-coated pork tenderloin in batches in a single layer in the pan and spritz with cooking spray.
5. Bake for 12 minutes or until the pork is golden brown and crispy. Flip the pork halfway through. Repeat with remaining pork sections.
6. Serve immediately.

BBQ Sausage with Pineapple and Bell Peppers
Prep time: 15 minutes | Cook time: 12 minutes | Serves 2 to 4

¾ pound (340 g) kielbasa sausage, cut into ½-inch slices
1 (8-ounce / 227-g) can pineapple chunks in juice, drained
1 cup bell pepper chunks
1 tablespoon barbecue seasoning
1 tablespoon soy sauce
Cooking spray

1. Preheat the Oster to 425°F (218°C). Spritz the baking pan with cooking spray.
2. Combine all the ingredients in a large bowl. Toss to mix well.
3. Pour the sausage mixture in the preheated Oster.
4. Bake for 12 minutes or until the sausage is lightly browned and the bell pepper and pineapple are soft.
5. Serve immediately.

Balsamic Ribeye Steaks with Rosemary
Prep time: 10 minutes | Cook time: 18 minutes | Serves 2

¼ cup butter
1 clove garlic, minced
Salt and ground black pepper, to taste
1½ tablespoons balsamic vinegar
¼ cup rosemary, chopped
2 ribeye steaks

1. Melt the butter in a skillet over medium heat. Add the garlic and fry until fragrant.
2. Remove the skillet from the heat and add the salt, pepper, and vinegar. Allow it to cool.
3. Add the rosemary, then pour the mixture into a Ziploc bag.
4. Put the ribeye steaks in the bag and shake well, coating the meat well. Refrigerate for an hour, then allow to sit for a further twenty minutes.
5. Preheat the Oster to 400°F (204°C).
6. Transfer the ribeye steaks to the baking pan. Bake for 18 minutes.
7. Take care when removing the steaks from the Oster and plate up.
8. Serve immediately.

Chipotle Flank Steak with Oregano
Prep time: 5 minutes | Cook time: 18 minutes | Serves 4

3 chipotle peppers in adobo, chopped
⅓ cup chopped fresh oregano
⅓ cup chopped fresh parsley
4 cloves garlic, minced
Juice of 2 limes
1 teaspoon ground cumin seeds
⅓ cup olive oil
1 to 1½ pounds (454 g to 680 g) flank steak
Salt, to taste

1. Combine the chipotle, oregano, parsley, garlic, lime juice, cumin, and olive oil in a large bowl. Stir to mix well.
2. Dunk the flank steak in the mixture and press to coat well. Wrap the bowl in plastic and marinate under room temperature for at least 30 minutes.
3. Preheat the Oster to 400°F (204°C).
4. Discard the marinade and place the steak in the preheated Oster. Sprinkle with salt.
5. Bake for 18 minutes or until the steak is medium-rare or it reaches your desired doneness. Flip the steak halfway through the cooking time.
6. Remove the steak from the Oster and slice to serve.

Beef, Kale and Tomato Omelet
Prep time: 15 minutes | Cook time: 18 minutes | Serves 4

½ pound (227 g) leftover beef, coarsely chopped
2 garlic cloves, pressed
1 cup kale, torn into pieces and wilted
1 tomato, chopped
¼ teaspoon sugar
4 eggs, beaten
4 tablespoons heavy cream
½ teaspoon turmeric powder
Salt and ground black pepper, to taste
⅛ teaspoon ground allspice
Cooking spray

1. Preheat the Oster to 385°F (196°C). Spritz four ramekins with cooking spray.
2. Put equal amounts of each of the ingredients into each ramekin and mix well.
3. Bake for 18 minutes. Serve immediately.

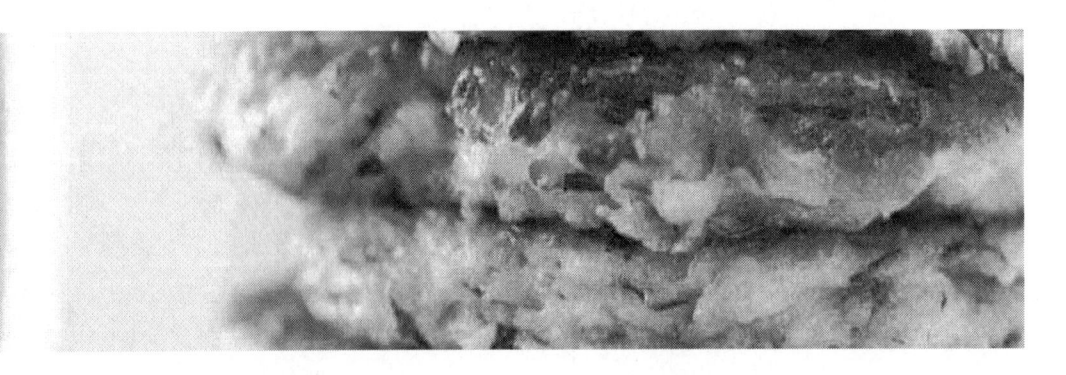

Beef and Mushroom Meatloaf
Prep time: 10 minutes | Cook time: 25 minutes | Serves 4

1 pound (454 g) ground beef
1 egg, beaten
1 mushrooms, sliced
1 tablespoon thyme
1 small onion, chopped
3 tablespoons bread crumbs
Ground black pepper, to taste

1. Preheat the Oster to 400°F (204°C).
2. Put all the ingredients into a large bowl and combine entirely.
3. Transfer the meatloaf mixture into the loaf pan.
4. Bake for 25 minutes. Slice up before serving.

Beef Meatloaf with Tomato Sauce
Prep time: 15 minutes | Cook time: 25 minutes | Serves 4

1½ pounds (680 g) ground beef
1 cup tomato sauce
½ cup bread crumbs
2 egg whites
½ cup grated Parmesan cheese
1 diced onion
2 tablespoons chopped parsley
2 tablespoons minced ginger
2 garlic cloves, minced
½ teaspoon dried basil
1 teaspoon cayenne pepper
Salt and ground black pepper, to taste
Cooking spray

1. Preheat the Oster to 360°F (182°C). Spritz a meatloaf pan with cooking spray.
2. Combine all the ingredients in a large bowl. Stir to mix well.
3. Pour the meat mixture in the prepared meatloaf pan and press with a spatula to make it firm.
4. Arrange the pan in the preheated Oster and bake for 25 minutes or until the beef is well browned.
5. Serve immediately.

Beef Stroganoff with Mushrooms
Prep time: 15 minutes | Cook time: 17 minutes | Serves 4

1 pound (454 g) beef steak, thinly sliced
8 ounces (227 g) mushrooms, sliced
1 whole onion, chopped
2 cups beef broth
1 cup sour cream
4 tablespoons butter, melted
2 cups cooked egg noodles

1. Preheat the Oster to 425°F (218°C).
2. Combine the mushrooms, onion, beef broth, sour cream and butter in a bowl until well blended. Add the beef steak to another bowl.
3. Spread the mushroom mixture over the steak and let marinate for 10 minutes.
4. Pour the marinated steak in a baking pan and bake in the preheated Oster for 17 minutes, or until the steak is browned and the vegetables are tender.
5. Serve hot with the cooked egg noodles.

Miso-Sake Marinated Flank Steak
Prep time: 5 minutes | Cook time: 15 minutes | Serves 4

¾ pound (340 g) flank steak
1½ tablespoons sake
1 tablespoon brown miso paste
1 teaspoon honey
2 cloves garlic, pressed
1 tablespoon olive oil

1. Put all the ingredients in a Ziploc bag. Shake to cover the steak well with the seasonings and refrigerate for at least 1 hour.
2. Preheat the Oster to 425°F (218°C). Coat all sides of the steak with cooking spray. Put the steak in the baking pan.
3. Bake for 15 minutes, turning the steak twice during the cooking time, then serve immediately.

Beef Kofta with Cinnamon
Prep time: 10 minutes | Cook time: 13 minutes per batch | Makes 12 koftas

1½ pounds (680 g) lean ground beef
1 teaspoon onion powder
¾ teaspoon ground cinnamon
¾ teaspoon ground dried turmeric
1 teaspoon ground cumin
¾ teaspoon salt
¼ teaspoon cayenne
12 (3½- to 4-inch-long) cinnamon sticks
Cooking spray

1. Preheat the Oster to 400°F (204°C). Spritz the baking pan with cooking spray.
2. Combine all the ingredients, except for the cinnamon sticks, in a large bowl. Toss to mix well.
3. Divide and shape the mixture into 12 balls, then wrap each ball around each cinnamon stick and leave a quarter of the length uncovered.
4. Arrange the beef-cinnamon sticks in the pan and spritz with cooking spray. Work in batches to avoid overcrowding.
5. Bake for 15 minutes or until the beef is browned. Flip the sticks halfway through.
6. Serve immediately.

Pork Ribs with Honey-Soy Sauce
Prep time: 5 minutes | Cook time: 36 minutes | Serves 4

¼ cup soy sauce
¼ cup honey
1 teaspoon garlic powder
1 teaspoon ground dried ginger
4 (8-ounce / 227-g) boneless country-style pork ribs
Cooking spray

1. Preheat the Oster to 375°F (191°C). Spritz the baking pan with cooking spray.
2. Make the teriyaki sauce: Combine the soy sauce, honey, garlic powder, and ginger in a bowl. Stir to mix well.
3. Brush the ribs with half of the teriyaki sauce, then arrange the ribs in the pan. Spritz with cooking spray. You may need to work in batches to avoid overcrowding.
4. Bake for 36 minutes or until the internal temperature of the ribs reaches at least 145°F (63°C). Brush the ribs with remaining teriyaki sauce and flip halfway through.
5. Serve immediately.

Lemongrass Pork Chops with Fish Sauce
Prep time: 15 minutes | Cook time: 15 minutes | Serves 2

1 tablespoon chopped shallot
1 tablespoon chopped garlic
1 tablespoon fish sauce
3 tablespoons lemongrass
1 teaspoon soy sauce
1 tablespoon brown sugar
1 tablespoon olive oil
1 teaspoon ground black pepper
2 pork chops

1. Combine shallot, garlic, fish sauce, lemongrass, soy sauce, brown sugar, olive oil, and pepper in a bowl. Stir to mix well.
2. Put the pork chops in the bowl. Toss to coat well. Place the bowl in the refrigerator to marinate for 2 hours.
3. Preheat the Oster to 425°F (218°C).
4. Remove the pork chops from the bowl and discard the marinade. Transfer the chops into the Oster.
5. Bake for 15 minutes or until lightly browned. Flip the pork chops halfway through the cooking time.
6. Remove the pork chops from the Oster and serve hot.

Lamb Kofta with Mint
Prep time: 25 minutes | Cook time: 12 minutes | Serves 4

1 pound (454 g) ground lamb
1 tablespoon ras el hanout (North African spice)
½ teaspoon ground coriander
1 teaspoon onion powder
1 teaspoon garlic powder
1 teaspoon cumin
2 tablespoons mint, chopped
Salt and ground black pepper, to taste

Special Equipment:
4 bamboo skewers

1. Combine the ground lamb, ras el hanout, coriander, onion powder, garlic powder, cumin, mint, salt, and ground black pepper in a large bowl. Stir to mix well.
2. Transfer the mixture into sausage molds and sit the bamboo skewers in the mixture. Refrigerate for 15 minutes.
3. Preheat Oster to 400°F (204°C). Spritz the baking pan with cooking spray.
4. Place the lamb skewers in the preheated Oster and spritz with cooking spray.
5. Bake for 12 minutes or until the lamb is well browned. Flip the lamb skewers halfway through.
6. Serve immediately.

Beef and Carrot Meatballs
Prep time: 10 minutes | Cook time: 14 minutes | Serves 8

1 pound (454 g) ground beef
1 egg, beaten
2 carrots, shredded
2 bread slices, crumbled
1 small onion, minced
½ teaspoons garlic salt
Pepper and salt, to taste
1 cup tomato sauce
2 cups pasta sauce

1. Preheat the Oster to 425°F (218°C).
2. In a bowl, combine the ground beef, egg, carrots, crumbled bread, onion, garlic salt, pepper and salt.
3. Divide the mixture into equal amounts and shape each one into a small meatball.
4. Put them in the baking pan and bake for 8 minutes.
5. Transfer the meatballs to an Oster-safe dish and top with the tomato sauce and pasta sauce.
6. Set the dish into the Oster and allow to bake at 350°F (177°C) for 6 more minutes. Serve hot.

Pork and Mushroom Rolls with Teriyaki
Prep time: 10 minutes | Cook time: 10 minutes | Serves 6

4 tablespoons brown sugar
4 tablespoons mirin
4 tablespoons soy sauce
1 teaspoon almond flour
2-inch ginger, chopped
6 (4-ounce / 113-g) pork belly slices
6 ounces (170 g) Enoki mushrooms

1. Mix the brown sugar, mirin, soy sauce, almond flour, and ginger together until brown sugar dissolves.
2. Take pork belly slices and wrap around a bundle of mushrooms. Brush each roll with teriyaki sauce. Chill for half an hour.
3. Preheat the Oster to 350°F (177°C) and add marinated pork rolls to the baking pan.
4. Bake for 10 minutes. Flip the rolls halfway through.
5. Serve immediately.

Beef and Spaghetti Squash Lasagna
Prep time: 5 minutes | Cook time: 1 hour 15 minutes | Serves 6

2 large spaghetti squash, cooked (about 2¾ pounds / 1.2 kg)
4 pounds (1.8 kg) ground beef
1 (2½-pound / 1.1-kg) large jar Marinara sauce
25 slices Mozzarella cheese
30 ounces whole-milk ricotta cheese

1. Preheat the Oster to 375°F (191°C).
2. Slice the spaghetti squash and place it face down inside a baking dish. Fill with water until covered.
3. Bake in the preheated Oster for 45 minutes until skin is soft.
4. Sear the ground beef in a skillet over medium-high heat for 5 minutes or until browned, then add the marinara sauce and heat until warm. Set aside.
5. Scrape the flesh off the cooked squash to resemble strands of spaghetti.
6. Layer the lasagna in a large greased pan in alternating layers of spaghetti squash, beef sauce, Mozzarella, ricotta. Repeat until all the ingredients have been used.
7. Bake for 30 minutes and serve!

Paprika Lamb Chops with Sage
Prep time: 5 minutes | Cook time: 30 minutes | Serves 4

1 cup all-purpose flour
2 teaspoons dried sage leaves
2 teaspoons garlic powder
1 tablespoon mild paprika
1 tablespoon salt
4 (6-ounce / 170-g) bone-in lamb shoulder chops, fat trimmed
Cooking spray

1. Preheat the Oster to 400°F (204°C) and spritz the baking pan with cooking spray.
2. Combine the flour, sage leaves, garlic powder, paprika, and salt in a large bowl. Stir to mix well. Dunk in the lamb chops and toss to coat well.
3. Arrange the lamb chops in a single layer in the pan and spritz with cooking spray. Bake for 30 minutes or until the chops are golden brown and reaches your desired doneness. Flip the chops halfway through.
4. Serve immediately.

Cheddar Prosciutto and Potato Salad
Prep time: 10 minutes | Cook time: 8 minutes | Serves 8

Salad:
4 pounds (1.8 kg) potatoes, boiled and cubed
15 slices prosciutto, diced
2 cups shredded Cheddar cheese
Dressing:
15 ounces (425 g) sour cream
2 tablespoons mayonnaise
1 teaspoon salt
1 teaspoon black pepper
1 teaspoon dried basil

1. Preheat the Oster to 375°F (191°C).
2. Put the potatoes, prosciutto, and Cheddar in a baking dish. Put it in the Oster and bake for 8 minutes.
3. In a separate bowl, mix the sour cream, mayonnaise, salt, pepper, and basil using a whisk.
4. Coat the salad with the dressing and serve.

Crispy Baked Venison
Prep time: 10 minutes | Cook time: 12 minutes | Serves 4

2 eggs
¼ cup milk
1 cup whole wheat flour
½ teaspoon salt
¼ teaspoon ground black pepper
1 pound (454 g) venison backstrap, sliced
Cooking spray

1. Preheat the Oster to 385°F (196°C) and spritz the baking pan with cooking spray.
2. Whisk the eggs with milk in a large bowl. Combine the flour with salt and ground black pepper in a shallow dish.
3. Dredge the venison in the flour first, then into the egg mixture. Shake the excess off and roll the venison back over the flour to coat well.
4. Arrange half of the venison in the pan and spritz with cooking spray.
5. Bake for 12 minutes or until the internal temperature of the venison reaches at least 145°F (63°C) for medium rare. Flip the venison halfway through. Repeat with remaining venison.
6. Serve immediately.

Panko Breaded Wasabi Spam
Prep time: 5 minutes | Cook time: 12 minutes | Serves 3

⅔ cup all-purpose flour
2 large eggs
1½ tablespoons wasabi paste
2 cups panko bread crumbs
6½-inch-thick spam slices
Cooking spray

1. Preheat the Oster to 425°F (218°C) and spritz the baking pan with cooking spray.
2. Pour the flour in a shallow plate. Whisk the eggs with wasabi in a large bowl. Pour the panko in a separate shallow plate.
3. Dredge the spam slices in the flour first, then dunk in the egg mixture, and then roll the spam over the panko to coat well. Shake the excess off.
4. Arrange the spam slices in a single layer in the pan and spritz with cooking spray.
5. Bake for 15 minutes or until the spam slices are golden and crispy. Flip the spam slices halfway through.
6. Serve immediately.

Smoky Beef with Jalapeño Peppers
Prep time: 10 minutes | Cook time: 45 minutes | Serves 8

2 pounds (907 g) beef, at room temperature
2 tablespoons extra-virgin olive oil
1 teaspoon sea salt flakes
1 teaspoon ground black pepper
1 teaspoon smoked paprika
Few dashes of liquid smoke
2 jalapeño peppers, thinly sliced

1. Preheat the Oster to 330°F (166°C).
2. With kitchen towels, pat the beef dry.
3. Massage the extra-virgin olive oil, salt, black pepper, and paprika into the meat. Cover with liquid smoke.
4. Put the beef in the Oster and bake for 30 minutes. Flip the beef over and allow to bake for another 15 minutes.
5. When cooked through, serve topped with sliced jalapeños.

Orange Pork Ribs with Garlic

Prep time: 1 hour 10 minutes | Cook time: 30 minutes | Serves 6

2½ pounds (1.1 kg) boneless country-style pork ribs, cut into 2-inch pieces
3 tablespoons olive brine
1 tablespoon minced fresh oregano leaves
⅓ cup orange juice
1 teaspoon ground cumin
1 tablespoon minced garlic
1 teaspoon salt
1 teaspoon ground black pepper
Cooking spray

1. Combine all the ingredients in a large bowl. Toss to coat the pork ribs well. Wrap the bowl in plastic and refrigerate for at least an hour to marinate.
2. Preheat the Oster to 425°F (218°C) and spritz the baking pan with cooking spray.
3. Arrange the marinated pork ribs in a single layer in the pan and spritz with cooking spray.
4. Bake for 30 minutes or until well browned. Flip the ribs halfway through.
5. Serve immediately.

Chapter 6
Poultry

Chicken Cordon Bleu with Swiss Cheese
Prep time: 15 minutes | Cook time: 13 to 15 minutes | Serves 4

4 chicken breast fillets
¼ cup chopped ham
⅓ cup grated Swiss or Gruyère cheese
¼ cup flour
Pinch salt
Freshly ground black pepper, to taste
½ teaspoon dried marjoram
1 egg
1 cup panko bread crumbs
Olive oil for misting

1. Preheat the Oster to 380°F (193°C).
2. Put the chicken breast fillets on a work surface and gently press them with the palm of your hand to make them a bit thinner. Don't tear the meat.
3. In a small bowl, combine the ham and cheese. Divide this mixture among the chicken fillets. Wrap the chicken around the filling to enclose it, using toothpicks to hold the chicken together.
4. In a shallow bowl, mix the flour, salt, pepper, and marjoram. In another bowl, beat the egg. Spread the bread crumbs out on a plate.
5. Dip the chicken into the flour mixture, then into the egg, then into the bread crumbs to coat thoroughly.
6. Put the chicken in the baking pan and mist with olive oil.
7. Bake for 13 to 15 minutes or until the chicken is thoroughly cooked to 165°F (74°C). Carefully remove the toothpicks and serve.

Curried Chicken with Orange and Honey
Prep time: 10 minutes | Cook time: 16 to 19 minutes | Serves 4

¾ pound (340 g) boneless, skinless chicken thighs, cut into 1-inch pieces
1 yellow bell pepper, cut into 1½-inch pieces
1 small red onion, sliced
Olive oil for misting
¼ cup chicken stock
2 tablespoons honey
¼ cup orange juice
1 tablespoon cornstarch
2 to 3 teaspoons curry powder

1. Preheat the Oster to 370°F (188°C).
2. Put the chicken thighs, pepper, and red onion in the baking pan and mist with olive oil.
3. Bake for 12 to 14 minutes or until the chicken is cooked to 165°F (74°C), stirring halfway through cooking time.
4. Remove the chicken and vegetables from the Oster and set aside.
5. In a metal bowl, combine the stock, honey, orange juice, cornstarch, and curry powder, and mix well. Add the chicken and vegetables, stir, and put the bowl in the Oster.
6. Bake for 2 minutes. Remove and stir, then bake for 2 to 3 minutes or until the sauce is thickened and bubbly.
1. Serve warm.

Chicken and Bell Pepper Fajitas
Prep time: 15 minutes | Cook time: 10 to 15 minutes | Serves 4

4 (5-ounce / 142-g) low-sodium boneless, skinless chicken breasts, cut into 4-by-½-inch strips
1 tablespoon freshly squeezed lemon juice
2 teaspoons olive oil
2 teaspoons chili powder
2 red bell peppers, sliced
4 low-sodium whole-wheat tortillas
⅓ cup nonfat sour cream
1 cup grape tomatoes, sliced

1. Preheat the Oster to 380°F (193°C).
2. In a large bowl, mix the chicken, lemon juice, olive oil, and chili powder. Toss to coat. Transfer the chicken to the baking pan. Add the red bell peppers. Bake for 10 to 15 minutes, or until the chicken reaches an internal temperature of 165°F (74°C) on a meat thermometer.
3. Assemble the fajitas with the tortillas, chicken, bell peppers, sour cream, and tomatoes. Serve immediately.

Curried Cinnamon Chicken
Prep time: 5 minutes | Cook time: 18 to 23 minutes | Serves 4

⅔ cup plain low-fat yogurt
2 tablespoons freshly squeezed lemon juice
2 teaspoons curry powder
½ teaspoon ground cinnamon
2 garlic cloves, minced
2 teaspoons olive oil
4 (5-ounce / 142-g) low-sodium boneless, skinless chicken breasts

1. In a medium bowl, whisk the yogurt, lemon juice, curry powder, cinnamon, garlic, and olive oil.
2. With a sharp knife, cut thin slashes into the chicken. Add it to the yogurt mixture and turn to coat. Let stand for 10 minutes at room temperature. You can also prepare this ahead of time and marinate the chicken in the refrigerator for up to 24 hours.
3. Preheat the Oster to 360°F (182°C).
4. Remove the chicken from the marinade and shake off any excess liquid. Discard any remaining marinade. Place in the baking pan.
5. Bake the chicken for 10 minutes. With tongs, carefully turn each piece. Bake for 8 to 13 minutes more, or until the chicken reaches an internal temperature of 165°F (74°C) on a meat thermometer. Serve immediately.

Chicken Lettuce Tacos with Peanut Sauce
Prep time: 10 minutes | Cook time: 6 minutes | Serves 4

1 pound (454 g) ground chicken
2 cloves garlic, minced
¼ cup diced onions
¼ teaspoon sea salt
Cooking spray
Peanut Sauce:
¼ cup creamy peanut butter, at room temperature
2 tablespoons tamari
1½ teaspoons hot sauce
2 tablespoons lime juice
2 tablespoons grated fresh ginger
2 tablespoons chicken broth
2 teaspoons sugar
2 small heads butter lettuce, leaves separated
Lime slices (optional)

1. Preheat the Oster to 350°F (177°C). Spritz a baking pan with cooking spray.
2. Combine the ground chicken, garlic, and onions in the baking pan, then sprinkle with salt. Use a fork to break the ground chicken and combine them well.
3. Place the pan in the preheated Oster. Bake in the preheated Oster for 5 minutes or until the chicken is lightly browned. Stir them halfway through the cooking time.
4. Meanwhile, combine the ingredients for the sauce in a small bowl. Stir to mix well.
5. Pour the sauce in the pan of chicken, then cook for 1 more minute or until heated through.
6. Unfold the lettuce leaves on a large serving plate, then divide the chicken mixture on the lettuce leaves. Drizzle with lime juice and serve immediately.

Curried Cranberry and Apple Chicken
Prep time: 12 minutes | Cook time: 18 minutes | Serves 4

3 (5-ounce / 142-g) low-sodium boneless, skinless chicken breasts, cut into 1½-inch cubes
2 teaspoons olive oil
2 tablespoons cornstarch
1 tablespoon curry powder
1 tart apple, chopped
½ cup low-sodium chicken broth
⅓ cup dried cranberries
2 tablespoons freshly squeezed orange juice
Brown rice, cooked (optional)

1. Preheat the Oster to 380°F (193°C).
2. In a medium bowl, mix the chicken and olive oil. Sprinkle with the cornstarch and curry powder. Toss to coat. Stir in the apple and transfer to a metal pan. Bake in the Oster for 8 minutes, stirring once during cooking.
3. Add the chicken broth, cranberries, and orange juice. Bake for about 10 minutes more, or until the sauce is slightly thickened and the chicken reaches an internal temperature of 165°F (74°C) on a meat thermometer. Serve over hot cooked brown rice, if desired.

Chicken Nuggets with Almond Crust
Prep time: 10 minutes | Cook time: 10 to 13 minutes | Serves 4

1 egg white
1 tablespoon freshly squeezed lemon juice
½ teaspoon dried basil
½ teaspoon ground paprika
1 pound (454 g) low-sodium boneless, skinless chicken breasts, cut into 1½-inch cubes
½ cup ground almonds
2 slices low-sodium whole-wheat bread, crumbled

1. Preheat the Oster to 400°F (204°C).
2. In a shallow bowl, beat the egg white, lemon juice, basil, and paprika with a fork until foamy.
3. Add the chicken and stir to coat.
4. On a plate, mix the almonds and bread crumbs.
5. Toss the chicken cubes in the almond and bread crumb mixture until coated.
6. Bake the nuggets in the Oster, in two batches, for 10 to 13 minutes, or until the chicken reaches an internal temperature of 165°F (74°C) on a meat thermometer. Serve immediately.

Chili-Garlic Chicken Tenders
Prep time: 5 minutes | Cook time: 7 minutes | Serves 4

Seasoning:
1 teaspoon kosher salt
½ teaspoon garlic powder
½ teaspoon onion powder
½ teaspoon chili powder
¼ teaspoon sweet paprika
¼ teaspoon freshly ground black pepper
Chicken:
8 chicken breast tenders (1 pound / 454 g total)
2 tablespoons mayonnaise

1. Preheat the Oster to 400°F (204°C).
2. For the seasoning: In a small bowl, combine the salt, garlic powder, onion powder, chili powder, paprika, and pepper.
3. For the chicken: Place the chicken in a medium bowl and add the mayonnaise. Mix well to coat all over, then sprinkle with the seasoning mix.
4. Working in batches, arrange a single layer of the chicken in the baking pan. Bake for 7 minutes, flipping halfway, until cooked through in the center. Serve immediately.

Chicken Manchurian with Ketchup Sauce
Prep time: 10 minutes | Cook time: 20 minutes | Serves 2

1 pound (454 g) boneless, skinless chicken breasts, cut into 1-inch pieces
¼ cup ketchup
1 tablespoon tomato-based chili sauce, such as Heinz
1 tablespoon soy sauce
1 tablespoon rice vinegar
2 teaspoons vegetable oil
1 teaspoon hot sauce, such as Tabasco
½ teaspoon garlic powder
¼ teaspoon cayenne pepper
2 scallions, thinly sliced
Cooked white rice, for serving

1. Preheat the Oster to 350°F (177°C).
2. In a bowl, combine the chicken, ketchup, chili sauce, soy sauce, vinegar, oil, hot sauce, garlic powder, cayenne, and three-quarters of the scallions and toss until evenly coated.
3. Scrape the chicken and sauce into a metal cake pan and place the pan in the Oster. Bake until the chicken is cooked through and the sauce is reduced to a thick glaze, about 20 minutes, flipping the chicken pieces halfway through.
4. Remove the pan from the Oster. Spoon the chicken and sauce over rice and top with the remaining scallions. Serve immediately.

Havarti Chicken and Ham Burgers
Prep time: 10 minutes | Cook time: 13 to 16 minutes | Serves 4

⅓ cup soft bread crumbs
3 tablespoons milk
1 egg, beaten
½ teaspoon dried thyme
Pinch salt
Freshly ground black pepper, to taste
1¼ pounds (567 g) ground chicken
¼ cup finely chopped ham
⅓ cup grated Havarti cheese
Olive oil for misting

1. Preheat the Oster to 350°F (177°C).
2. In a medium bowl, combine the bread crumbs, milk, egg, thyme, salt, and pepper. Add the chicken and mix gently but thoroughly with clean hands.
3. Form the chicken into eight thin patties and place on waxed paper.
4. Top four of the patties with the ham and cheese. Top with remaining four patties and gently press the edges together to seal, so the ham and cheese mixture is in the middle of the burger.
5. Place the burgers in the baking pan and mist with olive oil. Bake for 13 to 16 minutes or until the chicken is thoroughly cooked to 165°F (74°C) as measured with a meat thermometer. Serve immediately.

Cilantro Chicken with Lime
Prep time: 35 minutes | Cook time: 12 minutes | Serves 4

4 (4-ounce / 113-g) boneless, skinless chicken breasts
½ cup chopped fresh cilantro
Juice of 1 lime
Chicken seasoning or rub, to taste
Salt and ground black pepper, to taste
Cooking spray

1. Put the chicken breasts in the large bowl, then add the cilantro, lime juice, chicken seasoning, salt, and black pepper. Toss to coat well.
2. Wrap the bowl in plastic and refrigerate to marinate for at least 30 minutes.
3. Preheat the Oster to 425°F (218°C). Spritz the baking pan with cooking spray.
4. Remove the marinated chicken breasts from the bowl and place in the preheated Oster. Spritz with cooking spray. You may need to work in batches to avoid overcrowding.
5. Bake for 12 minutes or until the internal temperature of the chicken reaches at least 165°F (74°C). Flip the breasts halfway through.
6. Serve immediately.

Pineapple and Peach Chicken Breasts
Prep time: 10 minutes | Cook time: 14 to 15 minutes | Serves 4

1 pound (454 g) low-sodium boneless, skinless chicken breasts, cut into 1-inch pieces
1 medium red onion, chopped
1 (8-ounce / 227-g) can pineapple chunks, drained, ¼ cup juice reserved
1 tablespoon peanut oil or safflower oil
1 peach, peeled, pitted, and cubed
1 tablespoon cornstarch
½ teaspoon ground ginger
¼ teaspoon ground allspice
Brown rice, cooked (optional)

1. Preheat the Oster to 380°F (193°C).
2. In a medium metal bowl, mix the chicken, red onion, pineapple, and peanut oil. Bake in the Oster for 9 minutes. Remove and stir.
3. Add the peach and return the bowl to the Oster. Bake for 3 minutes more. Remove and stir again.
4. In a small bowl, whisk the reserved pineapple juice, the cornstarch, ginger, and allspice well. Add to the chicken mixture and stir to combine.
5. Bake for 2 to 3 minutes more, or until the chicken reaches an internal temperature of 165°F (74°C) on a meat thermometer and the sauce is slightly thickened.
6. Serve immediately over hot cooked brown rice, if desired.

BBQ Chicken Breast with Creamy Coleslaw
Prep time: 10 minutes | Cook time: 20 minutes | Serves 2

3 cups shredded coleslaw mix
Salt and pepper
2 (12-ounce / 340-g) bone-in split chicken breasts, trimmed
1 teaspoon vegetable oil
2 tablespoons barbecue sauce, plus extra for serving
2 tablespoons mayonnaise
2 tablespoons sour cream
1 teaspoon distilled white vinegar, plus extra for seasoning
¼ teaspoon sugar

1. Preheat the Oster to 350°F (177°C).
2. Toss coleslaw mix and ¼ teaspoon salt in a colander set over bowl. Let sit until wilted slightly, about 30 minutes. Rinse, drain, and dry well with a dish towel.
3. Meanwhile, pat chicken dry with paper towels, rub with oil, and season with salt and pepper. Arrange breasts skin-side down the baking pan, spaced evenly apart, alternating ends. Bake for 10 minutes. Flip breasts and brush skin side with barbecue sauce. Return the pan to Oster and bake until well browned and chicken registers 160°F (71°C), 10 to 15 minutes.
4. Transfer chicken to serving platter, tent loosely with aluminum foil, and let rest for 5 minutes. While chicken rests, whisk mayonnaise, sour cream, vinegar, sugar, and pinch pepper together in a large bowl. Stir in coleslaw mix and season with salt, pepper, and additional vinegar to taste. Serve chicken with coleslaw, passing extra barbecue sauce separately.

Smoked Paprika Chicken Wings
Prep time: 15 minutes | Cook time: 24 minutes | Serves 4

1 pound (454 g) chicken wings
3 tablespoons vegetable oil
½ cup all-purpose flour
½ teaspoon smoked paprika
½ teaspoon garlic powder
½ teaspoon kosher salt
1½ teaspoons freshly cracked black pepper

1. Preheat the Oster to 425°F (218°C).
2. Place the chicken wings in a large bowl. Drizzle the vegetable oil over wings and toss to coat.
3. In a separate bowl, whisk together the flour, paprika, garlic powder, salt, and pepper until combined.
4. Dredge the wings in the flour mixture one at a time, coating them well, and place in the baking pan. Bake for 24 minutes, turning the wings halfway through the cooking time, until the breading is browned and crunchy.
5. Serve hot.

Dill Chicken Strips with Italian Dressing
Prep time: 15 minutes | Cook time: 10 minutes | Serves 4

2 whole boneless, skinless chicken breasts, halved lengthwise
1 cup Italian dressing
3 cups finely crushed potato chips
1 tablespoon dried dill weed
1 tablespoon garlic powder
1 large egg, beaten
Cooking spray

1. In a large resealable bag, combine the chicken and Italian dressing. Seal the bag and refrigerate to marinate at least 1 hour.
2. In a shallow dish, stir together the potato chips, dill, and garlic powder. Place the beaten egg in a second shallow dish.
3. Remove the chicken from the marinade. Roll the chicken pieces in the egg and the potato chip mixture, coating thoroughly.
4. Preheat the Oster to 325°F (163°C). Line the baking pan with parchment paper.
5. Place the coated chicken on the parchment and spritz with cooking spray.
6. Bake for 5 minutes. Flip the chicken, spritz it with cooking spray, and bake for 5 minutes more until the outsides are crispy and the insides are no longer pink. Serve immediately.

Fajita Chicken Strips with Bell Peppers
Prep time: 10 minutes | Cook time: 16 minutes | Serves 4

1 pound (454 g) boneless, skinless chicken tenderloins, cut into strips
3 bell peppers, any color, cut into chunks
1 onion, cut into chunks
1 tablespoon olive oil
1 tablespoon fajita seasoning mix
Cooking spray

1. Preheat the Oster to 395°F (202°C).
2. In a large bowl, mix together the chicken, bell peppers, onion, olive oil, and fajita seasoning mix until completely coated.
3. Spray the baking pan lightly with cooking spray.
4. Place the chicken and vegetables in the pan and lightly spray with cooking spray.
5. Bake for 8 minutes. Stir and bake for an additional 8 minutes, until the chicken is cooked through and the veggies are starting to char.
6. Serve warm.

Garlic Chicken Thighs with Scallions
Prep time: 10 minutes | Cook time: 30 minutes | Serves 1 to 2

2 tablespoons chicken stock
2 tablespoons reduced-sodium soy sauce
1½ tablespoons sugar
4 garlic cloves, smashed and peeled
2 large scallions, cut into 2- to 3-inch batons, plus more, thinly sliced, for garnish
2 bone-in, skin-on chicken thighs (7 to 8 ounces / 198 to 227 g each)

1. Preheat the Oster to 375°F (191°C).
2. In a metal cake pan, combine the chicken stock, soy sauce, and sugar and stir until the sugar dissolves. Add the garlic cloves, scallions, and chicken thighs, turning the thighs to coat them in the marinade, then resting them skin-side up. Place the pan in the Oster and bake, flipping the thighs every 5 minutes after the first 10 minutes, until the chicken is cooked through and the marinade is reduced to a sticky glaze over the chicken, about 30 minutes.
3. Remove the pan from the Oster and serve the chicken thighs warm, with any remaining glaze spooned over top and sprinkled with more sliced scallions.

Ginger Chicken Thighs with Cilantro
Prep time: 10 minutes | Cook time: 10 minutes | Serves 4

¼ cup julienned peeled fresh ginger
2 tablespoons vegetable oil
1 tablespoon honey
1 tablespoon soy sauce
1 tablespoon ketchup
1 teaspoon garam masala
1 teaspoon ground turmeric
¼ teaspoon kosher salt
½ teaspoon cayenne pepper
Vegetable oil spray
1 pound (454 g) boneless, skinless chicken thighs, cut crosswise into thirds
¼ cup chopped fresh cilantro, for garnish

1. In a small bowl, combine the ginger, oil, honey, soy sauce, ketchup, garam masala, turmeric, salt, and cayenne. Whisk until well combined. Place the chicken in a resealable plastic bag and pour the marinade over. Seal the bag and massage to cover all of the chicken with the marinade. Marinate at room temperature for 30 minutes or in the refrigerator for up to 24 hours.
2. Preheat the Oster to 350°F (177°C).
3. Spray the baking pan with vegetable oil spray and add the chicken and as much of the marinade and julienned ginger as possible. Bake for 10 minutes. Use a meat thermometer to ensure the chicken has reached an internal temperature of 165°F (74°C).
4. To serve, garnish with cilantro.

Turkey, Cauliflower and Onion Meatloaf
Prep time: 15 minutes | Cook time: 50 minutes | Serves 6

2 pounds (907 g) lean ground turkey
1⅓ cups riced cauliflower
2 large eggs, lightly beaten
¼ cup almond flour
⅔ cup chopped yellow or white onion
1 teaspoon ground dried turmeric
1 teaspoon ground cumin
1 teaspoon ground coriander
1 tablespoon minced garlic
1 teaspoon salt
1 teaspoon ground black pepper
Cooking spray

1. Preheat the Oster to 350°F (177°C). Spritz a loaf pan with cooking spray.
2. Combine all the ingredients in a large bowl. Stir to mix well. Pour half of the mixture in the prepared loaf pan and press with a spatula to coat the bottom evenly. Spritz the mixture with cooking spray.
3. Arrange the loaf pan in the preheated Oster and bake for 25 minutes or until the meat is well browned and the internal temperature reaches at least 165°F (74°C). Repeat with remaining mixture.
4. Remove the loaf pan from the Oster and serve immediately.

Garlic Whole Chicken Bake
Prep time: 10 minutes | Cook time: 1 hour | Serves 2 to 4

½ cup melted butter
3 tablespoons garlic, minced
Salt, to taste
1 teaspoon ground black pepper
1 (1-pound / 454-g) whole chicken

1. Preheat the Oster to 350°F (177°C).
2. Combine the butter with garlic, salt, and ground black pepper in a small bowl.
3. Brush the butter mixture over the whole chicken, then place the chicken in the preheated Oster, skin side down.
4. Bake the chicken for an hour or until an instant-read thermometer inserted in the thickest part of the chicken registers at least 165°F (74°C). Flip the chicken halfway through.
5. Remove the chicken from the Oster and allow to cool for 15 minutes before serving.

Garlic Baked Chicken Wings
Prep time: 10 minutes | Cook time: 18 minutes | Serves 4

1 tablespoon olive oil
8 whole chicken wings
Chicken seasoning or rub, to taste
1 teaspoon garlic powder
Freshly ground black pepper, to taste

1. Preheat the Oster to 425°F (218°C). Grease the baking pan with olive oil.
2. On a clean work surface, rub the chicken wings with chicken seasoning and rub, garlic powder, and ground black pepper.
3. Arrange the well-coated chicken wings in the preheated Oster. Bake for 18 minutes or until the internal temperature of the chicken wings reaches at least 165°F (74°C). Flip the chicken wings halfway through.
4. Remove the chicken wings from the Oster. Serve immediately.

Pineapple Chicken Thighs with Ginger
Prep time: 10 minutes | Cook time: 15 minutes | Serves 4

4 boneless, skinless chicken thighs (about 1½ pounds / 680 g)
1 (8-ounce / 227-g) can pineapple chunks in juice, drained, ¼ cup juice reserved
¼ cup soy sauce
¼ cup sugar
2 tablespoons ketchup
1 tablespoon minced fresh ginger
1 tablespoon minced garlic
¼ cup chopped scallions

1. Use a fork to pierce the chicken all over to allow the marinade to penetrate better. Place the chicken in a large bowl or large resealable plastic bag.
2. Set the drained pineapple chunks aside. In a small microwave-safe bowl, combine the pineapple juice, soy sauce, sugar, ketchup, ginger, and garlic. Pour half the sauce over the chicken; toss to coat. Reserve the remaining sauce. Marinate the chicken at room temperature for 30 minutes, or cover and refrigerate for up to 24 hours.
3. Preheat the Oster to 350°F (177°C).
4. Place the chicken in the baking pan, discarding marinade. Bake for 15 minutes, turning halfway through the cooking time.
5. Meanwhile, microwave the reserved sauce on high for 45 to 60 seconds, stirring every 15 seconds, until the sauce has the consistency of a thick glaze.
6. At the end of the cooking time, use a meat thermometer to ensure the chicken has reached an internal temperature of 165°F (74°C).
7. Transfer the chicken to a serving platter. Pour the sauce over the chicken. Garnish with the pineapple chunks and scallions before serving.

Panko Breaded Chicken Nuggets
Prep time: 10 minutes | Cook time: 10 minutes | Serves 4

1 pound (454 g) boneless, skinless chicken breasts, cut into 1-inch pieces
2 tablespoons panko bread crumbs
6 tablespoons bread crumbs
Chicken seasoning or rub, to taste
Salt and ground black pepper, to taste
2 eggs
Cooking spray

1. Preheat the Oster to 425°F (218°C). Spritz the baking pan with cooking spray.
2. Combine the bread crumbs, chicken seasoning, salt, and black pepper in a large bowl. Stir to mix well. Whisk the eggs in a separate bowl.
3. Dunk the chicken pieces in the egg mixture, then in the bread crumb mixture. Shake the excess off.
4. Arrange the well-coated chicken pieces in the pan. Spritz with cooking spray and bake for 10 minutes or until crispy and golden brown. You may need to work in batches to avoid overcrowding.
5. Serve immediately.

Buttermilk-Marinated Chicken Breast
Prep time: 5 minutes | Cook time: 40 minutes | Serves 2

1 large bone-in, skin-on chicken breast
1 cup buttermilk
1½ teaspoons dried parsley
1½ teaspoons dried chives
¾ teaspoon kosher salt
½ teaspoon dried dill
½ teaspoon onion powder
¼ teaspoon garlic powder
¼ teaspoon dried tarragon
Cooking spray

1. Place the chicken breast in a bowl and pour over the buttermilk, turning the chicken in it to make sure it's completely covered. Let the chicken stand at room temperature for at least 20 minutes or in the refrigerator for up to 4 hours.
2. Meanwhile, in a bowl, stir together the parsley, chives, salt, dill, onion powder, garlic powder, and tarragon.
3. Preheat the Oster to 300°F (149°C).
4. Remove the chicken from the buttermilk, letting the excess drip off, then place the chicken skin-side up directly in the Oster. Sprinkle the seasoning mix all over the top of the chicken breast, then let stand until the herb mix soaks into the buttermilk, at least 5 minutes.
5. Spray the top of the chicken with cooking spray. Bake for 10 minutes, then increase the temperature to 350°F (177°C) and bake until an instant-read thermometer inserted into the thickest part of the breast reads 160°F (71°C) and the chicken is deep golden brown, 30 to 35 minutes.
6. Transfer the chicken breast to a cutting board, let rest for 10 minutes, then cut the meat off the bone and cut into thick slices for serving.

Spice-Marinated Chicken Drumsticks

Prep time: 10 minutes | Cook time: 17 minutes | Serves 4

8 (4- to 5-ounce / 113- to 142-g) skinless bone-in chicken drumsticks
½ cup plain full-fat or low-fat yogurt
¼ cup buttermilk
2 teaspoons minced garlic
2 teaspoons minced fresh ginger
2 teaspoons ground cinnamon
2 teaspoons ground coriander
2 teaspoons mild paprika
1 teaspoon salt
1 teaspoon Tabasco hot red pepper sauce

1. Preheat the Oster to 400°F (204°C).
2. In a large bowl, stir together all the ingredients except for chicken drumsticks until well combined. Add the chicken drumsticks to the bowl and toss until well coated. Cover in plastic and set in the refrigerator to marinate for 1 hour, tossing once.
3. Arrange the marinated drumsticks in a single layer in the baking pan, leaving enough space between them. Bake for 17 minutes, or until the internal temperature of the chicken drumsticks reaches 160°F (71°C) on a meat thermometer. Flip the drumsticks once halfway through to ensure even cooking.
4. Transfer the drumsticks to plates. Rest for 5 minutes before serving.

Chapter 7
Fish and Seafood

Honey-Glazed Cod with Sesame Seeds
Prep time: 5 minutes | Cook time: 7 to 9 minutes | Makes 1 fillet

1 tablespoon reduced-sodium soy sauce
2 teaspoons honey
Cooking spray
6 ounces (170 g) fresh cod fillet
1 teaspoon sesame seeds

1. Preheat the Oster to 360°F (182°C).
2. In a small bowl, combine the soy sauce and honey.
3. Spray the baking pan with cooking spray, then place the cod in the pan, brush with the soy mixture, and sprinkle sesame seeds on top. Bake for 7 to 9 minutes or until opaque.
4. Remove the fish and allow to cool on a wire rack for 5 minutes before serving.

Almond-Coconut Flounder Fillets
Prep time: 8 minutes | Cook time: 12 minutes | Serves 2

2 flounder fillets, patted dry
1 egg
½ teaspoon Worcestershire sauce
¼ cup almond flour
¼ cup coconut flour
½ teaspoon coarse sea salt
½ teaspoon lemon pepper
¼ teaspoon chili powder
Cooking spray

1. Preheat the Oster to 390°F (199°C). Spritz the baking pan with cooking spray.
2. In a shallow bowl, beat together the egg with Worcestershire sauce until well incorporated.
3. In another bowl, thoroughly combine the almond flour, coconut flour, sea salt, lemon pepper, and chili powder.
4. Dredge the fillets in the egg mixture, shaking off any excess, then roll in the flour mixture to coat well.
5. Place the fillets in the pan and bake for 7 minutes. Flip the fillets and spray with cooking spray. Continue cooking for 5 minutes, or until the fish is flaky.
6. Serve warm.

Lemon-Caper Salmon Burgers
Prep time: 15 minutes | Cook time: 15 minutes | Serves 5

Lemon-Caper Rémoulade:
½ cup mayonnaise
2 tablespoons minced drained capers
2 tablespoons chopped fresh parsley
2 teaspoons fresh lemon juice
Salmon Patties:
1 pound (454 g) wild salmon fillet, skinned and pin bones removed
6 tablespoons panko bread crumbs
¼ cup minced red onion plus ¼ cup slivered for serving
1 garlic clove, minced
1 large egg, lightly beaten
1 tablespoon Dijon mustard
1 teaspoon fresh lemon juice
1 tablespoon chopped fresh parsley
½ teaspoon kosher salt
For Serving:
5 whole wheat potato buns or gluten-free buns
10 butter lettuce leaves

1. For the lemon-caper rémoulade: In a small bowl, combine the mayonnaise, capers, parsley, and lemon juice and mix well.
2. For the salmon patties: Cut off a 4-ounce / 113-g piece of the salmon and transfer to a food processor. Pulse until it becomes pasty. With a sharp knife, chop the remaining salmon into small cubes.
3. In a medium bowl, combine the chopped and processed salmon with the panko, minced red onion, garlic, egg, mustard, lemon juice, parsley, and salt. Toss gently to combine. Form the mixture into 5 patties about ¾ inch thick. Refrigerate for at least 30 minutes.
4. Preheat the Oster to 425°F (218°C).
5. Working in batches, place the patties in the baking pan. Bake for about 15 minutes, gently flipping halfway, until golden and cooked through.
6. To serve, transfer each patty to a bun. Top each with 2 lettuce leaves, 2 tablespoons of the rémoulade, and the slivered red onions.

Almond-Lemon Crusted Fish
Prep time: 10 minutes | Cook time: 9 minutes | Serves 4

½ cup raw whole almonds
1 scallion, finely chopped
Grated zest and juice of 1 lemon
½ tablespoon extra-virgin olive oil
¾ teaspoon kosher salt, divided
Freshly ground black pepper, to taste
4 (6 ounces / 170 g each) skinless fish fillets
Cooking spray
1 teaspoon Dijon mustard

1. In a food processor, pulse the almonds to coarsely chop. Transfer to a small bowl and add the scallion, lemon zest, and olive oil. Season with ¼ teaspoon of the salt and pepper to taste and mix to combine.
2. Spray the top of the fish with oil and squeeze the lemon juice over the fish. Season with the remaining ½ teaspoon salt and pepper to taste. Spread the mustard on top of the fish. Dividing evenly, press the almond mixture onto the top of the fillets to adhere.
3. Preheat the Oster to 400°F (204°C).
4. Working in batches, place the fillets in the baking pan in a single layer. Bake for 9 minutes, until the crumbs start to brown and the fish is cooked through.
5. Serve immediately.

Italian-Style Salmon Patties
Prep time: 10 minutes | Cook time: 8 minutes | Serves 4

2 (5-ounce / 142 g) cans salmon, flaked
2 large eggs, beaten
⅓ cup minced onion
⅔ cup panko bread crumbs
1½ teaspoons Italian-Style seasoning
1 teaspoon garlic powder
Cooking spray

1. In a medium bowl, stir together the salmon, eggs, and onion.
2. In a small bowl, whisk the bread crumbs, Italian-Style seasoning, and garlic powder until blended. Add the bread crumb mixture to the salmon mixture and stir until blended. Shape the mixture into 8 patties.
3. Preheat the Oster to 350°F (177°C). Line the baking pan with parchment paper.
4. Working in batches as needed, place the patties on the parchment and spritz with oil.
5. Bake for 4 minutes. Flip, spritz the patties with oil, and bake for 4 to 8 minutes more, until browned and firm. Serve.

Old Bay Salmon Patty Bites
Prep time: 15 minutes | Cook time: 15 minutes | Serves 4

4 (5-ounce / 142-g) cans pink salmon, skinless, boneless in water, drained
2 eggs, beaten
1 cup whole-wheat panko bread crumbs
4 tablespoons finely minced red bell pepper
2 tablespoons parsley flakes
2 teaspoons Old Bay seasoning
Cooking spray

1. Preheat the Oster to 385°F (196°C).
2. Spray the baking pan lightly with cooking spray.
3. In a medium bowl, mix the salmon, eggs, panko bread crumbs, red bell pepper, parsley flakes, and Old Bay seasoning.
4. Using a small cookie scoop, form the mixture into 20 balls.
5. Place the salmon bites in the pan in a single layer and spray lightly with cooking spray. You may need to cook them in batches.
6. Bake for 15 minutes, stirring a couple of times for even cooking.
7. Serve immediately.

Garlic-Lemon Shrimp
Prep time: 10 minutes | Cook time: 14 minutes | Serves 4

2 teaspoons minced garlic
2 teaspoons lemon juice
2 teaspoons olive oil
½ to 1 teaspoon crushed red pepper
12 ounces (340 g) medium shrimp, deveined, with tails on
Cooking spray

1. In a medium bowl, mix together the garlic, lemon juice, olive oil, and crushed red pepper to make a marinade.
2. Add the shrimp and toss to coat in the marinade. Cover with plastic wrap and place the bowl in the refrigerator for 30 minutes.
3. Preheat the Oster to 425°F (218°C). Spray the baking pan lightly with cooking spray.
4. Place the shrimp in the pan. Bake for 6 minutes. Stir and bake until the shrimp are cooked through and nicely browned, an additional 8 minutes. Cool for 5 minutes before serving.

Trout Amandine with Lemon Butter Sauce
Prep time: 20 minutes | Cook time: 8 minutes | Serves 4

Trout Amandine:
⅔ cup toasted almonds
⅓ cup grated Parmesan cheese
1 teaspoon salt
½ teaspoon freshly ground black pepper
2 tablespoons butter, melted
4 (4-ounce / 113-g) trout fillets, or salmon fillets
Cooking spray
Lemon Butter Sauce:
8 tablespoons (1 stick) butter, melted
2 tablespoons freshly squeezed lemon juice
½ teaspoon Worcestershire sauce
½ teaspoon salt
½ teaspoon freshly ground black pepper
¼ teaspoon hot sauce

1. In a blender or food processor, pulse the almonds for 5 to 10 seconds until finely processed. Transfer to a shallow bowl and whisk in the Parmesan cheese, salt, and pepper. Place the melted butter in another shallow bowl.
2. One at a time, dip the fish in the melted butter, then the almond mixture, coating thoroughly.
3. Preheat the Oster to 300°F (149°C). Line the baking pan with parchment paper.
4. Place the coated fish on the parchment and spritz with oil.
5. Bake for 4 minutes. Flip the fish, spritz it with oil, and bake for 4 minutes more until the fish flakes easily with a fork.
6. In a small bowl, whisk the butter, lemon juice, Worcestershire sauce, salt, pepper, and hot sauce until blended.
7. Serve with the fish.

Parmesan Sriracha Tuna Patty Sliders
Prep time: 15 minutes | Cook time: 15 minutes | Serves 4

3 (5-ounce / 142-g) cans tuna, packed in water
⅔ cup whole-wheat panko bread crumbs
⅓ cup shredded Parmesan cheese
1 tablespoon sriracha
¾ teaspoon black pepper
10 whole-wheat slider buns
Cooking spray

1. Preheat the Oster to 375°F (191°C).
2. Spray the baking pan lightly with cooking spray.
3. In a medium bowl combine the tuna, bread crumbs, Parmesan cheese, sriracha, and black pepper and stir to combine.
4. Form the mixture into 10 patties.
5. Place the patties in the pan in a single layer. Spray the patties lightly with cooking spray. You may need to cook them in batches.
6. Bake for 8 minutes. Turn the patties over and lightly spray with cooking spray. Bake until golden brown and crisp, another 7 more minutes. Serve warm.

Paprika Tilapia with Garlic Aioli
Prep time: 5 minutes | Cook time: 15 minutes | Serves 4

Tilapia:
4 tilapia fillets
1 tablespoon extra-virgin olive oil
1 teaspoon garlic powder
1 teaspoon paprika
1 teaspoon dried basil
A pinch of lemon-pepper seasoning
Garlic Aioli:
2 garlic cloves, minced
1 tablespoon mayonnaise
Juice of ½ lemon
1 teaspoon extra-virgin olive oil
Salt and pepper, to taste

1. Preheat the Oster to 400°F (204°C).
2. On a clean work surface, brush both sides of each fillet with the olive oil. Sprinkle with the garlic powder, paprika, basil, and lemon-pepper seasoning.
3. Place the fillets in the baking pan and bake for 15 minutes, flipping the fillets halfway through, or until the fish flakes easily and is no longer translucent in the center.
4. Meanwhile, make the garlic aioli: Whisk together the garlic, mayo, lemon juice, olive oil, salt, and pepper in a small bowl until smooth.
5. Remove the fish from the pan and serve with the garlic aioli on the side.

Breaded Calamari Rings with Lemon
Prep time: 5 minutes | Cook time: 12 minutes | Serves 4

2 large eggs
2 garlic cloves, minced
½ cup cornstarch
1 cup bread crumbs
1 pound (454 g) calamari rings
Cooking spray
1 lemon, sliced

1. In a small bowl, whisk the eggs with minced garlic. Place the cornstarch and bread crumbs into separate shallow dishes.
2. Dredge the calamari rings in the cornstarch, then dip in the egg mixture, shaking off any excess, finally roll them in the bread crumbs to coat well. Let the calamari rings sit for 10 minutes in the refrigerator.
3. Preheat the Oster to 425°F (218°C). Spritz the baking pan with cooking spray.
4. Put the calamari rings in the pan and bake for 15 minutes until cooked through. Stir halfway through the cooking time.
5. Serve the calamari rings with the lemon slices sprinkled on top.

Baked Bacon-Wrapped Scallops

Prep time: 5 minutes | Cook time: 12 minutes | Serves 4

8 slices bacon, cut in half
16 sea scallops, patted dry
Cooking spray
Salt and freshly ground black pepper, to taste
16 toothpicks, soaked in water for at least 30 minutes

1. Preheat the Oster to 395°F (202°C).
2. On a clean work surface, wrap half of a slice of bacon around each scallop and secure with a toothpick.
3. Lay the bacon-wrapped scallops in the baking pan in a single layer. You may need to work in batches to avoid overcrowding.
4. Spritz the scallops with cooking spray and sprinkle the salt and pepper to season.
5. Bake for 12 minutes, flipping the scallops halfway through, or until the bacon is cooked through and the scallops are firm.
6. Remove the scallops from the Oster to a plate and repeat with the remaining scallops. Serve warm.

Breaded Fresh Scallops

Prep time: 5 minutes | Cook time: 10 minutes | Serves 4

1 egg
3 tablespoons flour
1 cup bread crumbs
1 pound (454 g) fresh scallops
2 tablespoons olive oil
Salt and black pepper, to taste

1. Preheat the Oster to 385°F (196°C).
2. In a bowl, lightly beat the egg. Place the flour and bread crumbs into separate shallow dishes.
3. Dredge the scallops in the flour and shake off any excess. Dip the flour-coated scallops in the beaten egg and roll in the bread crumbs.
4. Brush the scallops generously with olive oil and season with salt and pepper, to taste.
5. Arrange the scallops in the baking pan and bake for 10 minutes, or until the scallops are firm and reach an internal temperature of just 145°F (63°C) on a meat thermometer. Stir halfway through the cooking time.
6. Let the scallops cool for 5 minutes and serve.

Cajun Cod with Lemon Pepper

Prep time: 5 minutes | Cook time: 12 minutes | Makes 2 cod fillets

1 tablespoon Cajun seasoning
1 teaspoon salt
½ teaspoon lemon pepper
½ teaspoon freshly ground black pepper
2 (8-ounce / 227-g) cod fillets
Cooking spray
2 tablespoons unsalted butter, melted
1 lemon, cut into 4 wedges

1. Preheat the Oster to 360°F (182°C). Spritz the baking pan with cooking spray.
2. Thoroughly combine the Cajun seasoning, salt, lemon pepper, and black pepper in a small bowl. Rub this mixture all over the cod fillets until completely coated.
3. Put the fillets in the pan and brush the melted butter over both sides of each fillet.
4. Bake in the preheated Oster for 12 minutes, flipping the fillets halfway through, or until the fish flakes easily with a fork.
5. Remove the fillets from the Oster and serve with fresh lemon wedges.

Cayenne Prawns with Cumin

Prep time: 10 minutes | Cook time: 10 minutes | Serves 2

8 prawns, cleaned
Salt and black pepper, to taste
½ teaspoon ground cayenne pepper
½ teaspoon garlic powder
½ teaspoon ground cumin
½ teaspoon red chili flakes
Cooking spray

1. Preheat the Oster to 375°F (191°C). Spritz the baking pan with cooking spray.
2. Toss the remaining ingredients in a large bowl until the prawns are well coated.
3. Spread the coated prawns evenly in the pan and spray them with cooking spray.
4. Bake for 10 minutes, flipping the prawns halfway through, or until the prawns are pink.
5. Remove the prawns from the pan to a plate.

Tuna Casserole with Peppers
Prep time: 10 minutes | Cook time: 16 minutes | Serves 4

½ tablespoon sesame oil
⅓ cup yellow onions, chopped
½ bell pepper, seeded and chopped
2 cups canned tuna, chopped
Cooking spray
5 eggs, beaten
½ chili pepper, seeded and finely minced
1½ tablespoons sour cream
⅓ teaspoon dried basil
⅓ teaspoon dried oregano
Fine sea salt and ground black pepper, to taste

1. Heat the sesame oil in a nonstick skillet over medium heat until it shimmers.
2. Add the onions and bell pepper and sauté for 4 minutes, stirring occasionally, or until tender.
3. Add the canned tuna and keep stirring until the tuna is heated through.
4. Meanwhile, coat a baking dish lightly with cooking spray.
5. Transfer the tuna mixture to the baking dish, along with the beaten eggs, chili pepper, sour cream, basil, and oregano. Stir to combine well. Season with sea salt and black pepper.
6. Preheat the Oster to 325°F (160°C).
7. Place the baking dish in the Oster and bake for 12 minutes, or until the top is lightly browned and the eggs are completely set.
8. Remove from the Oster and serve on a plate.

Tomato Chili Fish Curry
Prep time: 10 minutes | Cook time: 24 minutes | Serves 4

2 tablespoons sunflower oil
1 pound (454 g) fish, chopped
1 ripe tomato, pureéd
2 red chilies, chopped
1 shallot, minced
1 garlic clove, minced
1 cup coconut milk
1 tablespoon coriander powder
1 teaspoon red curry paste
½ teaspoon fenugreek seeds
Salt and white pepper, to taste

1. Preheat the Oster to 400°F (204°C). Coat the baking pan with the sunflower oil.
2. Place the fish in the pan and bake for 12 minutes. Flip the fish halfway through the cooking time.
3. When done, stir in the remaining ingredients and return to the Oster.
4. Reduce the temperature to 350°F (177°C) and bake for another 12 minutes until heated through.
5. Cool for 5 to 8 minutes before serving.

Crab Ratatouille with Tomatoes and Eggplant
Prep time: 15 minutes | Cook time: 11 to 14 minutes | Serves 4

1½ cups peeled and cubed eggplant
2 large tomatoes, chopped
1 red bell pepper, chopped
1 onion, chopped
1 tablespoon olive oil
½ teaspoon dried basil
½ teaspoon dried thyme
Pinch salt
Freshly ground black pepper, to taste
1½ cups cooked crab meat

1. Preheat the Oster to 400°F (204°C).
2. In a metal bowl, stir together the eggplant, tomatoes, bell pepper, onion, olive oil, basil and thyme. Season with salt and pepper.
3. Place the bowl in the preheated Oster and bake for 9 minutes.
4. Remove the bowl from the Oster. Add the crab meat and stir well and bake for another 2 to 5 minutes, or until the vegetables are softened and the ratatouille is bubbling.
5. Serve warm.

Crab and Fish Cakes with Celery
Prep time: 20 minutes | Cook time: 10 to 12 minutes | Serves 4

8 ounces (227 g) imitation crab meat
4 ounces (113 g) leftover cooked fish (such as cod, pollock, or haddock)
2 tablespoons minced celery
2 tablespoons minced green onion
2 tablespoons light mayonnaise
1 tablespoon plus 2 teaspoons Worcestershire sauce
¾ cup crushed saltine cracker crumbs
2 teaspoons dried parsley flakes
1 teaspoon prepared yellow mustard
½ teaspoon garlic powder
½ teaspoon dried dill weed, crushed
½ teaspoon Old Bay seasoning
½ cup panko bread crumbs
Cooking spray

1. Preheat the Oster to 390°F (199°C).
2. Pulse the crab meat and fish in a food processor until finely chopped.
3. Transfer the meat mixture to a large bowl, along with the celery, green onion, mayo, Worcestershire sauce, cracker crumbs, parsley flakes, mustard, garlic powder, dill weed, and Old Bay seasoning. Stir to mix well.
4. Scoop out the meat mixture and form into 8 equal-sized patties with your hands.
5. Place the panko bread crumbs on a plate. Roll the patties in the bread crumbs until they are evenly coated on both sides. Spritz the patties with cooking spray.
6. Put the patties in the baking pan and bake for 10 to 12 minutes, flipping them halfway through, or until they are golden brown and cooked through.
7. Divide the patties among four plates and serve.

Salmon and Carrot Spring Rolls

Prep time: 20 minutes | Cook time: 15 to 19 minutes | Serves 4

½ pound (227 g) salmon fillet
1 teaspoon toasted sesame oil
1 onion, sliced
1 carrot, shredded
1 yellow bell pepper, thinly sliced
⅓ cup chopped fresh flat-leaf parsley
¼ cup chopped fresh basil
8 rice paper wrappers

1. Preheat the Oster to 370°F (188°C).
2. Arrange the salmon in the baking pan. Drizzle the sesame oil all over the salmon and scatter the onion on top. Bake for 8 to 10 minutes, or until the fish flakes when pressed lightly with a fork.
3. Meanwhile, fill a small shallow bowl with warm water. One by one, dip the rice paper wrappers into the water for a few seconds or just until moistened, then put them on a work surface.
4. Make the spring rolls: Place ⅛ of the salmon and onion mixture, carrot, bell pepper, parsley, and basil into the center of the rice wrapper and fold the sides over the filling. Roll up the wrapper carefully and tightly like you would a burrito. Repeat with the remaining wrappers and filling.
5. Transfer the rolls to the pan and bake at 380°F (193°C) for 7 to 9 minutes, or until the rolls are crispy and lightly browned.
6. Cut each roll in half and serve warm.

Swordfish Steaks with Jalapeño

Prep time: 10 minutes | Cook time: 13 minutes | Serves 4

4 (4-ounce / 113-g) swordfish steaks
½ teaspoon toasted sesame oil
1 jalapeño pepper, finely minced
2 garlic cloves, grated
2 tablespoons freshly squeezed lemon juice
1 tablespoon grated fresh ginger
½ teaspoon Chinese five-spice powder
⅛ teaspoon freshly ground black pepper

1. On a clean work surface, place the swordfish steaks and brush both sides of the fish with the sesame oil.
2. Combine the jalapeño, garlic, lemon juice, ginger, five-spice powder, and black pepper in a small bowl and stir to mix well. Rub the mixture all over the fish until completely coated. Allow to sit for 10 minutes.
3. Preheat the Oster to 410°F (210°C).
4. Arrange the swordfish steaks in the baking pan and bake for 13 minutes until cooked through, flipping the steaks halfway through.
5. Cool for 5 minutes before serving.

White Fish, Carrot and Cabbage Tacos

Prep time: 10 minutes | Cook time: 15 minutes | Serves 4

1 pound (454 g) white fish fillets
2 teaspoons olive oil
3 tablespoons freshly squeezed lemon juice, divided
1½ cups chopped red cabbage
1 large carrot, grated
½ cup low-sodium salsa
⅓ cup low-fat Greek yogurt
4 soft low-sodium whole-wheat tortillas

1. Preheat the Oster to 400°F (204°C).
2. Brush the fish with the olive oil and sprinkle with 1 tablespoon of lemon juice. Bake in the baking pan for 15 minutes, or until the fish just flakes when tested with a fork.
3. Meanwhile, in a medium bowl, stir together the remaining 2 tablespoons of lemon juice, the red cabbage, carrot, salsa, and yogurt.
4. When the fish is cooked, remove it from the pan and break it up into large pieces.
5. Offer the fish, tortillas, and the cabbage mixture, and let each person assemble a taco.
6. Serve immediately.

Mustard-Lemon Sole Fillets

Prep time: 5 minutes | Cook time: 8 to 11 minutes | Serves 4

5 teaspoons low-sodium yellow mustard
1 tablespoon freshly squeezed lemon juice
4 (3.5-ounce / 99-g) sole fillets
2 teaspoons olive oil
½ teaspoon dried marjoram
½ teaspoon dried thyme
⅛ teaspoon freshly ground black pepper
1 slice low-sodium whole-wheat bread, crumbled

1. Preheat the Oster to 320°F (160°C).
2. Whisk together the mustard and lemon juice in a small bowl until thoroughly mixed and smooth. Spread the mixture evenly over the sole fillets, then transfer to the baking pan.
3. In a separate bowl, combine the olive oil, marjoram, thyme, black pepper, and bread crumbs and stir to mix well. Gently but firmly press the mixture onto the top of fillets, coating them completely.
4. Bake in the preheated Oster for 8 to 11 minutes, or until the internal temperature reaches 145°F (63°C) on a meat thermometer and the outer coating is crisp.
5. Remove from the Oster and serve on a plate.

Salmon and Scallion Patties

Prep time: 5 minutes | Cook time: 12 minutes | Makes 6 patties

1 (14.75-ounce / 418-g) can Alaskan pink salmon, drained and bones removed
½ cup bread crumbs
1 egg, whisked
2 scallions, diced
1 teaspoon garlic powder
Salt and pepper, to taste
Cooking spray

1. Preheat the Oster to 425°F (218°C).
2. Stir together the salmon, bread crumbs, whisked egg, scallions, garlic powder, salt, and pepper in a large bowl until well incorporated.
3. Divide the salmon mixture into six equal portions and form each into a patty with your hands.
4. Arrange the salmon patties in the baking pan and spritz them with cooking spray. Bake for 12 minutes, flipping the patties once during cooking, or until the patties are golden brown and cooked through.
5. Remove the patties from the pan and serve on a plate.

Smoked Paprika Salmon in White Wine

Prep time: 5 minutes | Cook time: 12 minutes | Serves 4

4 tablespoons butter, melted
2 cloves garlic, minced
Sea salt and ground black pepper, to taste
¼ cup dry white wine
1 tablespoon lime juice
1 teaspoon smoked paprika
½ teaspoon onion powder
4 salmon steaks
Cooking spray

1. Place all the ingredients except the salmon and oil in a shallow dish and stir to mix well.
2. Add the salmon steaks, turning to coat well on both sides. Transfer the salmon to the refrigerator to marinate for 30 minutes.
3. Preheat the Oster to 385°F (196°C).
4. Place the salmon steaks in the baking pan, discarding any excess marinade. Spray the salmon steaks with cooking spray.
5. Bake for about 12 minutes, flipping the salmon steaks halfway through, or until cooked to your preferred doneness.
6. Divide the salmon steaks among four plates and serve.

Shrimp and Artichoke Paella

Prep time: 5 minutes | Cook time: 14 to 17 minutes | Serves 4

1 (10-ounce / 284-g) package frozen cooked rice, thawed
1 (6-ounce / 170-g) jar artichoke hearts, drained and chopped
¼ cup vegetable broth
½ teaspoon dried thyme
½ teaspoon turmeric
1 cup frozen cooked small shrimp
½ cup frozen baby peas
1 tomato, diced

1. Preheat the Oster to 340°F (171°C).
2. Mix together the cooked rice, chopped artichoke hearts, vegetable broth, thyme, and turmeric in a baking pan and stir to combine.
3. Put the baking pan in the preheated Oster and bake for about 9 minutes, or until the rice is heated through.
4. Remove the pan from the Oster and fold in the shrimp, baby peas, and diced tomato and mix well.
5. Return to the Oster and continue cooking for 5 to 8 minutes, or until the shrimp are done and the paella is bubbling.
6. Cool for 5 minutes before serving.

Chapter 8
Wraps and Sandwiches

BBQ Bacon and Bell Pepper Sandwich
Prep time: 10 minutes | Cook time: 6 minutes | Serves 4

⅓ cup spicy barbecue sauce
2 tablespoons honey
8 slices cooked bacon, cut into thirds
1 red bell pepper, sliced
1 yellow bell pepper, sliced
3 pita pockets, cut in half
1¼ cups torn butter lettuce leaves
2 tomatoes, sliced

1. Preheat the Oster to 350°F (177°C).
2. In a small bowl, combine the barbecue sauce and the honey. Brush this mixture lightly onto the bacon slices and the red and yellow pepper slices.
3. Put the peppers into the baking pan and bake for 4 minutes. Add the bacon, and bake for 2 minutes or until the bacon is browned and the peppers are tender.
4. Fill the pita halves with the bacon, peppers, any remaining barbecue sauce, lettuce, and tomatoes, and serve immediately.

Mozzarella Chicken and Cabbage Sandwich
Prep time: 10 minutes | Cook time: 5 to 7 minutes | Serves 1

⅓ cup chicken, cooked and shredded
2 Mozzarella slices
1 hamburger bun
¼ cup shredded cabbage
1 teaspoon mayonnaise
2 teaspoons butter, melted
1 teaspoon olive oil
½ teaspoon balsamic vinegar
¼ teaspoon smoked paprika
¼ teaspoon black pepper
¼ teaspoon garlic powder
Pinch of salt

1. Preheat the Oster to 370°F (188°C).
2. Brush some butter onto the outside of the hamburger bun.
3. In a bowl, coat the chicken with the garlic powder, salt, pepper, and paprika.
4. In a separate bowl, stir together the mayonnaise, olive oil, cabbage, and balsamic vinegar to make coleslaw.
5. Slice the bun in two. Start building the sandwich, starting with the chicken, followed by the Mozzarella, the coleslaw, and finally the top bun.
6. Transfer the sandwich to the Oster and bake for 5 to 7 minutes.
7. Serve immediately.

Swiss Greens Sandwich
Prep time: 15 minutes | Cook time: 13 minutes | Serves 4

1½ cups chopped mixed greens
2 garlic cloves, thinly sliced
2 teaspoons olive oil
2 slices low-sodium low-fat Swiss cheese
4 slices low-sodium whole-wheat bread
Cooking spray

1. Preheat the Oster to 425°F (218°C).
2. In a baking pan, mix the greens, garlic, and olive oil. Bake for 5 minutes, stirring once, until the vegetables are tender. Drain, if necessary.
3. Make 2 sandwiches, dividing half of the greens and 1 slice of Swiss cheese between 2 slices of bread. Lightly spray the outsides of the sandwiches with cooking spray.
4. Bake the sandwiches in the Oster for 8 minutes, turning with tongs halfway through, until the bread is toasted and the cheese melts.
5. Cut each sandwich in half and serve.

Beef Sloppy Joes
Prep time: 10 minutes | Cook time: 17 to 19 minutes | Makes 4 large sandwiches or 8 sliders

1 pound (454 g) very lean ground beef
1 teaspoon onion powder
⅓ cup ketchup
¼ cup water
½ teaspoon celery seed
1 tablespoon lemon juice
1½ teaspoons brown sugar
1¼ teaspoons low-sodium Worcestershire sauce
½ teaspoon salt (optional)
½ teaspoon vinegar
⅛ teaspoon dry mustard
Hamburger or slider buns, for serving
Cooking spray

1. Preheat the Oster to 390°F (199°C). Spray the baking pan with cooking spray.
2. Break raw ground beef into small chunks and pile into the pan. Bake for 5 minutes. Stir to break apart and bake for 3 minutes. Stir and bake for 2 to 4 minutes longer, or until meat is well done.
3. Remove the meat from the Oster, drain, and use a knife and fork to crumble into small pieces.
4. Give your pan a quick rinse to remove any bits of meat.
5. Place all the remaining ingredients, except for the buns, in the pan and mix together. Add the meat and stir well.
6. Bake at 330°F (166°C) for 5 minutes. Stir and bake for 2 minutes.
7. Scoop onto buns. Serve hot.

Colby Shrimp Sandwich with Mayo
Prep time: 10 minutes | Cook time: 7 minutes | Serves 4

1¼ cups shredded Colby, Cheddar, or Havarti cheese
1 (6-ounce / 170-g) can tiny shrimp, drained
3 tablespoons mayonnaise
2 tablespoons minced green onion
4 slices whole grain or whole-wheat bread
2 tablespoons softened butter

1. Preheat the Oster to 425°F (218°C).
2. In a medium bowl, combine the cheese, shrimp, mayonnaise, and green onion, and mix well.
3. Spread this mixture on two of the slices of bread. Top with the other slices of bread to make two sandwiches. Spread the sandwiches lightly with butter.
4. Bake for 7 minutes, or until the bread is browned and crisp and the cheese is melted.
5. Cut in half and serve warm.

Chicken and Lettuce Pita Sandwich
Prep time: 10 minutes | Cook time: 9 to 11 minutes | Serves 4

2 boneless, skinless chicken breasts, cut into 1-inch cubes
1 small red onion, sliced
1 red bell pepper, sliced
½ teaspoon dried thyme
4 pita pockets, split
2 cups torn butter lettuce
1 cup chopped cherry tomatoes

1. Preheat the Oster to 380°F (193°C).
2. Place the chicken, onion, and bell pepper in the baking pan. Drizzle with 1 tablespoon of the Italian salad dressing, add the thyme, and toss.
3. Transfer the chicken and vegetables to a bowl and toss with the remaining salad dressing.
4. Assemble sandwiches with the pita pockets, butter lettuce, and cherry tomatoes. Serve immediately.

Parmesan Eggplant Hoagies
Prep time: 15 minutes | Cook time: 14 minutes | Makes 3 hoagies

¼ cup jarred pizza sauce
6 tablespoons grated Parmesan cheese
3 Italian sub rolls, split open lengthwise, warmed
Cooking spray

1. Preheat the Oster to 375°F (191°C) and spritz the baking pan with cooking spray.
2. Arrange the eggplant slices in the pan and spritz with cooking spray.
3. Bake for 12 minutes or until lightly wilted and tender. Flip the slices halfway through.
4. Divide and spread the pizza sauce and cheese on top of the eggplant slice and bake for 2 more minutes or until the cheese melts.
5. Assemble each sub roll with two slices of eggplant and serve immediately.

Tilapia Tacos with Mayo
Prep time: 20 minutes | Cook time: 6 minutes | Serves 4

2 tablespoons milk
⅓ cup mayonnaise
¼ teaspoon garlic powder
1 teaspoon chili powder
1½ cups panko bread crumbs
½ teaspoon salt
4 teaspoons canola oil
1 pound (454 g) skinless tilapia fillets, cut into 3-inch-long and 1-inch-wide strips
4 small flour tortillas
Lemon wedges, for topping
Cooking spray

1. Preheat the Oster to 425°F (218°C). Spritz the baking pan with cooking spray.
2. Combine the milk, mayo, garlic powder, and chili powder in a bowl. Stir to mix well. Combine the panko with salt and canola oil in a separate bowl. Stir to mix well.
3. Dredge the tilapia strips in the milk mixture first, then dunk the strips in the panko mixture to coat well. Shake the excess off.
4. Arrange the tilapia strips in the pan. Bake for 6 minutes or until opaque on all sides and the panko is golden brown. Flip the strips halfway through. You may need to work in batches to avoid overcrowding.
5. Unfold the tortillas on a large plate, then divide the tilapia strips over the tortillas. Squeeze the lemon wedges on top before serving.

Turkey Sliders with Chive Mayo
Prep time: 10 minutes | Cook time: 18 minutes | Serves 6

12 burger buns
Cooking spray
For the Turkey Sliders:
¾ pound (340 g) turkey, minced
1 tablespoon chopped fresh cilantro
1 to 2 cloves garlic, minced
Sea salt and ground black pepper, to taste
For the Chive Mayo:
1 tablespoon chives
1 cup mayonnaise
Zest of 1 lime
1 teaspoon salt

1. Preheat the Oster to 380°F (193°C) and spritz the baking pan with cooking spray.
2. Arrange the patties in the pan and spritz with cooking spray. Bake for 18 minutes or until well browned. Flip the patties halfway through.
3. Meanwhile, combine the ingredients for the chive mayo in a small bowl. Stir to mix well.
4. Smear the patties with chive mayo, then assemble the patties between two buns to make the sliders. Serve immediately.

Turkey and Pepper Hamburger

Prep time: 10 minutes | Cook time: 20 minutes | Serves 4

1 cup leftover turkey, cut into bite-sized chunks
1 leek, sliced
1 Serrano pepper, deveined and chopped
2 bell peppers, deveined and chopped
2 tablespoons Tabasco sauce
½ cup sour cream
1 heaping tablespoon fresh cilantro, chopped
1 teaspoon hot paprika
¾ teaspoon kosher salt
½ teaspoon ground black pepper
4 hamburger buns
Cooking spray

1. Preheat the Oster to 385°F (196°C). Spritz a baking pan with cooking spray.
2. Mix all the ingredients, except for the buns, in a large bowl. Toss to combine well.
3. Pour the mixture in the baking pan and place in the Oster. Bake for 20 minutes or until the turkey is well browned and the leek is tender.
4. Assemble the hamburger buns with the turkey mixture and serve immediately.

Chapter 9
Desserts

Graham Cracker Chocolate Cheesecake
Prep time: 10 minutes | Cook time: 20 minutes | Serves 8

1 cup graham cracker crumbs
3 tablespoons softened butter
1½ (8-ounce / 227-g) packages cream cheese, softened
⅓ cup sugar
2 eggs
1 tablespoon flour
1 teaspoon vanilla
¼ cup chocolate syrup

1. For the crust, combine the graham cracker crumbs and butter in a small bowl and mix well. Press into the bottom of a baking pan and put in the freezer to set.
2. For the filling, combine the cream cheese and sugar in a medium bowl and mix well. Beat in the eggs, one at a time. Add the flour and vanilla.
3. Preheat the Oster to 450°F (232°C).
4. Remove ⅔ cup of the filling to a small bowl and stir in the chocolate syrup until combined.
5. Pour the vanilla filling into the pan with the crust. Drop the chocolate filling over the vanilla filling by the spoonful. With a clean butter knife, stir the fillings in a zigzag pattern to marbleize them.
6. Bake for 20 minutes or until the cheesecake is just set.
7. Cool on a wire rack for 1 hour, then chill in the refrigerator until the cheesecake is firm.
8. Serve immediately.

Honey-Glazed Pears with Walnuts
Prep time: 5 minutes | Cook time: 20 minutes | Serves 4

2 large Bosc pears, halved and deseeded
3 tablespoons honey
1 tablespoon unsalted butter
½ teaspoon ground cinnamon
¼ cup walnuts, chopped
¼ cup part skim low-fat ricotta cheese, divided

1. Preheat the Oster to 350°F (177°C).
2. In a baking pan, place the pears, cut side up.
3. In a small microwave-safe bowl, melt the honey, butter, and cinnamon. Brush this mixture over the cut sides of the pears.
4. Pour 3 tablespoons of water around the pears in the pan. Bake the pears for 20 minutes, or until tender when pierced with a fork and slightly crisp on the edges, basting once with the liquid in the pan.
5. Carefully remove the pears from the pan and place on a serving plate. Drizzle each with some liquid from the pan, sprinkle the walnuts on top, and serve with a spoonful of ricotta cheese.

Brown Sugar-Lemon Applesauce
Prep time: 10 minutes | Cook time: 1 hour | Makes 1¼ cups

Cooking spray
2 cups unsweetened applesauce
⅔ cup packed light brown sugar
3 tablespoons fresh lemon juice
½ teaspoon kosher salt
¼ teaspoon ground cinnamon
⅛ teaspoon ground allspice

1. Preheat the Oster to 340°F (171°C).
2. Spray a metal cake pan with cooking spray. Whisk together all the ingredients in a bowl until smooth, then pour into the greased pan. Set the pan in the Oster and bake until the apple mixture is caramelized, reduced to a thick purée, and fragrant, about 1 hour.
3. Remove the pan from the Oster, stir to combine the caramelized bits at the edge with the rest, then let cool completely to thicken.
4. Serve immediately.

Blueberry Chocolate Cupcakes
Prep time: 5 minutes | Cook time: 15 minutes | Serves 6

¾ cup granulated erythritol
1¼ cups almond flour
1 teaspoon unsweetened baking powder
3 teaspoons cocoa powder
½ teaspoon baking soda
½ teaspoon ground cinnamon
¼ teaspoon grated nutmeg
⅛ teaspoon salt
½ cup milk
1 stick butter, at room temperature
3 eggs, whisked
1 teaspoon pure rum extract
½ cup blueberries
Cooking spray

1. Preheat the Oster to 345°F (174°C). Spray a 6-cup muffin tin with cooking spray.
2. In a mixing bowl, combine the erythritol, almond flour, baking powder, cocoa powder, baking soda, cinnamon, nutmeg, and salt and stir until well blended.
3. In another mixing bowl, mix together the milk, butter, egg, and rum extract until thoroughly combined. Slowly and carefully pour this mixture into the bowl of dry mixture. Stir in the blueberries.
4. Spoon the batter into the greased muffin cups, filling each about three-quarters full.
5. Bake for 15 minutes, or until the center is springy and a toothpick inserted in the middle comes out clean.
6. Remove from the Oster and place on a wire rack to cool. Serve immediately.

Lemon Blackberry and Granola Crisp
Prep time: 5 minutes | Cook time: 20 minutes | Serves 1

2 tablespoons lemon juice
⅓ cup powdered erythritol
¼ teaspoon xantham gum
2 cup blackberries
1 cup crunchy granola

1. Preheat the Oster to 350°F (177°C).
2. In a bowl, combine the lemon juice, erythritol, xantham gum, and blackberries. Transfer to a round baking dish and cover with aluminum foil.
3. Put the dish in the Oster and bake for 12 minutes.
4. Take care when removing the dish from the Oster. Give the blackberries a stir and top with the granola.
5. Return the dish to the Oster and bake for an additional 3 minutes, this time at 320°F (160°C). Serve once the granola has turned brown and enjoy.

Apple Cinnamon Fritters
Prep time: 30 minutes | Cook time: 7 to 8 minutes | Serves 6

1 cup chopped, peeled Granny Smith apple
½ cup granulated sugar
1 teaspoon ground cinnamon
1 cup all-purpose flour
1 teaspoon baking powder
1 teaspoon salt
2 tablespoons milk
2 tablespoons butter, melted
1 large egg, beaten
Cooking spray
¼ cup confectioners' sugar (optional)

1. Mix together the apple, granulated sugar, and cinnamon in a small bowl. Allow to sit for 30 minutes.
2. Combine the flour, baking powder, and salt in a medium bowl. Add the milk, butter, and egg and stir to incorporate.
3. Pour the apple mixture into the bowl of flour mixture and stir with a spatula until a dough forms.
4. Make the fritters: On a clean work surface, divide the dough into 12 equal portions and shape into 1-inch balls. Flatten them into patties with your hands.
5. Preheat the Oster to 350°F (177°C). Line the baking pan with parchment paper and spray it with cooking spray.
6. Transfer the apple fritters onto the parchment paper, evenly spaced but not too close together. Spray the fritters with cooking spray.
7. Bake for 7 to 8 minutes until lightly browned. Flip the fritters halfway through the cooking time.
8. Remove from the pan to a plate and serve with the confectioners' sugar sprinkled on top, if desired.

Raisin Oatmeal Bars
Prep time: 15 minutes | Cook time: 15 minutes | Serves 8

⅓ cup all-purpose flour
¼ teaspoon kosher salt
¼ teaspoon baking powder
¼ teaspoon ground cinnamon
¼ cup light brown sugar, lightly packed
¼ cup granulated sugar
½ cup canola oil
1 large egg
1 teaspoon vanilla extract
1⅓ cups quick-cooking oats
⅓ cup raisins

1. Preheat the Oster to 360°F (182°C).
2. In a large bowl, combine the all-purpose flour, kosher salt, baking powder, ground cinnamon, light brown sugar, granulated sugar, canola oil, egg, vanilla extract, quick-cooking oats, and raisins.
3. Spray a baking pan with nonstick cooking spray, then pour the oat mixture into the pan and press down to evenly distribute. Place the pan in the Oster and bake for 15 minutes or until golden brown.
4. Remove from the Oster and allow to cool in the pan on a wire rack for 20 minutes before slicing and serving.

Orange Cornmeal Cake
Prep time: 10 minutes | Cook time: 23 minutes | Serves 8

Nonstick baking spray with flour
1¼ cups all-purpose flour
⅓ cup yellow cornmeal
¾ cup white sugar
1 teaspoon baking soda
¼ cup safflower oil
1¼ cups orange juice, divided
1 teaspoon vanilla
¼ cup powdered sugar

1. Preheat the Oster to 350°F (177°C).
2. Spray a baking pan with nonstick spray and set aside.
3. In a medium bowl, combine the flour, cornmeal, sugar, baking soda, safflower oil, 1 cup of the orange juice, and vanilla, and mix well.
4. Pour the batter into the baking pan and place in the Oster. Bake for 23 minutes or until a toothpick inserted in the center of the cake comes out clean.
5. Remove the cake from the Oster and place on a cooling rack. Using a toothpick, make about 20 holes in the cake.
6. In a small bowl, combine remaining ¼ cup of orange juice and the powdered sugar and stir well. Drizzle this mixture over the hot cake slowly so the cake absorbs it.
7. Cool completely, then cut into wedges to serve.

Apple and Pear Crisp with Walnuts
Prep time: 10 minutes | Cook time: 20 minutes | Serves 6

½ pound (227 g) apples, cored and chopped
½ pound (227 g) pears, cored and chopped
1 cup flour
1 cup sugar
1 tablespoon butter
1 teaspoon ground cinnamon
¼ teaspoon ground cloves
1 teaspoon vanilla extract
¼ cup chopped walnuts
Whipped cream, for serving

1. Preheat the Oster to 340°F (171°C).
2. Lightly grease a baking dish and place the apples and pears inside.
3. Combine the rest of the ingredients, minus the walnuts and the whipped cream, until a coarse, crumbly texture is achieved.
4. Pour the mixture over the fruits and spread it evenly. Top with the chopped walnuts.
5. Bake for 20 minutes or until the top turns golden brown.
6. Serve at room temperature with whipped cream.

Chocolate Pineapple Cake
Prep time: 10 minutes | Cook time: 35 to 40 minutes | Serves 4

2 cups flour
4 ounces (113 g) butter, melted
¼ cup sugar
½ pound (227 g) pineapple, chopped
½ cup pineapple juice
1 ounce (28 g) dark chocolate, grated
1 large egg
2 tablespoons skimmed milk

1. Preheat the Oster to 370°F (188°C).
2. Grease a cake tin with a little oil or butter.
3. In a bowl, combine the butter and flour to create a crumbly consistency.
4. Add the sugar, chopped pineapple, juice, and grated dark chocolate and mix well.
5. In a separate bowl, combine the egg and milk. Add this mixture to the flour mixture and stir well until a soft dough forms.
6. Pour the mixture into the cake tin and transfer to the Oster.
7. Bake for 35 to 40 minutes.
8. Serve immediately.

Carrot, Cherry and Oatmeal Cups
Prep time: 10 minutes | Cook time: 8 minutes | Makes 16 cups

3 tablespoons unsalted butter, at room temperature
¼ cup packed brown sugar
1 tablespoon honey
1 egg white
½ teaspoon vanilla extract
⅓ cup finely grated carrot
½ cup quick-cooking oatmeal
⅓ cup whole-wheat pastry flour
½ teaspoon baking soda
¼ cup dried cherries

1. Preheat the Oster to 350°F (177°C)
2. In a medium bowl, beat the butter, brown sugar, and honey until well combined.
3. Add the egg white, vanilla, and carrot. Beat to combine.
4. Stir in the oatmeal, pastry flour, and baking soda.
5. Stir in the dried cherries.
6. Double up 32 mini muffin foil cups to make 16 cups. Fill each with about 4 teaspoons of dough. Bake the cookie cups, 8 at a time, for 8 minutes, or until light golden brown and just set. Serve warm.

Ginger Pumpkin Pudding
Prep time: 10 minutes | Cook time: 15 minutes | Serves 4

3 cups pumpkin purée
3 tablespoons honey
1 tablespoon ginger
1 tablespoon cinnamon
1 teaspoon clove
1 teaspoon nutmeg
1 cup full-fat cream
2 eggs
1 cup sugar

1. Preheat the Oster to 390°F (199°C).
2. In a bowl, stir all the ingredients together to combine.
3. Scrape the mixture into the a greased dish and transfer to the Oster. Bake for 15 minutes. Serve warm.

Vanilla Chocolate Cookie
Prep time: 10 minutes | Cook time: 9 minutes | Serves 4

Nonstick baking spray with flour
3 tablespoons softened butter
⅓ cup plus 1 tablespoon brown sugar
1 egg yolk
½ cup flour
2 tablespoons ground white chocolate
¼ teaspoon baking soda
½ teaspoon vanilla
¾ cup chocolate chips

1. Preheat the Oster to 350°F (177°C).
2. In a medium bowl, beat the butter and brown sugar together until fluffy. Stir in the egg yolk.
3. Add the flour, white chocolate, baking soda, and vanilla, and mix well. Stir in the chocolate chips.
4. Line a baking pan with parchment paper. Spray the parchment paper with nonstick baking spray with flour.
5. Spread the batter into the prepared pan, leaving a ½-inch border on all sides.
6. Bake for about 9 minutes or until the cookie is light brown and just barely set.
7. Remove the pan from the Oster and let cool for 10 minutes. Remove the cookie from the pan, remove the parchment paper, and let cool on a wire rack.
8. Serve immediately.

Vanilla Pound Cake
Prep time: 5 minutes | Cook time: 30 minutes | Serves 8

1 stick butter, at room temperature
1 cup Swerve
4 eggs
1½ cups coconut flour
½ cup buttermilk
½ teaspoon baking soda
½ teaspoon baking powder
¼ teaspoon salt
1 teaspoon vanilla essence
A pinch of ground star anise
A pinch of freshly grated nutmeg
Cooking spray

1. Preheat the Oster to 320°F (160°C). Spray a baking pan with cooking spray.
2. With an electric mixer or hand mixer, beat the butter and Swerve until creamy. One at a time, mix in the eggs and whisk until fluffy. Add the remaining ingredients and stir to combine.
3. Transfer the batter to the prepared baking pan. Bake in the preheated Oster for 30 minutes until the center of the cake is springy. Rotate the pan halfway through the cooking time.
4. Allow the cake to cool in the pan for 10 minutes before removing and serving.

Vanilla Chocolate Brownies
Prep time: 10 minutes | Cook time: 20 minutes | Makes 1 dozen brownies

1 egg
¼ cup brown sugar
2 tablespoons white sugar
2 tablespoons safflower oil
1 teaspoon vanilla
⅓ cup all-purpose flour
¼ cup cocoa powder
¼ cup white chocolate chips
Nonstick cooking spray

1. Preheat the Oster to 340°F (171°C). Spritz a baking pan with nonstick cooking spray.
2. Whisk together the egg, brown sugar, and white sugar in a medium bowl. Mix in the safflower oil and vanilla and stir to combine.
3. Add the flour and cocoa powder and stir just until incorporated. Fold in the white chocolate chips.
4. Scrape the batter into the prepared baking pan.
5. Bake in the preheated Oster for 20 minutes, or until the brownie springs back when touched lightly with your fingers.
6. Transfer to a wire rack and let cool for 30 minutes before slicing to serve.

Vanilla-Rum Pineapple Galette
Prep time: 10 minutes | Cook time: 40 minutes | Serves 2

¼ medium-size pineapple, peeled, cored, and cut crosswise into ¼-inch-thick slices
2 tablespoons dark rum
1 teaspoon vanilla extract
½ teaspoon kosher salt
Finely grated zest of ½ lime
1 store-bought sheet puff pastry, cut into an 8-inch round
3 tablespoons granulated sugar
2 tablespoons unsalted butter, cubed and chilled
Coconut ice cream, for serving

1. Preheat the Oster to 310°F (154°C).
2. In a small bowl, combine the pineapple slices, rum, vanilla, salt, and lime zest and let stand for at least 10 minutes to allow the pineapple to soak in the rum.
3. Meanwhile, press the puff pastry round into the bottom and up the sides of a round metal cake pan and use the tines of a fork to dock the bottom and sides.
4. Arrange the pineapple slices on the bottom of the pastry in more or less a single layer, then sprinkle with the sugar and dot with the butter. Drizzle with the leftover juices from the bowl. Put the pan in the Oster and bake until the pastry is puffed and golden brown and the pineapple is lightly caramelized on top, about 40 minutes.
5. Transfer the pan to a wire rack to cool for 15 minutes. Unmold the galette from the pan and serve warm with coconut ice cream.

Vanilla Peaches with Fresh Blueberries
Prep time: 10 minutes | **Cook time:** 7 to 11 minutes | **Serves 6**

3 peaches, peeled, halved, and pitted
2 tablespoons packed brown sugar
1 cup plain Greek yogurt
¼ teaspoon ground cinnamon
1 teaspoon pure vanilla extract
1 cup fresh blueberries

1. Preheat the Oster to 380°F (193°C).
2. Arrange the peaches in the baking pan, cut-side up. Top with a generous sprinkle of brown sugar.
3. Bake in the preheated Oster for 7 to 11 minutes, or until the peaches are lightly browned and caramelized.
4. Meanwhile, whisk together the yogurt, cinnamon, and vanilla in a small bowl until smooth.
5. Remove the peaches from the pan to a plate. Serve topped with the yogurt mixture and fresh blueberries.

Lemon Poppy Seed Cake
Prep time: 15 minutes | **Cook time:** 55 minutes | **Serves 4**

Unsalted butter, at room temperature
1 cup almond flour
½ cup sugar
3 large eggs
¼ cup heavy cream
¼ cup full-fat ricotta cheese
¼ cup coconut oil, melted
2 tablespoons poppy seeds
1 teaspoon baking powder
1 teaspoon pure lemon extract
Grated zest and juice of 1 lemon, plus more zest for garnish

1. Preheat the Oster to 325°F (163°C).
2. Generously butter a round baking pan. Line the bottom of the pan with parchment paper cut to fit.
3. In a large bowl, combine the almond flour, sugar, eggs, cream, ricotta, coconut oil, poppy seeds, baking powder, lemon extract, lemon zest, and lemon juice. Beat with a hand mixer on medium speed until well blended and fluffy.
4. Pour the batter into the prepared pan. Cover the pan tightly with aluminum foil. Set the pan in the Oster and bake for 45 minutes. Remove the foil and bake for 10 to 15 minutes more until a knife (do not use a toothpick) inserted into the center of the cake comes out clean.
5. Let the cake cool in the pan on a wire rack for 10 minutes. Remove the cake from pan and let it cool on the rack for 15 minutes before slicing.
6. Top with additional lemon zest, slice and serve.

Ginger Cinnamon Cookies
Prep time: 15 minutes | **Cook time:** 12 minutes | **Serves 4**

4 tablespoons (½ stick) unsalted butter, at room temperature
2 tablespoons agave nectar
1 large egg
2 tablespoons water
2½ cups almond flour
½ cup sugar
2 teaspoons ground ginger
1 teaspoon ground cinnamon
½ teaspoon freshly grated nutmeg
1 teaspoon baking soda
¼ teaspoon kosher salt

1. Preheat the Oster to 325°F (163°C).
2. Line the baking pan with parchment paper cut to fit.
3. In a large bowl using a hand mixer, beat together the butter, agave, egg, and water on medium speed until fluffy.
4. Add the almond flour, sugar, ginger, cinnamon, nutmeg, baking soda, and salt. Beat on low speed until well combined.
5. Roll the dough into 2-tablespoon balls and arrange them on the parchment paper. (They don't really spread too much, but try to leave a little room between them.) Bake for 12 minutes, or until the tops of cookies are lightly browned.
6. Transfer to a wire rack and let cool completely.
7. Serve immediately

Chocolate Cake with Fresh Blackberries
Prep time: 10 minutes | **Cook time:** 22 minutes | **Serves 8**

½ cup butter, at room temperature
2 ounces (57 g) Swerve
4 eggs
1 cup almond flour
1 teaspoon baking soda
⅓ teaspoon baking powder
½ cup cocoa powder
1 teaspoon orange zest
⅓ cup fresh blackberries

1. Preheat the Oster to 335°F (168°C).
2. With an electric mixer or hand mixer, beat the butter and Swerve until creamy.
3. One at a time, mix in the eggs and beat again until fluffy.
4. Add the almond flour, baking soda, baking powder, cocoa powder, orange zest and mix well. Add the butter mixture to the almond flour mixture and stir until well blended. Fold in the blackberries.
5. Scrape the batter to a baking pan and bake in the preheated Oster for 22 minutes. Check the cake for doneness: If a toothpick inserted into the center of the cake comes out clean, it's done.
6. Allow the cake cool on a wire rack to room temperature. Serve immediately.

Peach Blackberry Cobbler with Oats
Prep time: 10 minutes | Cook time: 20 minutes | Serves 4

Filling:
1 (6-ounce / 170-g) package blackberries
1½ cups chopped peaches, cut into ½-inch thick slices
2 teaspoons arrowroot or cornstarch
2 tablespoons coconut sugar
1 teaspoon lemon juice
Topping:
2 tablespoons sunflower oil
1 tablespoon maple syrup
1 teaspoon vanilla
3 tablespoons coconut sugar
½ cup rolled oats
⅓ cup whole-wheat pastry flour
1 teaspoon cinnamon
¼ teaspoon nutmeg
⅛ teaspoon sea salt

Make the Filling:
1. Combine the blackberries, peaches, arrowroot, coconut sugar, and lemon juice in a baking pan.
2. Using a rubber spatula, stir until well incorporated. Set aside.

Make the Topping:
3. Preheat the Oster to 320ºF (160ºC)
4. Combine the oil, maple syrup, and vanilla in a mixing bowl and stir well. Whisk in the remaining ingredients. Spread this mixture evenly over the filling.
5. Place the pan in the Oster and bake for 20 minutes, or until the topping is crispy and golden brown. Serve warm

Coconut Chia Pudding
Prep time: 5 minutes | Cook time: 4 minutes | Serves 2

1 cup chia seeds
1 cup unsweetened coconut milk
1 teaspoon liquid stevia
1 tablespoon coconut oil
1 teaspoon butter, melted

1. Preheat the fryer to 360ºF (182ºC).
2. Mix together the chia seeds, coconut milk, and stevia in a large bowl. Add the coconut oil and melted butter and stir until well blended.
3. Divide the mixture evenly between the ramekins, filling only about ⅔ of the way.
4. Bake in the preheated Oster for 4 minutes.
5. Allow to cool for 5 minutes and serve warm.

Coconut Chocolate Cake
Prep time: 5 minutes | Cook time: 15 minutes | Serves 6

½ cup unsweetened chocolate, chopped
½ stick butter, at room temperature
1 tablespoon liquid stevia
1½ cups coconut flour
2 eggs, whisked
½ teaspoon vanilla extract
A pinch of fine sea salt
Cooking spray

1. Place the chocolate, butter, and stevia in a microwave-safe bowl. Microwave for about 30 seconds until melted.
2. Let the chocolate mixture cool for 5 to 10 minutes.
3. Add the remaining ingredients to the bowl of chocolate mixture and whisk to incorporate.
4. Preheat the Oster to 330ºF (166ºC). Lightly spray a baking pan with cooking spray.
5. Scrape the chocolate mixture into the prepared baking pan.
6. Place the baking pan in the Oster and bake for 15 minutes, or until the top springs back lightly when gently pressed with your fingers.
7. Let the cake cool for 5 minutes and serve.

Chocolate Pie with Pecans
Prep time: 20 minutes | Cook time: 25 minutes | Serves 8

1 (9-inch) unbaked pie crust
Filling:
2 large eggs
⅓ cup butter, melted
1 cup sugar
½ cup all-purpose flour
1 cup milk chocolate chips
1½ cups coarsely chopped pecans
2 tablespoons bourbon

1. Preheat the Oster to 350ºF (177ºC).
2. Whisk the eggs and melted butter in a large bowl until creamy.
3. Add the sugar and flour and stir to incorporate. Mix in the milk chocolate chips, pecans, and bourbon and stir until well combined.
4. Use a fork to prick holes in the bottom and sides of the pie crust. Pour the prepared filling into the pie crust. Place the pie crust in the baking pan.
5. Bake for 25 minutes until a toothpick inserted in the center comes out clean.
6. Allow the pie cool for 10 minutes in the pan before serving.

Pumpkin Apple Turnovers
Prep time: 10 minutes | Cook time: 10 minutes | Serves 4

1 apple, peeled, quartered, and thinly sliced
½ teaspoon pumpkin pie spice
Juice of ½ lemon
1 tablespoon granulated sugar
Pinch of kosher salt
6 sheets phyllo dough

1. Preheat the Oster to 330°F (166°C).
2. In a medium bowl, combine the apple, pumpkin pie spice, lemon juice, granulated sugar, and kosher salt.
3. Cut the phyllo dough sheets into 4 equal pieces and place individual tablespoons of apple filling in the center of each piece, then fold in both sides and roll from front to back.
4. Spray the baking pan with nonstick cooking spray, then place the turnovers in the pan and bake for 10 minutes or until golden brown.
5. Remove the turnovers from the Oster and allow to cool on a wire rack for 10 minutes before serving.

Peppermint Chocolate Cheesecake
Prep time: 5 minutes | Cook time: 18 minutes | Serves 6

Crust:
½ cup butter, melted
½ cup coconut flour
2 tablespoons stevia
Cooking spray
Topping:
4 ounces (113 g) unsweetened baker's chocolate
1 cup mascarpone cheese, at room temperature
1 teaspoon vanilla extract
2 drops peppermint extract

1. Preheat the Oster to 350°F (177°C). Lightly coat a baking pan with cooking spray.
2. In a mixing bowl, whisk together the butter, flour, and stevia until well combined. Transfer the mixture to the prepared baking pan.
3. Place the baking pan in the Oster and bake for 18 minutes until a toothpick inserted in the center comes out clean.
4. Remove the crust from the Oster to a wire rack to cool.
5. Once cooled completely, place it in the freezer for 20 minutes.
6. When ready, combine all the ingredients for the topping in a small bowl and stir to incorporate.
7. Spread this topping over the crust and let it sit for another 15 minutes in the freezer.
8. Serve chilled.

Coffee Coconut Chocolate Cake
Prep time: 5 minutes | Cook time: 30 minutes | Serves 8

Dry Ingredients:
1½ cups almond flour
½ cup coconut meal
⅔ cup Swerve
1 teaspoon baking powder
¼ teaspoon salt
Wet Ingredients:
1 egg
1 stick butter, melted
½ cup hot strongly brewed coffee
Topping:
½ cup confectioner's Swerve
¼ cup coconut flour
3 tablespoons coconut oil
1 teaspoon ground cinnamon
½ teaspoon ground cardamom

1. Preheat the Oster to 330°F (166°C).
2. In a medium bowl, combine the almond flour, coconut meal, Swerve, baking powder, and salt.
3. In a large bowl, whisk the egg, melted butter, and coffee until smooth.
4. Add the dry mixture to the wet and stir until well incorporated. Transfer the batter to a greased baking pan.
5. Stir together all the ingredients for the topping in a small bowl. Spread the topping over the batter and smooth the top with a spatula.
6. Bake in the preheated Oster for 30 minutes, or until the cake springs back when gently pressed with your fingers.
7. Rest for 10 minutes before serving.

Candied Cinnamon Apples
Prep time: 15 minutes | Cook time: 12 minutes | Serves 4

1 cup packed light brown sugar
2 teaspoons ground cinnamon
2 medium Granny Smith apples, peeled and diced

1. Preheat the Oster to 350°F (177°C).
2. Thoroughly combine the brown sugar and cinnamon in a medium bowl.
3. Add the apples to the bowl and stir until well coated. Transfer the apples to a baking pan.
4. Bake in the preheated Oster for 9 minutes. Stir the apples once and bake for an additional 3 minutes until softened.
5. Serve warm.

Cinnamon S'mores
Prep time: 5 minutes | Cook time: 10 minutes | Makes 12 s'mores

12 whole cinnamon graham crackers, halved
2 (1.55-ounce / 44-g) chocolate bars, cut into 12 pieces
12 marshmallows

1. Preheat the Oster to 350°F (177°C)
2. Working in batches, arrange 6 graham cracker squares in the baking pan in a single layer.
3. Top each square with a piece of chocolate and bake for 2 minutes.
4. Remove the pan and place a marshmallow on each piece of melted chocolate. Bake for another 1 minute.
5. Remove from the pan to a serving plate. Repeat with the remaining 6 graham cracker squares, chocolate pieces, and marshmallows.
6. Serve topped with the remaining graham cracker squares

Mixed Berry Crisp with Coconut Chips
Prep time: 5 minutes | Cook time: 20 minutes | Serves 6

1 tablespoon butter, melted
12 ounces (340 g) mixed berries
⅓ cup granulated Swerve
1 teaspoon pure vanilla extract
½ teaspoon ground cinnamon
¼ teaspoon ground cloves
¼ teaspoon grated nutmeg
½ cup coconut chips, for garnish

1. Preheat the Oster to 330°F (166°C). Coat a baking pan with melted butter.
2. Put the remaining ingredients except the coconut chips in the prepared baking pan.
3. Bake in the preheated Oster for 20 minutes.
4. Serve garnished with the coconut chips.

Chapter 10
Appetizers and Snacks

Almond-Stuffed Dates with Turkey Bacon
Prep time: 10 minutes | Cook time: 8 minutes | Makes 16 appetizers

16 whole dates, pitted
16 whole almonds
6 to 8 strips turkey bacon, cut in half

Special Equipment:
16 toothpicks, soaked in water for at least 30 minutes

1. Preheat the Oster to 400°F (204°C).
2. On a flat work surface, stuff each pitted date with a whole almond.
3. Wrap half slice of bacon around each date and secure it with a toothpick.
4. Place the bacon-wrapped dates in the baking pan and bake for 8 minutes, or until the bacon is cooked to your desired crispiness.
5. Transfer the dates to a paper towel-lined plate to drain. Serve hot.

Paprika-Mustard Pork Spareribs
Prep time: 5 minutes | Cook time: 35 minutes | Serves 2

1 tablespoon kosher salt
1 tablespoon dark brown sugar
1 tablespoon sweet paprika
1 teaspoon garlic powder
1 teaspoon onion powder
1 teaspoon poultry seasoning
½ teaspoon mustard powder
½ teaspoon freshly ground black pepper
2¼ pounds (1 kg) individually cut St. Louis–style pork spareribs

1. Preheat the Oster to 350°F (177°C).
2. In a large bowl, whisk together the salt, brown sugar, paprika, garlic powder, onion powder, poultry seasoning, mustard powder, and pepper. Add the ribs and toss. Rub the seasonings into them with your hands until they're fully coated.
3. Arrange the ribs in the baking pan. Bake for 35 minutes, or until the ribs are tender inside and golden brown and crisp on the outside. Transfer the ribs to plates and serve hot.

Baked Bacon-Wrapped Dates
Prep time: 10 minutes | Cook time: 10 to 14 minutes | Serves 6

12 dates, pitted
6 slices high-quality bacon, cut in half
Cooking spray

1. Preheat the Oster to 360°F (182°C).
2. Wrap each date with half a bacon slice and secure with a toothpick.
3. Spray the baking pan with cooking spray, then place 6 bacon-wrapped dates in the pan and bake for 5 to 7 minutes or until the bacon is crispy. Repeat this process with the remaining dates.
4. Remove the dates and allow to cool on a wire rack for 5 minutes before serving.

Balsamic Mango and Beef Skewers
Prep time: 10 minutes | Cook time: 4 to 7 minutes | Serves 4

¾ pound (340 g) beef sirloin tip, cut into 1-inch cubes
2 tablespoons balsamic vinegar
1 tablespoon olive oil
1 tablespoon honey
½ teaspoon dried marjoram
Pinch of salt
Freshly ground black pepper, to taste
1 mango

1. Preheat the Oster to 390°F (199°C).
2. Thread metal skewers alternating with three beef cubes and two mango cubes.
3. Bake the skewers in the Oster for 4 to 7 minutes, or until the beef is browned and at least 145°F (63°C).
4. Serve hot.

Beef Cubes with Cheese Pasta Sauce
Prep time: 10 minutes | Cook time: 12 to 16 minutes | Serves 4

1 pound (454 g) sirloin tip, cut into 1-inch cubes
1 cup cheese pasta sauce
1½ cups soft bread crumbs
2 tablespoons olive oil
½ teaspoon dried marjoram

1. Preheat the Oster to 380°F (193°C).
2. In a medium bowl, toss the beef with the pasta sauce to coat.
3. In a shallow bowl, combine the bread crumbs, oil, and marjoram, and mix well. Drop the beef cubes, one at a time, into the bread crumb mixture to coat thoroughly. Transfer to the baking pan.
4. Bake the beef in two batches for 10 minutes, or until the beef is at least 145°F (63°C) and the outside is crisp and brown.
5. Serve hot.

Mozzarella Bruschetta with Basil Pesto
Prep time: 10 minutes | Cook time: 5 to 11 minutes | Serves 4

8 slices French bread, ½ inch thick
2 tablespoons softened butter
1 cup shredded Mozzarella cheese
½ cup basil pesto
1 cup chopped grape tomatoes
2 green onions, thinly sliced

1. Preheat the Oster to 350°F (177°C).
2. Remove the bread from the pan and top each piece with some of the cheese. Return to the pan in 2 batches and bake for 1 to 3 minutes, or until the cheese melts.
3. Meanwhile, combine the pesto, tomatoes, and green onions in a small bowl.
4. When the cheese has melted, remove the bread from the Oster and place on a serving plate. Top each slice with some of the pesto mixture and serve.

Cayenne Mixed Nuts with Sesame Seeds
Prep time: 10 minutes | Cook time: 2 minutes | Makes 4 cups

1 tablespoon buttery spread, melted
2 teaspoons honey
¼ teaspoon cayenne pepper
2 teaspoons sesame seeds
¼ teaspoon kosher salt
¼ teaspoon freshly ground black pepper
1 cup cashews
1 cup almonds
1 cup mini pretzels
1 cup rice squares cereal
Cooking spray

1. Preheat the Oster to 360°F (182°C).
2. In a large bowl, combine the buttery spread, honey, cayenne pepper, sesame seeds, kosher salt, and black pepper, then add the cashews, almonds, pretzels, and rice squares, tossing to coat.
3. Spray a baking pan with cooking spray, then pour the mixture into the pan and bake for 2 minutes.
4. Remove the sesame mix from the Oster and allow to cool in the pan on a wire rack for 5 minutes before serving.

Cheesy Salsa Stuffed Mushrooms
Prep time: 10 minutes | Cook time: 15 minutes | Serves 4

16 medium button mushrooms, rinsed and patted dry
⅓ cup low-sodium salsa
3 garlic cloves, minced
1 medium onion, finely chopped
1 jalapeño pepper, minced
⅛ teaspoon cayenne pepper
3 tablespoons shredded Pepper Jack cheese
2 teaspoons olive oil

1. Preheat the Oster to 375°F (191°C).
2. Remove the stems from the mushrooms and finely chop them, reserving the whole caps.
3. In a medium bowl, mix the salsa, garlic, onion, jalapeño, cayenne, and Pepper Jack cheese. Stir in the chopped mushroom stems.
4. Stuff this mixture into the mushroom caps, mounding the filling. Drizzle the olive oil on the mushrooms. Bake the mushrooms in the baking pan for 15 minutes, or until the filling is hot and the mushrooms are tender.
5. Serve immediately.

Mozzarella Hash Brown Bruschetta
Prep time: 5 minutes | Cook time: 6 to 8 minutes | Serves 4

4 frozen hash brown patties
1 tablespoon olive oil
⅓ cup chopped cherry tomatoes
3 tablespoons diced fresh Mozzarella
2 tablespoons grated Parmesan cheese
1 tablespoon balsamic vinegar
1 tablespoon minced fresh basil

1. Preheat the Oster to 425°F (218°C).
2. Place the hash brown patties in the baking pan in a single layer. Bake for 8 minutes, or until the potatoes are crisp, hot, and golden brown.
3. Meanwhile, combine the olive oil, tomatoes, Mozzarella, Parmesan, vinegar, and basil in a small bowl.
4. When the potatoes are done, carefully remove from the pan and arrange on a serving plate. Top with the tomato mixture and serve.

Broccoli, Spinach and Bell Pepper Dip
Prep time: 10 minutes | Cook time: 9 to 14 minutes | Serves 4

½ cup low-fat Greek yogurt
¼ cup nonfat cream cheese
½ cup frozen chopped broccoli, thawed and drained
½ cup frozen chopped spinach, thawed and drained
⅓ cup chopped red bell pepper
1 garlic clove, minced
½ teaspoon dried oregano
2 tablespoons grated low-sodium Parmesan cheese

1. Preheat the Oster to 340°F (171°C).
2. In a medium bowl, blend the yogurt and cream cheese until well combined.
3. Stir in the broccoli, spinach, red bell pepper, garlic, and oregano. Transfer to a baking pan. Sprinkle with the Parmesan cheese.
4. Place the pan in the Oster. Bake for 9 to 14 minutes, or until the dip is bubbly and the top starts to brown.
5. Serve immediately.

Apple Chips
Prep time: 5 minutes | Cook time: 35 minutes | Serves 1

1 Honeycrisp or Pink Lady apple

1. Preheat the Oster to 325°F (163°C).
2. Core the apple with an apple corer, leaving apple whole. Cut the apple into ⅛-inch-thick slices.
3. Arrange the apple slices in the baking pan, staggering slices as much as possible. Bake for 35 minutes, or until the chips are dry and some are lightly browned, turning 4 times with tongs to separate and rotate them from top to bottom.
4. Place the chips in a single layer on a wire rack to cool. Apples will become crisper as they cool. Serve immediately.

Ricotta Phyllo Artichoke Triangles
Prep time: 15 minutes | Cook time: 9 to 12 minutes | Makes 18 triangles

¼ cup Ricotta cheese
1 egg white
⅓ cup minced and drained artichoke hearts
3 tablespoons grated Mozzarella cheese
½ teaspoon dried thyme
6 sheets frozen phyllo dough, thawed
2 tablespoons melted butter

1. Preheat the Oster to 400°F (204°C).
2. In a small bowl, combine the Ricotta cheese, egg white, artichoke hearts, Mozzarella cheese, and thyme, and mix well.
3. Put about 1½ teaspoons of the filling on each strip at the base. Fold the bottom right-hand tip of phyllo over the filling to meet the other side in a triangle, then continue folding in a triangle. Brush each triangle with butter to seal the edges. Repeat with the remaining phyllo dough and filling.
4. Place the triangles in the baking pan. Bake, 6 at a time, for about 3 to 4 minutes, or until the phyllo is golden brown and crisp.
5. Serve hot.

Prosciutto-Wrapped Asparagus Spears
Prep time: 5 minutes | Cook time: 5 minutes | Serves 6

12 asparagus spears, woody ends trimmed
24 pieces thinly sliced prosciutto
Cooking spray

1. Preheat the Oster to 380°F (193°C).
2. Wrap each asparagus spear with 2 slices of prosciutto, then repeat this process with the remaining asparagus and prosciutto.
3. Spray the baking pan with cooking spray, then place 2 to 3 bundles in the pan and bake for 5 minutes. Repeat this process with the remaining asparagus bundles.
4. Remove the bundles and allow to cool on a wire rack for 5 minutes before serving.

Chili Kale Chips with Sesame Seeds
Prep time: 15 minutes | Cook time: 10 minutes | Serves 5

8 cups deribbed kale leaves, torn into 2-inch pieces
1½ tablespoons olive oil
¾ teaspoon chili powder
¼ teaspoon garlic powder
½ teaspoon paprika
2 teaspoons sesame seeds

1. Preheat Oster to 375°F (191°C).
2. In a large bowl, toss the kale with the olive oil, chili powder, garlic powder, paprika, and sesame seeds until well coated.
3. Put the kale in the baking pan and bake for 10 minutes, flipping the kale twice during cooking, or until the kale is crispy.
4. Serve warm.

Garlic-Paprika Potato Chips
Prep time: 5 minutes | Cook time: 25 minutes | Serves 3

2 medium potatoes, preferably Yukon Gold, scrubbed
Cooking spray
2 teaspoons olive oil
½ teaspoon garlic granules
¼ teaspoon paprika
¼ teaspoon plus ⅛ teaspoon sea salt
Ketchup or hot sauce, for serving

1. Preheat the Oster to 425°F (218°C). Spritz the baking pan with cooking spray.
2. Put the potato slices in the pan and bake for 25 minutes until tender and nicely browned.
3. Remove from the pan and serve alongside the ketchup for dipping.

Paprika Deviled Eggs with Dill Pickle
Prep time: 20 minutes | Cook time: 16 minutes | Serves 12

3 cups ice
12 large eggs
½ cup mayonnaise
10 hamburger dill pickle chips, diced
¼ cup diced onion
2 teaspoons salt
2 teaspoons yellow mustard
1 teaspoon freshly ground black pepper
½ teaspoon paprika

1. Preheat the Oster to 250°F (121°C).
2. Put the ice in a large bowl.
3. Place the eggs in the baking pan and bake for 16 minutes.
4. Remove the eggs from the pan to the large bowl of ice to cool.
5. When cool enough to handle, peel the eggs. Slice them in half lengthwise and scoop out yolks into a small bowl. Stir in the mayonnaise, pickles, onion, salt, mustard, and pepper. Mash the mixture with a fork until well combined.
6. Fill each egg white half with 1 to 2 teaspoons of the egg yolk mixture.
7. Sprinkle the paprika on top and serve immediately.

Parmesan Cauliflower with Turmeric
Prep time: 15 minutes | Cook time: 15 minutes | Makes 5 cups

8 cups small cauliflower florets (about 1¼ pounds / 567 g)
1 teaspoon garlic powder
½ teaspoon salt
½ teaspoon turmeric
¼ cup shredded Parmesan cheese

1. Preheat the Oster to 425°F (218°C).
2. In a bowl, combine the cauliflower florets, olive oil, garlic powder, salt, and turmeric and toss to coat.
3. Transfer to the baking and bake for 18 minutes, or until the florets are crisp-tender.
4. Remove from the pan to a plate. Sprinkle with the shredded Parmesan cheese and toss well. Serve warm.

Spanish Mango Pastry
Prep time: 15 minutes | Cook time: 5 minutes | serves 8

3 large mangoes, pitted, peeled, chopped, and pureed (about 3 cups)
2 tablespoons sugar
1 teaspoon finely grated lime zest
2 tablespoons fresh lime juice
¼ teaspoon red chile powder (such as ancho)
CHURROS
1¼ cups sugar
3 tablespoons unsalted butter
1 teaspoon pure vanilla extract
½ teaspoon kosher salt
2 cups all-purpose flour
2 large eggs
1 tablespoon ground cinnamon
Vegetable oil, for deep-frying

1. Make the mango-chile sauce: In a medium saucepan, stir together the mango puree, sugar, lime zest, and lime juice. Bring to a simmer over medium heat, then partially cover and cook, stirring occasionally, until reduced to about 1 cup, about 30 minutes. Stir in the chile powder.
2. Transfer the sauce to a bowl and let cool to room temperature. Cover with plastic wrap and refrigerate until chilled, at least 1 hour or for up to 3 days.
3. Cook the mixture, stirring constantly, until the dough forms into a sticky ball and pulls away from the sides of the pan, 30 seconds to 1 minute. Remove the pan from the heat and transfer the dough to a large bowl. Let cool for 5 minutes. Using an electric mixer, add the eggs one at a time and beat on medium speed until the dough is smooth after each addition. Spoon the dough into a pastry bag fitted with a large star tip.
4. Preheat the Oster to 200°F (93°C). In a large bowl, whisk together the remaining 1 cup sugar and the cinnamon and set aside. Line a wire rack with paper towels and have it nearby.
5. Pour at least 2 inches of vegetable oil into a large, deep, heavy-bottomed pot and heat the oil over medium-high heat until a pinch of flour sizzles when you drop it into the oil or a candy thermometer reads around 360°F (182°C). Holding the pastry bag over the hot oil, squeeze about 3 inches of dough from the pastry bag, slicing it off at the tip end with a paring knife, and carefully let the dough fall into the hot oil.
6. Repeat to make 5 churros. Fry the churros, using a fork or frying spider to turn them often, until they are evenly golden brown and cooked through, about 5 minutes. Using a fork or a frying spider, transfer the churros to the paper towels to drain, then transfer them to a baking sheet and place in the Oster to keep warm while you fry the remaining dough.
7. While the churros are still warm, toss them in the cinnamon-sugar mixture until well coated, shaking off any excess. Stir the chilled mango sauce to loosen.
8. Serve the churros immediately, with the mango-chile sauce alongside for dipping.

Sweet Butter Puffs
Prep time: 5 minutes | Cook time: 40 minutes | Makes 50 mini Puffs

1 sticks (4 ounces) unsalted butter, cubed
2 tablespoons granulated sugar (optional, for the sweet version)
½ to 1 teaspoon kosher salt (½ teaspoon for sweet version; 1 teaspoon for savory version)
1¼ cups all-purpose flour
4 large eggs

1. In a medium saucepan, combine the butter, sugar (if using), salt, and 1 cup water. Bring to a simmer over medium heat, stirring until the butter melts. Add the flour all at once and stir vigorously with a wooden spoon.
2. Cook, stirring constantly, until there is a thin film of dough on the bottom of the pan and the dough forms a sticky ball and pulls away from the sides of the pan, 30 seconds to 1 minute. Remove the pan from the heat and let the dough cool for 5 minutes.
3. Transfer the dough to a large bowl. Add the eggs one at a time and beat using an electric mixer with the whisk attachment on medium speed after each addition until the dough is smooth. Immediately transfer the dough to a pastry bag fitted with a large plain tip, or covers with plastic wrap and refrigerate for up to 2 days.
4. Preheat the Oster to 425°F (218°C). Line two baking sheets with parchment paper. Pipe the dough onto the parchment in the shape of your choice, leaving 1½ inches between them.
5. Bake for 15 minutes, and then reduce the Oster temperature to 375°F(191°C) (191°C)and bake until the pastries are golden and puffed and sound hollow when you tap on them, about 25 minutes more. Immediately pierce the shells with a small, sharp knife to release steam (this helps them stay crispy) and transfer them to a wire rack to cool.
6. Fill as directed or store unfilled shells in an airtight container for up to 2 days. Before serving, stuff with the filling of your choice.

Cinnamon Nut Mix
Prep time: 5 minutes | Cook time: 20 minutes | Serves 6

2 cups mixed nuts (walnuts, pecans, and almonds)
2 tablespoons egg white
2 tablespoons sugar
1 teaspoon paprika
1 teaspoon ground cinnamon
Cooking spray

1. Preheat the Oster to 300°F (149°C). Spray the baking pan with cooking spray.
2. Stir together the mixed nuts, egg white, sugar, paprika, and cinnamon in a small bowl until the nuts are fully coated.
3. Put the nuts in the pan and bake for 20 minutes. Stir halfway through the cooking time for even cooking.
4. Transfer the nuts to a bowl and serve warm.

Golden Choux Pastry
Prep time: 5 minutes | Cook time: 40 minutes | serves 8

1½ cups granulated sugar
½ cup light corn syrup
½ cup confectioners' sugar

1. Preheat the Oster to 425°F (218°C). Line two baking sheets with parchment paper. Prepare the sweet pâte à choux as directed through step 3. Pipe the batter onto the baking sheets into 1-inch rounds and bake for 15 minutes, then reduce the Oster temperature to 375°F(191°C).
2. Bake until the pastries are golden and puffed and sound hollow when you tap on them, about 25 minutes more. Pierce one side of each puff with a small, sharp knife to release steam (this helps the cream puffs stay crispy) and transfer to a wire rack to cool. (After they have cooled, the puffs can be stored in an airtight container for up to 2 days.)
3. Prepare and chill the pastry cream as directed on this page. Just before you're ready to assemble the croquembouche, spoon the chilled pastry cream into a pastry bag fitted with a small plain tip. Holding a cream puff in your palm, poke the tip of the pastry bag into the side where you made the steam vent and squeeze until filled.
4. Repeat with the remaining cream puffs. (Refrigerate filled cream puffs until you begin assembly.)
5. In a medium saucepan, whisk together the sugar, corn syrup, and ½ cup water, stirring until the sugar has dissolved. Bring the mixture to a boil over medium heat and cook, without stirring, until the syrup turns a deep golden amber color and a candy thermometer inserted into the mixture reads 340°F, 6 to 8 minutes. Immediately get ready to assemble the croquembouche.
6. Set a cake stand or round serving platter on your work surface. Hold the cream puffs at the rounded tip and very, very carefully dip the flat end of one cream puff into the warm caramel until just lightly coated (the caramel is very hot—take care not to accidently dip your fingertips in the hot caramel—be sure a grown-up is nearby in case you need help).
7. Place the cream puff, caramel-side down, at the edge of the cake stand. Continue dipping and placing cream puffs until you have formed a roughly 8-inch circle of cream puffs around the perimeter of the cake stand. (You'll need about 12 cream puffs for the first layer.) Next make a smaller layer on top of the first, dipping and placing the cream puffs so that they are staggered with the layer below. Continue dipping and placing cream puffs, building circles on top of each other, until you have formed a pyramid-shaped tower that narrows at the top.
8. Finish with a single cream puff at the top. Dust with the confectioners' sugar and serve.

Chocolate Drizzled Cocoa Puffs
Prep time: 10 minutes | Cook time: 40 minutes | serves 8

COCOA-CREAM FILLING
⅔ cup confectioners' sugar
⅓ cup unsweetened Dutch-process cocoa powder
2 cups heavy cream
1 tablespoon pure vanilla extract
DARK CHOCOLATE GLAZE
½ cup bittersweet chocolate chips
¼ cup heavy cream
1 tablespoon light corn syrup
⅓ cup confectioners' sugar, for dusting

1. Preheat the Oster to 425°F (218°C). Line two baking sheets with parchment paper. Prepare the sweet pâte à choux as directed through step 3. Pipe the batter onto the baking sheets into 2-inch rounds.
2. Bake for 15 minutes, and then reduce the Oster temperature to 375°F(191°C) (191°C)and bake until the pastries are golden and puffed and sound hollow when you tap on them, about 25 minutes more.
3. Pierce one side of each puff with a small, sharp knife to release steam (this helps the cream puffs stay crispy) and transfer them to a wire rack to cool. (After they have cooled, the puffs can be stored in an airtight container for up to 2 days.)
4. Make the cocoa-cream filling: In a small bowl, whisk together the confectioners' sugar and cocoa powder until combined. In a large bowl, using an electric mixer fitted with the whisk attachment, beat the cream on medium-high speed until frothy, about 1 minute. With the mixer running, reduce the speed to medium-low, slowly sprinkle in the vanilla and the sugar-cocoa mixture, and beat until the cream holds stiff, smooth peaks, 1 to 1½ minutes more.
5. Make the dark chocolate glaze: Place the chocolate chips in a heatproof medium bowl. In a small saucepan, bring the cream and corn syrup to a simmer over medium heat, whisking to combine. Pour the hot cream mixture over the chocolate chips. Let stand for 1 minute, then stir until smooth. Set aside while you assemble the cream puffs.
6. To assemble the puffs, halve the cream puffs horizontally. Using a small spoon, fill the bottom halves with the cocoa-cream, then cover with the tops and drizzle each one with chocolate glaze.
7. Chill until the glaze sets, about 30 minutes. Just before serving, dust the puffs with the confectioners' sugar.

Meringue Dessert with Whipped Cream
Prep time: 20 minutes | Cook time: 0 minutes | serves 8

MERINGUES
6 large egg whites, at room temperature
⅛ teaspoon kosher salt
1 teaspoon cream of tartar
1½ cups superfine sugar
2 tablespoons cornstarch
1 teaspoon pure vanilla extract
RASPBERRY SAUCE
1 cup fresh or frozen raspberries
¼ cup granulated sugar
¾ cup seedless raspberry jam
PEACHES
4 large peaches, pitted and thinly sliced (about 3 cups)
2 tablespoons granulated sugar
½ teaspoon ground ginger
YOGURT WHIPPED CREAM
2 cups heavy cream
1 cup plain whole-milk yogurt
2 teaspoons pure vanilla extract
2 tablespoons confectioners' sugar
⅛ teaspoon kosher salt
Fresh mint, for garnish

1. Make the meringues: Position racks in the center and lower third of the Oster and preheat the Oster to 250°F (121°C). Line two baking sheets with parchment paper. In the center of each sheet of parchment, use a pencil to draw a 9-inch-diameter circle (the easiest way to do this is to trace a 9-inch cake pan). Flip the parchment pencil-side down.
2. In a large bowl, using an electric mixer fitted with the whisk attachment, beat the egg whites and salt on medium-high speed until foamy, about 1 minute.
3. Turn off the Oster and let the meringues cool and dry completely in the Oster until they are no longer tacky to the touch, about 1½ hours. When they are done, they will be stiff and crisp on the outside and tender and chewy inside. (The meringue layers can be prepared up to 3 days ahead and stored lightly wrapped in parchment paper at room temperature until you're ready to assemble the Pavlova. Do not refrigerate.)
4. Make the raspberry sauce: In a small saucepan, combine the raspberries, granulated sugar, and 2 tablespoons water. Bring to a simmer and cook, stirring occasionally, until soft and jammy, about 5 minutes.
5. Transfer the raspberry mixture to a blender, add the raspberry jam, and puree until mostly smooth but with a few small pieces of raspberry still visible, about 30 seconds.
6. Transfer the sauce to a small measuring cup and refrigerate until cool, about 1 hour. (The sauce can be prepared up to 3 days ahead and stored, covered, in the refrigerator.)
7. Prepare the peaches: In a medium bowl, gently toss together the peaches, granulated sugar, and ginger. Cover and refrigerate until ready to use.
8. Just before assembling, make the yogurt whipped cream: In a large bowl, using an electric mixer fitted with the whisk attachment, beat the cream, yogurt, vanilla, confectioners' sugar, and salt on medium-high speed until it holds soft peaks, 2 to 3 minutes.
9. Assemble the Pavlov: Place one of the meringue rounds on a large platter. Spoon half the yogurt whipped cream into the center of the round and smooth it slightly with the back of a spoon.
10. Serve the Pavlova immediately, with the extra sauce on the side.

Cinnamon Pumpkin Bread
Prep time: 10 minutes | Cook time: 60 minutes | Makes 1 loaf

1 ½ cups all-purpose flour
½ teaspoon baking powder
½ teaspoon baking soda
1 teaspoon ground cinnamon
¼ teaspoon ground cloves
⅔ cup granulated white sugar
¼ cup packed dark brown sugar
⅓ cup grape seed oil
¾ teaspoon kosher salt
½ teaspoon vanilla extract
2 large eggs
1 ½ cups canned pumpkin purée
½ cup semisweet chocolate chips
BAKING EQUIPMENT
Measuring cups and spoons
Can opener
9 x 5-inch loaf pan
Parchment paper
Nonstick cooking spray
Sifter
2 mixing bowls
Whisk
Rubber spatula
Oster-safe gloves
Knife

1. Preheat your Oster to 350°F (177°C). Line a 9 x 5-inch loaf pan with parchment paper, and then spray with cooking spray.
2. Sift the flour, baking powder, baking soda, cinnamon, and cloves into a mixing bowl.
3. Add the granulated white sugar, brown sugar, oil, salt, and vanilla. Whisk together.
4. Whisk in the eggs one at a time.
5. Add the pumpkin purée, and whisk until incorporated.
6. Using a spatula, fold in the chocolate chips. Transfer the batter to the prepared loaf pan.
7. Put the loaf pan in the Oster. Bake for 50 minutes, or until a toothpick inserted into the center of the loaf comes out clean.
8. Using Oster-safe gloves, remove the loaf pan from the Oster. Let the loaf cool for 1 hour, then slice and serve. Leftover pumpkin bread can be kept in an airtight container lined at the bottom with a paper towel. It can be stored at room temperature for up to 4 days.

Butter Choco Soufflé
Prep time: 15 minutes | Cook time: 20 minutes | Makes 8

3 tablespoons unsalted butter, at room temperature
¾ cup granulated sugar, divided
4 large egg yolks
1¼ cups whole milk
2 tablespoons corn starch
1 tablespoon unsweetened Dutch-process cocoa powder
¼ teaspoon kosher salt
4 ounces bittersweet chocolate, finely chopped (about ⅔ cup)
1 teaspoon pure vanilla extract
8 large egg whites, at room temperature
½ teaspoon cream of tartar
¼ cup confectioners' sugar, plus more for dusting

1. Position a rack in the lower third of the Oster and preheat the Oster to 375°F(191°C). Use 2 tablespoons of the butter to lightly grease eight 6-ounce straight-sided ramekins. Use ¼ cup of the granulated sugar to coat the insides of the ramekins, turning them to coat the sides and bottom evenly, then tap out any excess.
2. Make an ice bath by filling a large bowl with ice cubes and 1 cup water. Set aside. In a medium saucepan, whisk together the egg yolks, milk, remaining ½ cup granulated sugar, the corn starch, cocoa powder, and salt.
3. Cook over medium heat, whisking often, as the mixture comes to a low simmer and thickens, about 4 minutes (be sure to get the whisk—or a wooden spoon—into the corners of the pan so the mixture doesn't cook on the bottom!).
4. Cook, whisking, until the mixture is smooth and thick, 1 to 2 minutes more. Remove from the heat and whisk in the chocolate, the remaining 1 tablespoon butter, and the vanilla until the mixture looks smooth and shiny.
5. Scrape the chocolate mixture into a medium bowl. Set the bottom of the bowl in the prepared ice bath, taking care not to let any water spill into the bowl. Let the mixture cool, whisking occasionally, until the chocolate base is smooth and cooled to room temperature, 10 to 12 minutes.
6. In a large, clean, dry bowl, using an electric mixer fitted with the whisk attachment beat the egg whites and cream of tartar on medium-high speed until they form soft peaks, about 1½ to 2 minutes. Slowly sprinkle in the confectioners' sugar, a tablespoon or two at a time, and beat until the egg whites are glossy and form stiff peaks, about 1 minute more.
7. Using a rubber spatula, very gently fold half the egg whites into the cooled chocolate base. Repeat with the remaining egg whites, folding just enough to combine.
8. Divide the mixture evenly among the prepared ramekins and very carefully place them on a baking sheet. Lightly set the baking sheet on the Oster rack and gently close the Oster door.
9. Bake until the soufflés rise and crack on top but are still slightly wobbly in the center, 15 to 20 minutes. Take care not to jump around or open the Oster door before the soufflés are ready—any big movements or sudden changes in temperature can make them deflate!

Basil Egg Frittata
Prep time: 10 minutes | Cook time: 50 minutes | serves 6

Nonstick cooking spray
1 tablespoon butter
1 bunch (about 1 pound) thin asparagus, trimmed and cut into 1-inch lengths
5 sheets matzo, broken into large chunks
5 large eggs
1 cup fresh basil leaves, chopped
1 cup frozen peas, thawed
1 tablespoon freshly grated lemon peel
1 teaspoon salt
½ teaspoon ground black pepper

1. Preheat Oster to 350°F(177°C). Spray 8 x 8-inch baking dish with nonstick cooking spray.
2. In 12-inch skillet over medium heat, melt butter. Add asparagus and cook for 5 to 8 minutes or until crisp-tender. Remove skillet from heat and cool.
3. Meanwhile, in medium bowl, pour 1 cup warm water over matzo. Let stand for 5 minutes or until softened. Drain.
4. In large bowl with wire whisk, beat eggs. Stir in asparagus, matzo, basil, peas, lemon peel, salt, and pepper.
5. Pour into prepared baking dish. Bake for 40 minutes or until top is golden brown and center is set. Cooled frittata may be made ahead, covered with plastic wrap, and refrigerated for up to 3 days.

Butter Loaf with Dried Currants
Prep time: 10 minutes | Cook time: 1 hour 15 minutes | serves 12

4 cups all-purpose flour
¼ cup sugar
1 tablespoon baking powder
1½ teaspoons salt
1 teaspoon baking soda
6 tablespoons butter
1 cup dried currants
2 teaspoons caraway seeds
1½ cups low-fat buttermilk

1. Preheat Oster to 350°F(177°C). Grease large cookie sheet.
2. In large bowl with wire whisk, mix flour, sugar, baking powder, salt, and baking soda. With pastry blender or 2 knives used scissors-fashion, cut in butter until mixture resembles coarse crumbs. Stir in currants and caraway seeds, then buttermilk, until flour is moistened.
3. Turn dough onto well-floured surface; knead dough 8 to 10 times, just until combined. Shape into flattened ball; transfer to prepared cookie sheet. Cut ¼-inch-deep X into top using a knife.
4. Bake 1 hour or until toothpick inserted in center of loaf comes out clean. Cool loaf completely on wire rack.

Cinnamon Oats Granola

Prep time: 10 minutes | **Cook time:** 45 minutes | **Makes 3 cups**

⅓ cup maple syrup
¼ cup coconut oil
¼ cup packed light brown sugar
½ teaspoon vanilla extract
¼ teaspoon ground cinnamon
¼ teaspoon kosher salt
2 cups old-fashioned rolled oats
⅔ cup chopped walnuts or other nuts, such as almonds and pecans
⅓ cup pumpkin seeds or other seeds, such as chia seeds or flaxseed

BAKING EQUIPMENT
Measuring cups and spoons
Sheet pan
Parchment paper
Large mixing bowl
Rubber spatula
Oster-safe gloves

1. Preheat your Oster to 350°F(177°C). Line a sheet pan with parchment paper.
2. In a large mixing bowl, combine the maple syrup, coconut oil, brown sugar, vanilla, cinnamon, and salt. Mix well with a spatula. Don't worry about any coconut oil lumps. They will melt when you bake.
3. Add the oats, nuts, and seeds. Stir well so that every morsel in your granola is coated with the maple syrup mixture.
4. Pour the granola onto the prepared sheet pan. Make sure to scrape every last bit out of your bowl. Spread out the granola mixture evenly.
5. Put the sheet pan in the Oster. Bake for 10 minutes. Using Oster-safe gloves, remove the pan, stir the granola, and return it to the Oster. Bake for 15 minutes, or until the granola is a beautiful golden brown color.
6. Remove the sheet pan from the Oster. Let the granola cool for 30 to 45 minutes, or until completely cool. Use your hands to break up the granola if there are large chunks. This will make some clumps, which is my favorite part!
7. Once cooled, pour yourself a bowl with some milk, and enjoy! The rest can be stored in an airtight jar in a cool, dry place for up to 1 month.

TIP: Instead of maple syrup, you can use honey or agave nectar.

Creamy Choco Cookies

Prep time: 10 minutes | **Cook time:** 40 minutes | **Makes 24 cups**

1 cup (2 sticks) unsalted butter, softened
1 cup packed dark brown sugar
1 cup granulated white sugar
1 ½ tablespoons heavy cream
2 eggs, at room temperature
½ teaspoon kosher salt
1 ½ teaspoons vanilla extract
3 cups all-purpose flour
¾ teaspoon baking soda
½ teaspoon baking powder
2 cups semisweet chocolate chips

BAKING EQUIPMENT
Measuring cups and spoons
Sheet pan
Parchment paper
Electric hand mixer
Mixing bowl
Ice-cream scoop
Oster-safe gloves
Offset spatula
Wire rack

1. Preheat your Oster to 375°F(191°C). Line a sheet pan with parchment paper.
2. Using an electric hand mixer in a mixing bowl, cream together the butter, brown sugar, and granulated white sugar for 2 minutes on high speed
3. Add the cream, eggs, salt, and vanilla. Mix until combined and glossy.
4. Add the flour, baking soda, and baking powder. Mix until there are no visible dry spots.
5. Reduce the mixer speed to low, and fold in the chocolate chips.
6. Using an ice-cream scoop, scoop about 12 dough balls onto the sheet pan. Give them some room because they will expand and flatten
7. Put the sheet pan in the Oster. Bake for 10 to 12 minutes, or until the edges of the cookies are golden brown and they look delicious.
8. Using Oster-safe gloves, remove the sheet pan from the Oster. Transfer the cookies using an offset spatula to a wire rack to cool for about 10 minutes.
9. Repeat with the remaining dough or keep it in an airtight container in the refrigerator for up to 3 days or in the freezer for up to 3 months.

TIP: Putting the dough in the refrigerator for at least 30 minutes before baking can help you have chewier, tastier cookies.

Rich Blackberry Cupcake
Prep time: 10 minutes | **Cook time:** 45 minutes | **Makes 12 muffins**

1 ⅓ cups all-purpose flour
½ teaspoon baking powder
½ teaspoon baking soda
¾ cup granulated white sugar
½ cup grape seed oil
½ teaspoon vanilla extract
½ teaspoon salt
1 large egg
⅓ cup milk
1 ¼ cups berries, such as blueberries, blackberries, and raspberries

BAKING EQUIPMENT
Measuring cups and spoons
Cupcake tin
Cupcake liners
Nonstick cooking spray
Sifter
2 mixing bowls
Electric hand mixer
Rubber spatula
Oster-safe gloves

1. Preheat your Oster to 400°F (204°C). Line your cupcake tin with cupcake liners, then spray the liners with cooking spray.
2. Sift together the flour, baking powder, and baking soda into a mixing bowl.
3. Using an electric hand mixer in another mixing bowl, mix together the sugar, oil, vanilla, and salt on medium speed for 1 minute.
4. Add the egg and milk. Mix for 1 minute.
5. Add the flour mixture into the liquid mixture. Mix until incorporated.
6. Turn off the mixer. Using a spatula, fold your berries into the batter.
7. Scoop your batter into the prepared cupcake tin. Fill only two-thirds full because the batter will expand.
8. Put the cupcake tin in the Oster. Bake for 20 minutes, or until a toothpick inserted into the center of a muffin comes out clean.
9. Using Oster-safe gloves, remove the tin from the Oster. Let the cupcakes cool for 20 minutes. Remove the cupcakes from the tin. Leftover muffins can be stored in an airtight container at room temperature for up to 2 days.

TIP: Berries naturally start to sink to the bottom of muffins because they are heavy. However, if you dust them with flour before folding them into the batter, it will help them float.

Vanilla flavored Choco sweets
Prep time: 10 minutes | **Cook time:** 1 hour 30 minutes | **Makes 12 cookies**

3 large eggs, cold
½ teaspoon cream of tartar
1 cup granulated white sugar
1 teaspoon vanilla extract
¼ cup cocoa powder (optional)

BAKING EQUIPMENT
Measuring cups and spoons
Sheet pan
Parchment paper
Mixing bowl, plus 2 small bowls for separating the eggs
Electric hand mixer
Oster-safe gloves
Sifter or fine-mesh sieve

1. Preheat your Oster to 225°F (107°C). Line a sheet pan with parchment paper.
2. Separate the egg whites from the yolks, placing the whites in a super clean mixing .
3. Add the cream of tartar to the egg whites. Using an electric hand mixer, mix on low speed. Once you get some foam, raise the speed to medium. Once the mixture turns white, raise the speed to high.
4. Add the sugar 1 tablespoon at a time so the egg whites can get big, fluffy, and glossy. If you see any sugar grains, keep mixing! You want your egg white mixture to be smooth.
5. Once the mixture is fluffy, add the vanilla. Continue whisking until fully mixed.
6. Turn off the mixer. Take 1 heaping tablespoon of your meringue, and spoon onto the prepared baking sheet. Repeat with the remaining meringue, leaving room in between.
7. Put the sheet pan in the Oster. Bake for 1 hour. Don't peek!
8. Turn off the Oster. Leave the sheet pan inside for 1 hour to completely dry the meringues. Keep the Oster door closed as it could deflate and crack them.
9. Using Oster-safe gloves, remove the sheet pan from the Oster. Let cool for 45 minutes. Dust the meringues with the cocoa powder (if using).

Rich Vanilla Butter Cake
Prep time: 10 minutes | Cook time: 1 hour 15 minutes | makes one 9 x 13-inch cake

For the cake:
½ cup (1 stick) unsalted butter, softened, plus more for greasing the pan
1 ½ cups all-purpose flour
1 teaspoon baking powder
½ cup buttermilk, at room temperature
½ cup grape seed oil
1 tablespoon vanilla extract
¾ teaspoon kosher salt
For the frosting:
4 ½ cups powdered sugar
1 cup (2 sticks) unsalted butter, softened
1 teaspoon vanilla extract
3 tablespoons whole milk
Sprinkles, for decorating (optional)
BAKING EQUIPMENT
Measuring cups and spoons
9 x 13-inch cake pan
Parchment paper
Sifter
3 mixing bowls
Electric hand mixer
Oster-safe gloves
Whisk attachment for mixer
Offset spatula

To make the cake:
1. Preheat your Oster to 350°F (177°C). Line a 9 x 13-inch cake pan with parchment paper, and grease the parchment paper with butter
2. Using an electric hand mixer in another mixing bowl, beat together the butter, granulated white sugar, and brown sugar on medium speed for 2 minutes
3. Add the eggs. Beat for about 4 minutes, or until the mixture is pale yellow, fluffy, and doubled in size.
4. Combine the buttermilk and oil in a measuring cup with a spout, and stream them into the batter while still beating. Add the vanilla and salt.
5. Add the flour mixture, and mix until there are no dry spots in the batter.
6. Turn off the mixer. Pour the batter into the prepared pan.
7. Put the cake pan in the Oster. Bake for 20 to 25 minutes, or until a toothpick inserted into the center of the cake comes out clean and the edges are slightly browned.
8. Using Oster-safe gloves, remove the cake pan from the Oster, and let cool.

To make the frosting:
1. Sift the powdered sugar into a mixing bowl to remove any lumps.
2. Add the butter and vanilla. Using an electric hand mixer, whisk on medium speed until smooth and thick.
3. Whisk in the milk 1 tablespoon at a time until you get a smooth, soft texture.

Cocoa Butter Brownies
Prep time: 10 minutes | Cook time: 50 minutes | Makes 8 brownies

¾ cup all-purpose flour
¼ cup Dutch-processed cocoa powder
1 cup semisweet chocolate chips
⅓ cup unsalted butter
¾ cup granulated white sugar
1 tablespoon packed dark brown sugar
1 teaspoon vanilla extract
½ teaspoon kosher salt
2 large eggs, at room temperature
1 large egg yolk, at room temperature
BAKING EQUIPMENT
Measuring cups and spoons
8 x 8-inch glass baking pan
Parchment paper
Nonstick cooking spray
Sifter
2 mixing bowls
Microwave-safe bowls
Rubber spatula
Electric hand mixer
Oster-safe gloves
Knife

1. Preheat your Oster to 325°F (163°C). Line an 8 x 8-inch glass baking pan with parchment paper, then spray the parchment paper with cooking spray. Make sure you have some extra parchment paper hanging off all the sides to make it easy to take the brownies out of the pan later.
2. Sift the flour and cocoa powder into a mixing bowl
3. In a microwave-safe bowl, melt ½ cup of chocolate chips. In another microwave-safe bowl, melt the butter. Combine both bowls and mix until smooth and silky.
4. In another mixing bowl, combine the granulated white sugar, brown sugar, vanilla, salt, eggs, and yolk. Using an electric hand mixer, mix on medium speed for 1 minute.
5. Add the butter and chocolate mixture to the egg mixture. Mix until fully combined.
6. Reduce the mixer speed to low. Add the flour mixture. Mix until there are no dry flour bits.
7. Slowly mix in the remaining ½ cup of chocolate chips.
8. Transfer the batter to the prepared baking pan. Tap the pan on the counter lightly a few times to get rid of any air bubbles. Put the baking pan in the Oster.
9. Bake for 25 to 30 minutes or until the top is crackly and the sides are fully baked.
10. Using Oster-safe gloves, remove the baking pan from the Oster. Let the brownies cool, and then remove from the pan. Cut into 8 pieces, and serve.

TIP: You can store brownie squares in an airtight container at room temperature for up to 2 days.

Cheesy Garlic Bake
Prep time: 10 minutes | Cook time: 50 minutes | Makes 2 cups of crackers

1 cup all-purpose flour, plus more for rolling the dough
1 teaspoon Italian seasoning
1 teaspoon kosher salt
½ teaspoon garlic powder
½ teaspoon dried minced garlic
¼ teaspoon baking powder
¾ cup ice water
2 tablespoons olive oil
BAKING EQUIPMENT
Measuring cups and spoons
Sheet pan
Parchment paper
Nonstick cooking spray
Mixing bowl
Wooden spoon
Rolling pin
Oster-safe gloves
2 metal or plastic spatulas
Wire rack

1. Preheat your Oster to 400°F(204°C). Line a sheet pan with parchment paper, and then spray it with cooking spray.
2. In a mixing bowl, combine the flour, Italian seasoning, salt, garlic powder, dried minced garlic, and baking powder.
3. Lightly flour a clean work surface and rolling pin. Turn out the dough onto the surface, and roll out until it is ¼ to ½ inch thick. With your hands, transfer the whole sheet of rolled out dough to the prepared sheet pan. You may need to ask for help to move the dough.
4. Using Oster-safe gloves, remove the sheet pan from the Oster. With two spatulas, transfer the baked dough to a wire rack. It will crisp as it cools.
5. Using the rolling pin, break the baked dough until you get some cool, jagged crackers!
6. You can serve crackers with soft cheese. Any leftovers can be stored in an airtight container at room temperature for up to a week.

Cheese and Herb mixed Breadsticks
Prep time: 10 minutes | Cook time: 1 hour 25 minutes | Makes 10 breadsticks

1 cup all-purpose flour, plus more for preparing the work surface
2 tablespoons shredded parmesan cheese
¼ teaspoon cracked black pepper
¼ teaspoon granulated white sugar
1 tablespoon olive oil
1 tablespoon unsalted butter, softened
¼ cup ice-cold water
BAKING EQUIPMENT
Measuring cups and spoons
Sheet pan
Parchment paper
Nonstick cooking spray
Mixing bowl
Wooden spoon
Dish towel or plastic wrap
Rolling pin
Oster-safe gloves

1. Preheat your Oster to 350°F(177°C). Line a sheet pan with parchment paper, then spray the parchment paper with cooking spray.
2. In a mixing bowl, add the flour, cheese, salt, parsley, pepper, and granulated white sugar. Stir until combined.
3. Divide the dough into 10 equal balls. Let them rest for 10 minutes, covered loosely with a dish towel or plastic wrap.
4. Roll each dough ball out to about 10 inches long. (You want them long and thin to fit the length of your sheet pan. I like to use my hands to make them cylindrical.) Place on the prepared sheet pan.
5. Put the sheet pan in the Oster. Bake for 35 to 40 minutes, or until the breadsticks are a beautiful golden brown color.
6. Using Oster-safe gloves, remove the sheet pan from the Oster. Let the breadsticks cool for 30 minutes.

Moms Special Apple Crisp
Prep time: 10 minutes | Cook time: 1 hour 15 minutes | Makes 9x3 inch dish

For the streusel topping:
1 ½ cups (3 sticks) unsalted butter, melted, plus more for greasing the baking dish
2 ½ cups rolled oats
1 cup packed light brown sugar
1 cup all-purpose flour
1 teaspoon vanilla extract
½ teaspoon kosher salt
½ teaspoon ground cinnamon
For the baked apple mix:
7 to 8 cups cored, peeled, diced apples, such as a Granny Smith and Gala about 5 large apples)
½ cup granulated white sugar
2 tablespoons water
1 ½ teaspoons cornstarch
1 teaspoon ground cinnamon
Juice of ½ lemon
BAKING EQUIPMENT
Knife
Measuring cups and spoons
9 x 13-inch baking pan
2 large mixing bowls
Wooden spoon
Oster-safe gloves
To make the streusel topping:
1. Preheat your Oster to 375°F(191°C). Grease a 9 x 13-inch baking pan with butter.
2. In a large mixing bowl, using a wooden spoon, combine the melted butter, oats, brown sugar, flour, vanilla, salt, and cinnamon. Set aside.
3. To make the baked apple mix:
4. In another large mixing bowl, combine the apples, granulated white sugar, water, cornstarch, cinnamon, and lemon juice. Stir until fully combined and the apples are well coated.
5. Pour the apples into the prepared baking pan. Top with the streusel.
6. Put the baking pan in the Oster. Bake for 35 to 40 minutes, or until bubbly and golden brown.

Grandma's Best Ever Chocolate Cake
Prep time: 10 minutes | Cook time: 1 hour 15 minutes | Makes 9x3 inch cake

For the chocolate cake:
1 cup (2 sticks) unsalted butter, plus more for greasing the pan
1 cup water
⅓ cup cocoa powder
2 cups all-purpose flour
1 teaspoon baking powder
1 teaspoon baking soda
2 cups granulated white sugar
¼ teaspoons kosher salt
½ cup buttermilk
2 large eggs, at room temperature
1 teaspoon vanilla extract
For the ganache icing:
1 cup dark or semisweet chocolate chips
½ cup heavy cream
BAKING EQUIPMENT
Measuring cups and spoons
9 x 13-inch baking pan
Parchment paper
Saucepan
Wooden spoon
2 mixing bowls
Microwave-safe bowl
Rubber spatula
Oster-safe gloves
Knife
Whisk
Offset spatula

To make the chocolate cake:
1. Preheat your Oster to 375°F(191°C). Line a 9 x 13-inch cake pan with parchment paper, and grease the parchment paper with butter.
2. In a saucepan, bring the butter and water to a boil over medium-high heat. Remove from the heat.
3. Add the cocoa powder, and stir until it is smooth. Set aside for about 10 minutes, or until cooled.
4. In a mixing bowl, combine the flour, baking powder, baking soda, sugar, and salt.
5. In a microwave-safe bowl, warm the buttermilk in the microwave for 10 seconds at a time, at 20 percent power, until it reaches room temperature (about 30 seconds total). Stir each time you remove the buttermilk from the microwave.
6. Add the buttermilk, eggs, and vanilla to the dry ingredients. Using a wooden spoon, stir to combine.
7. Add the cocoa powder and butter mixture. Stir until fully mixed.
8. Transfer the batter to the prepared baking pan.
9. Put the baking pan in the Oster. Bake for 25 to 30 minutes, or until a toothpick inserted into the center of the cake comes out clean.
10. Using Oster-safe gloves, remove the pan from the Oster. Let the cake cool completely.

To make the ganache icing:
11. Put the chocolate chips in a mixing bowl and set aside.
12. In a microwave-safe bowl, warm the heavy cream in the microwave on 100 percent power for about 45 seconds, or until it starts to bubble. Make sure it doesn't boil or bubble over.
13. Pour the warm cream over the chocolate chips. Allow it to sit for about 3 to 4 minutes then gently stir the cream and chocolate with a whisk until smooth.
14. Using an offset spatula, ice the top of the cake until the ganache reaches the edges.

Easy Vanilla Square Cakes
Prep time: 10 minutes | Cook time: 50 minutes | Makes 8 square cakes
1 cup all-purpose flour
½ teaspoon baking powder
¼ teaspoon baking soda
1 cup packed dark brown sugar
½ cup (1 stick) unsalted butter, at room temperature
1 ½ teaspoons vanilla extract
½ teaspoon kosher salt
2 large eggs, at room temperature
⅓ cup white chocolate chips
BAKING EQUIPMENT
Measuring cups and spoons
8 x 8-inch glass baking pan
Parchment paper
Nonstick cooking spray
Sifter
2 mixing bowls
Electric hand mixer
Rubber spatula
Oster-safe gloves
Knife

1. Preheat your Oster to 350°F(177°C). Line an 8 x 8-inch glass baking pan with parchment paper, then spray the parchment paper with cooking spray.
2. Make sure you have some extra parchment hanging off all the sides to make it easy to take the blondies out of the pan later.
3. Sift the flour, baking powder, and baking soda into a mixing bowl.
4. Using an electric hand mixer in another mixing bowl, mix the brown sugar, butter, vanilla, and salt on high speed for about 2 minutes, or until combined.
5. Reduce the speed to low and add the eggs one at a time. Mix until fully combined.
6. Add the flour, baking powder, and baking soda, and mix until there aren't any dry bits.
7. Add the chocolate chips and gently mix them in.
8. Turn off the mixer. Pour the batter into the prepared baking pan. Using a spatula, smooth out the top of the batter. Tap the pan on the counter lightly a few times to get rid of any air bubbles.
9. Put the baking pan in the Oster. Bake for 25 to 30 minutes, or until the edges and top are set and slightly browned.
10. Using Oster-safe gloves, remove the baking pan from the Oster. Let the Blondie cool, and then remove from the pan.
11. Cut into 8 pieces, and serve. Store leftover Blondie squares in an airtight container at room temperature for up to 2 days.

Enticing Blueberry Crumble Pie

Prep time: 10 minutes | Cook time: 1 hour | Makes 9x3 inch crumble

For the blueberries:
6 cups fresh blueberries
Juice of 1 lemon
2 tablespoons granulated white sugar
¼ cup all-purpose flour
1 tablespoon vanilla extract
For the crumble topping:
3 full-size Graham crackers
½ cup granulated white sugar
1 tablespoon packed light brown sugar
1 teaspoon vanilla extract
¼ teaspoon salt
BAKING EQUIPMENT
Measuring cups and spoons
Zip-top bag
Rolling pin
9 x 13-inch baking pan
Wooden spoon
Mixing bowl
Fork
Oster-safe gloves

To make the blueberries:

1. Preheat your Oster to 350°F(177°C). In a 9 x 13-inch baking pan combine the blueberries, lemon juice, granulated white sugar, flour, and vanilla. Stir well. Set aside.
2. To make the crumble topping: Put the graham crackers in a zip-top bag, and seal it. Using a rolling pin, smash the crackers. They do not have to be super fine crumbs.
3. In a mixing bowl, using a fork, mix together the granulated white sugar, flour, graham cracker crumbs, butter, brown sugar, vanilla, and salt until a crumbly mixture forms.
4. Pour the crumble on top of the blueberry mixture. Put the baking pan in the Oster. Bake for 35 minutes, until the center is bubbling.
5. Using Oster-safe gloves, remove the baking pan from the Oster. Serve the crumble warm with ice-cream.

Healthy Banana Bread

Prep time: 10 minutes | Cook time: 1 hour 20 minutes | Makes 1 loaf

2 bananas, brown or freckled
2 large eggs, at room temperature
1 cup granulated white sugar
½ cup packed dark brown sugar
¾ cup grape seed oil
1 ½ teaspoons vanilla extract
½ teaspoon kosher salt
1 ¾ cups all-purpose flour
1 ½ teaspoons baking powder
¾ cup walnuts (optional)
BAKING EQUIPMENT
Measuring cups and spoons
9 x 5-inch metal loaf pan
Parchment paper
Nonstick cooking spray
Mixing bowl
Fork
Electric hand mixer
Rubber spatula
Oster-safe gloves
Knife

1. Preheat your Oster to 350°F(177°C). Line a 9 x 5-inch metal loaf pan with parchment paper, and then spray it with cooking spray.
2. Add the flour and baking powder. Mix to combine well.
3. Using a spatula, fold in the walnuts (if using).
4. Transfer the dough to the prepared loaf pan.
5. Put the loaf pan in the Oster. Bake for 1 hour to 1 hour and 5 minutes, or until a toothpick inserted into the center of the bread comes out clean.
6. Remove the bread from the pan, and slice. Place leftover banana bread in an airtight container lined at the bottom with a paper towel. It can be stored at room temperature for up to 4 days.

Easy Buttermilk Bread

Prep time: 10 minutes | Cook time: 1 hour 30 minutes | Makes 1 loaf

4 cups all-purpose flour, plus more for rolling the dough
¼ cup granulated white sugar
½ teaspoon kosher salt
1 tablespoon baking powder
1 teaspoon baking soda
½ cup (1 stick) unsalted butter, softened
1 large egg
1 cup plus 1 tablespoon buttermilk
BAKING EQUIPMENT
Measuring cups and spoons
Sheet pan
Parchment paper
Mixing bowl
Rubber spatula
Knife
Pastry brush
Oster-safe gloves

1. Preheat your Oster to 375°F(191°C). Line a sheet pan with parchment paper.
2. In a mixing bowl, use a spatula to stir together the flour, sugar, salt, baking powder, and baking soda.
3. Add the butter, egg, and 1 cup of buttermilk. Stir until a wet dough forms.
4. Lightly flour a clean work surface and your hands. Pour the dough out onto the surface, and knead for about 2 minutes, or until it is no longer wet and sticky.
5. Shape the dough into a dome about 8 inches across, and score it with a knife.
6. Brush the dough with the remaining 1 tablespoon of buttermilk. Transfer to the prepared sheet pan.
7. Put the sheet pan in the Oster. Bake for 1 hour, or until a toothpick inserted into the center of the bread comes out clean.
8. Using Oster-safe gloves, remove the sheet pan from the Oster. Let the bread cool for 1 hour.

Homemade Coconut Tart
Prep time: 10 minutes | Cook time: 25 minutes | serves 8

1 cup shredded sweetened coconut
1 cup salted gluten-free pretzels, crushed into small pieces
½ cup rice flour
½ cup coconut oil, melted
3 tablespoons brown sugar
2 tablespoons unsweetened cocoa
1 cup coconut milk
6 ounces (170 g) dark chocolate, finely chopped
Pinch salt
Pomegranate seeds, for garnish, optional

1. Preheat Oster to 375°F (191°C). Grease 9-inch tart pan with removable bottom.
2. In large bowl, combine shredded coconut, pretzels, rice flour, melted coconut oil, sugar, and cocoa. Transfer to prepared tart pan. With your hands, firmly press mixture into bottom and up side of pan in even layer; place on cookie sheet. Bake for 10 minutes. Cool crust completely on wire rack.
3. In small saucepan, heat coconut milk over medium heat until just bubbling at edges, whisking occasionally. Place chocolate and salt in medium heatproof bowl.
4. Pour hot coconut milk over chocolate. Let stand for 5 minutes. Gently whisk until smooth.
5. Pour into tart shell. Refrigerate, uncovered, for 2 hours or until set. Once set, tart can be made ahead, covered with plastic wrap, for up to 2 days. To serve, garnish with pomegranate seeds, if using.

Milky Bread and Honeyed Butter
Prep time: 10 minutes | Cook time: 55 minutes | Makes 1 9 inch loaf

For the cornbread:
¼ cup (½ stick) unsalted butter, melted, plus more for greasing the pan
1 cup all-purpose flour
1 cup cornmeal
¼ cup granulated white sugar
1 teaspoon baking powder
¼ teaspoon baking soda
½ teaspoon kosher salt
1 cup milk
1 large egg
¼ cup grape seed oil
For the honey butter:
½ cup (1 stick) unsalted butter, softened
¼ cup honey
BAKING EQUIPMENT
Measuring cups and spoons
9-inch cake pan
Parchment paper
2 mixing bowls
Whisk
Oster-safe gloves
Wooden spoon

To make the cornbread:
1. Preheat your Oster to 400°F (204°C). Line a 9-inch cake pan with parchment paper, and grease the paper with butter.
2. In a mixing bowl, combine the flour, cornmeal, granulated white sugar, baking powder, baking soda, and salt. Whisk well.
3. Add the milk, egg, melted butter, and oil. Whisk until there are no dry bits and no lumps left. Pour the batter into the prepared cake pan.
4. Put the cake pan in the Oster. Bake for 22 minutes, or until a toothpick inserted into the center of the bread comes out dry.
5. Using Oster-safe gloves, remove the pan from the Oster. Let the cornbread cool for 15 minutes.
6. To make the honey butter: While the cornbread is cooling, in another mixing bowl, stir together the softened butter and honey until fully incorporated.
7. Serve the cornbread warm with the honey butter. Cooled cornbread can be tightly wrapped in plastic wrap, and stored at room temperature for up to 3 days.

Mini Apple Muffins
Prep time: 10 minutes | Cook time: 45 minutes | Makes 36 mini muffins

¾ cup applesauce
½ cup granulated white sugar
½ cup packed light brown sugar
1 large egg
1 ¼ cups all-purpose flour
½ teaspoon baking powder
1 teaspoon ground cinnamon
2 cups peeled, cored, and diced apples, such as Granny Smith and Fuji (about 4 large apples)
BAKING EQUIPMENT
Knife
Cutting board
Measuring cups and spoons
Mixing bowl
Whisk
Rubber spatula
Silicone mini muffin mold
Oster-safe gloves

1. Preheat your Oster to 350°F (177°C).
2. In a mixing bowl, whisk together the applesauce, granulated white sugar, brown sugar, and egg until combined and light yellow.
3. Add the flour, baking powder, cinnamon, and nutmeg. Whisk until you get a smooth batter.
4. Fold in the apples using a spatula.
5. Fill the cups in a silicone mini muffin mold three-quarters full with the batter.
6. Put the muffin mold in the Oster. Bake for 15 minutes until golden brown on top.
7. Using Oster-safe gloves, remove the muffin mold from the Oster. Let the muffins cool for 30 minutes. Leftover muffins can be stored in an airtight container at room temperature for up to 2 days.

TIP: You can use a metal muffin tin, but be sure to grease the pan. Using a silicone mold allows your mini muffins to pop out cleanly for fast removal. However, a silicone mold is less firm, so ask an adult for help when placing it in the Oster.

Milk Chocolate Cookies
Prep time: 10 minutes | Cook time: 60 minutes | Makes 20 cookies

2 cups all-purpose flour
½ cup cocoa powder
1 teaspoon baking powder
1 cup (2 sticks) unsalted butter, softened
1 ¾ cups powdered sugar
¼ cup granulated white sugar
½ cup packed dark brown sugar
1 teaspoon vanilla extract
¼ teaspoon kosher salt
2 large eggs
2 cups milk chocolate and semisweet
BAKING EQUIPMENT
Measuring cups and spoons
Sheet pan
Parchment paper
2 mixing bowls
Electric hand mixer
Ice-cream scoop
Oster-safe gloves
Metal spatula
Wire rack

1. Preheat your Oster to 375°F(191°C). Line a sheet pan with parchment paper. Sift together the flour, cocoa powder, and baking soda into a mixing bowl.
2. In another mixing bowl, combine the butter, powdered sugar, granulated white sugar, brown sugar, vanilla, and salt. Using an electric hand mixer, mix on high speed for 3 minutes, or until pale yellow in color.
3. Add the eggs one at a time, and mix until fully incorporated. Add the flour mixture. Mix until there are no dry bits. Reduce the mixer speed to low. Slowly mix in the chocolate chips.
4. Turn off the mixer. Using an ice-cream scoop, scoop 10 dough balls out and place them onto the prepared sheet pan. Make sure to leave space between them because they will spread a bit.
5. Put the sheet pan in the Oster. Bake for 12 minutes.
6. Using Oster-safe gloves, remove the sheet pan from the Oster. Using a metal spatula, transfer the cookies to a wire rack to cool for 15 minutes.
7. Repeat with the remaining dough or keep the remaining dough in an airtight container in the refrigerator for up to 3 days or in the freezer for up to 3 months.

Sweet and Citrus Pastry
Prep time: 10 minutes | Cook time: 40 minutes | serves 12

Pastry Cream
¼ cup Meyer lemon juice (from about 2 Meyer lemons)
Sweet Pâte à Choux
MEYER LEMON GLAZE
2 cups confectioners' sugar
1 tablespoon finely grated Meyer lemon zest
2 to 3 tablespoons Meyer lemon juice
1 or 2 drops yellow gel food coloring (optional)
2 teaspoons finely grated Meyer lemon zest, for garnish

1. Prepare and chill the pastry cream as directed on this page, slowly stirring in the Meyer lemon juice with the butter in step 2.
2. Preheat the Oster to 425°F (218°C). Line two baking sheets with parchment paper.
3. Make the sweet pâte à choux as directed through step 3. Pipe the batter onto the prepared baking sheets in strips that are 5 inches long and 1 inch wide. Run a moistened fingertip along the surface of the strips, smoothing out any peaks or rough edges.
4. Bake for 15 minutes, and then reduce the Oster temperature to 375°F(191°C) (191°C)and bake until the pastries are golden and puffed and sound hollow when you tap on them, about 25 minutes more.
5. Pierce the pastries at one end with a thin, sharp knife to release steam (this helps them stay crispy), and transfer to a wire rack to cool completely. (After they've cooled, they can be stored in an airtight container for up to 2 days.)
6. Make the glaze: In a medium bowl, whisk together the confectioners' sugar, lemon zest, 2 tablespoons of the lemon juice, and the food coloring (if using) until smooth. The glaze should be very shiny, thick, and almost pasty; if needed, add a bit more juice or confectioners' sugar until it reaches the right consistency.
7. Assemble the éclairs: Split the pastries in half horizontally. Fill the bottom half with chilled pastry cream and replace the top. Carefully spoon the glaze over the tops. Garnish with zest. Chill for 30 minutes to set, and then serve.

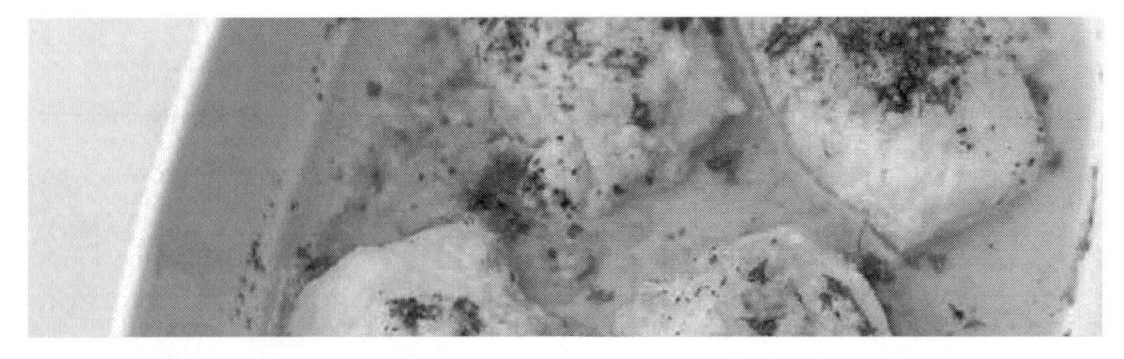

Sweet Butter Cookies

Prep time: 10 minutes | Cook time: 45 minutes | Makes 20 cookies

For the cinnamon-sugar coating:
¼ cup granulated white sugar
1 teaspoon ground cinnamon
¼ teaspoon kosher salt
For the cookies:
3 ⅓ cups all-purpose flour
2 teaspoons cream of tartar
1 teaspoon baking soda
1 teaspoon ground cinnamon
1 cup unsalted butter, softened
1 cup granulated white sugar
1 teaspoon vanilla extract
½ teaspoon kosher salt
⅔ cup cookie butter
1 large egg, at room temperature
Baking equipment
Measuring cups and spoons
3 mixing bowls
Wooden spoon
Sheet pan
Parchment paper
Sifter
Electric hand mixer
Ice-cream scoop
Oster-safe gloves
Metal spatula
Wire rack

To make the cinnamon-sugar coating:
1. In a mixing bowl, stir together the sugar, cinnamon, and salt. Set aside.

To make the cookies:
2. Preheat your Oster to 375°F(191°C). Line a sheet pan with parchment paper.
3. Sift together the flour, cream of tartar, baking soda, and cinnamon into a mixing bowl.
4. Using an electric hand mixer in another mixing bowl, cream together the butter, granulated white sugar, vanilla, and salt at high speed for 5 minutes, or until smooth and fluffy. Add the cookie butter and egg. Mix well.
5. Add the flour mixture. Mix until there are no more dry flour bits left.
6. Turn off the mixer. Using an ice-cream scoop, form the dough into balls, and roll in the cinnamon-sugar coating until fully coated. Place 10 balls on the prepared sheet pan. Give them some room because they will spread and flatten.
7. Put the sheet pan in the Oster. Bake for 10 to 12 minutes, or until the edges are lightly browned.
8. Using Oster-safe gloves, remove the baking sheets from the Oster. Transfer the cookies to a wire rack to cool for 20 minutes.
9. Repeat with the remaining dough or keep it in an airtight container in the refrigerator for up to 3 days or in the freezer for up to 3 months.

Simple Bread Dessert

Prep time: 10 minutes | Cook time: 1 hour 15 minutes | Makes one 9 inch cake pan

1 tablespoon unsalted butter, plus more for greasing the pan
½ cup raisins
1 cup milk
1 cup heavy cream
⅔ cup granulated white sugar
4 large eggs
1 ½ teaspoons vanilla extract
1 teaspoon ground cinnamon
6 cups torn day-old bread, such as a country loaf
BAKING EQUIPMENT
Measuring cups and spoons
9-inch cake pan
Parchment paper
Small bowl
Colander
Mixing bowl
Whisk
Oster-safe gloves

1. Preheat your Oster to 350°F(177°C). Line a 9-inch cake pan with parchment paper, and grease the parchment paper well with butter.
2. In a small bowl of warm water, steep the raisins for 5 minutes, or until nice and plump. Drain well in a colander.
3. In a mixing bowl, whisk together the milk, cream, sugar, butter, and eggs until a well-blended custard forms.
4. Add the vanilla and cinnamon and whisk to combine. Put the bread in the prepared cake pan. Sprinkle the raisins over the bread. Drizzle the custard on top.
5. Put the cake pan in the Oster. Bake for 45 minutes, or until the bread is golden brown and crispy on top.
6. Using Oster-safe gloves, remove the pan from the Oster. Let the bread pudding cool for 15 minutes. Serve warm with ice cream, if desired.

Orange Almond Cookies
Prep time: 10 minutes | Cook time: 1 hour 10 minutes | makes 4 dozen cookies

3¾ cups all-purpose flour
2 teaspoons baking powder
½ teaspoon salt
3 large eggs
1 cup sugar
¾ cup vegetable oil
2 teaspoons vanilla extract
¼ teaspoon almond extract
1 teaspoon freshly grated orange peel
1 cup slivered blanched almonds, toasted and coarsely chopped

1. Preheat Oster to 350°F(177°C). In large bowl with wire whisk, mix flour, baking powder, and salt.
2. In large bowl with mixer on medium speed, beat eggs and sugar until light lemon-colored. Add oil, extracts, and orange peel, and beat until blended. With wooden spoon, beat in flour mixture until combined. Stir in almonds.
3. Divide dough in half. On large ungreased cookie sheet, drop each half of dough by spoonfuls down length of cookie sheet. With lightly floured hands, shape each half of dough into 12-inch-long log, 4 inches apart (dough will be slightly sticky).
4. Bake for 30 minutes or until dough is light-colored and firm. Cool logs on cookie sheet on wire rack for 10 minutes or until easy to handle. Arrange Oster racks in top and bottom thirds of Oster.
5. Transfer logs to cutting board. With serrated knife, cut each log crosswise into ½-inch-thick slices. Place slices, cut side down, on 2 ungreased cookie sheets.
6. Bake for 7 to 8 minutes or until golden, rotating cookie sheets between upper and lower racks halfway through baking. With metal spatula, transfer cookies to wire racks to cool completely.

The Best Orange Choco Cake
Prep time: 10 minutes | Cook time: 1 hour | makes 6

Nonstick cooking spray
1 (15.25-ounce/ 432 g) box yellow or chocolate cake mix
Orange gel food coloring
2 cups confectioners' sugar
Orange and green crystal sugar or candy decorations
Pretzel rods or sticks
Marzipan, for leaves

1. Preheat Oster to 350°F(177°C). Spray 12 mini Bundt pans with nonstick cooking spray.
2. Prepare cake mix (tint with food coloring, if desired) and bake as directed, filling pans halfway with batter.
3. When cakes are done, unmold them onto wire rack and cool completely.
4. In 4-cup measuring cup, mix confectioners' sugar and 3 to 4 tablespoons water to make thick glaze. With sharp knife, trim bottom of each cake flat; assemble into pairs. Using a small amount of glaze drizzled on flat sides of cakes, attach pairs to form 6 pumpkins.
5. Drizzle pumpkin cakes with glaze and/or sprinkle with crystal sugar or candy decorations. Break pretzel rods to fit as stems. Moisten pretzels with water and roll in crystal sugar. Insert into centers of pumpkins.
6. Tint marzipan with green food coloring for leaves. Roll and cut as desired and place around pretzel stems. Let cakes stand until glaze is set.

Vanilla Butter Biscuits
Prep time: 10 minutes | Cook time: 35 minutes | Makes 20 cookies

¾ cup (1 ½ sticks) unsalted butter, softened
¾ cup granulated white sugar
1 large egg, at room temperature
1 teaspoon vanilla extract
¼ teaspoon kosher salt
2 cups all-purpose flour
½ teaspoon baking powder
½ teaspoon baking soda
BAKING EQUIPMENT:
Measuring cups and spoons
Sheet pan
Parchment paper
Electric hand mixer
Mixing bowl
Rubber spatula
Plastic wrap
Knife
Oster-safe gloves
Metal spatula
Wire rack

1. Preheat your Oster to 325°F(163°C). Line a sheet pan with parchment paper.
2. Using an electric hand mixer on medium-high speed in a mixing bowl, cream the butter and granulated white sugar together for about 5 minutes, or until fluffy.
3. Add the egg, vanilla, and salt. Mix for 1 minute. Add the flour, baking powder, and baking soda. Mix until fully combined.
4. Turn off the mixer. Using a spatula, turn out the cookie dough onto a large sheet of plastic wrap. Wrap the dough, forming it into a log. Refrigerate for 1 to 2 hours, or until firm.
5. Remove the dough log from the refrigerator and remove the plastic wrap. Cut the dough into about 20 equal slices, and place 10 on the prepared sheet pan. Refrigerate the rest.
6. Put the sheet pan in the Oster. Bake for 10 to 12 minutes, or until the cookies are very lightly browned on the edges and the bottoms.
7. Using Oster-safe gloves, remove the sheet pan from the Oster. Transfer the cookies to a wire rack to cool.
8. Repeat for remaining cookie slices or keep them in an airtight container in the refrigerator for up to 3 days or in the freezer for up to 3 months.

Chapter 11
Custards and Puddings

Custard Dessert with Caramelized Sugar
Prep time: 10 minutes | Cook time: 60 minutes | serves 6

4 large egg yolks
⅓ cup granulated sugar
2½ cups heavy cream
3 tablespoons malted milk powder
1 vanilla bean, split lengthwise
½ cup citrus marmalade, such as orange or grapefruit
6 tablespoons superfine sugar

1. Preheat the Oster to 300°F (149°C). In a large bowl, using an electric mixer fitted with the whisk attachment, beat the egg yolks and granulated sugar until pale and thick, about 2 minutes.
2. In a small saucepan, bring the cream to a simmer over medium heat. Add the malted milk powder and, using the tip of a small paring knife, scrape the vanilla seeds out of the vanilla bean into the pan; add the vanilla pod to the pan as well. Reduce the heat and cook, whisking occasionally, until the powder has dissolved, about 5 minutes. Discard the vanilla pod.
3. With the mixer running on low speed, very slowly beat ¼ cup of the warm cream mixture into the egg mixture. Beat in the cream mixture ¼ cup at a time until it is fully combined.
4. Spoon the marmalade evenly over the bottoms of six 6-ounce ramekins (about 1 heaping tablespoon for each ramekin). Top with the custard mixture, filling the ramekins to the top.
5. Bring a teakettle of water almost to a boil. Fold a kitchen towel so that it fits neatly inside a 9 × 13-inch baking dish and place the filled ramekins on top of it. (The towel will keep the ramekins from sliding as you move the pan.)
6. Transfer the pan to a pulled-out rack in the Oster. Pour enough hot water from the teakettle into the baking dish to come halfway up the sides of the ramekins.
7. Bake until the custards are just set (they should wobble just slightly when the pan is nudged), 50 to 55 minutes. Remove the baking dish from the Oster. Carefully transfer the ramekins out of the water bath and onto a wire rack to rest for 15 minutes, then cover the ramekins with plastic wrap and carefully transfer them to the refrigerator. Chill for at least 2 hours or up to 2 days.
8. Uncover the chilled ramekins and use a paper towel to gently dab away any condensation on the surface of the custard.
9. Sprinkle the top of each custard evenly with 1 tablespoon of the superfine sugar in a thin layer. Use a kitchen torch to toast the surface of each until the sugar is deeply golden and evenly caramelized. (If you do not have a torch, you can get similar results by placing the ramekins on a baking sheet and broiling them until the sugar melts and turns golden, about 4 minutes.) Let the custards rest for 10 minutes to allow the sugar to harden, then serve.

Sweet Savory Pastry with Figs
Prep time: 10 minutes | Cook time: 60 minutes | serves 6

3 large eggs
2 large egg yolks
1½ cups granulated sugar, divided
2 cups whole milk
1 teaspoon pure vanilla extract
⅛ teaspoon kosher salt
1 tablespoon honey
9 fresh black or green figs, halved lengthwise

1. Preheat the Oster to 325°F (163°C). In a medium bowl, whisk together the whole eggs and egg yolks until combined. Set aside.
2. In a small saucepan, combine 1 cup of the sugar and ⅓ cup water. Bring to a low simmer over medium heat, stirring just until the sugar dissolves, then cook, without stirring, until the sugar bubbles and turns a deep amber color, about 8 minutes. Quickly and carefully pour the caramel into six 6-ounce ramekins, tilting them to coat the bottoms evenly.
3. In a clean saucepan, combine the milk and remaining ½ cup sugar and cook over low heat, stirring, until the sugar has dissolved and the milk is warm but not boiling, 1 to 2 minutes. Whisking constantly, very slowly drizzle the warm milk mixture into the beaten eggs. Add the vanilla and salt and whisk to combine. Divide the mixture among the prepared ramekins.
4. Bring a teakettle of water almost to a boil. Fold a kitchen towel so that it fits neatly inside a 9 × 13-inch baking dish and place the filled ramekins on top of it. (The towel will keep the ramekins from sliding as you move the pan.)
5. Transfer the pan to a pulled-out rack in the Oster. Pour enough hot water from the teakettle into the baking dish to come halfway up the sides of the ramekins. Bake until the custards are set but still wobble slightly when the pan is tapped, 45 to 50 minutes.
6. Carefully transfer the ramekins out of the water bath and onto a wire rack to cool for 30 minutes, then cover each ramekin with plastic wrap and refrigerate until chilled, at least 3 hours or for up to 3 days.
7. Just before serving, in a large skillet, warm the honey over medium-high heat until runny, about 1 minute. Add the figs, cut-side down, and cook until soft and caramelized, about 5 minutes.
8. To unmold the flans, run a knife around the rim of each ramekin, then invert it onto a plate. The caramel syrup will come out, too—make sure you allow it all to spill out and over the flan.
9. Garnish each plate with some of the caramelized figs and serve.

Cheese Glazed Sweet Rolls

Prep time: 10 minutes | Cook time: 30 minutes | makes 24 rolls

For the rolls
1 tablespoon butter or nonstick cooking spray, for greasing the pan, plus ¼ cup butter (½ stick), melted
3 cups flour
½ cup sugar
¼ teaspoon salt
4 teaspoons baking powder
1½ cups milk
2 eggs
For the swirl filling
1 cup butter (2 sticks), softened*
1 tablespoon ground cinnamon
For the glaze
8 ounces cream cheese (1 brick), softened*
½ cup powdered sugar
1 tablespoon milk

1. Preheat the Oster and prepare the pan. Preheat the Oster to 350°F (177°C). Use a paper towel to spread 1 tablespoon of butter over the inside of each cup in the muffin pan.
2. Melt the butter. Using a microwave-safe bowl, melt ¼ cup of butter (about 25 seconds in the microwave). Set aside.
3. Prepare the swirl filling. Use the stand mixer to combine the softened butter, brown sugar, and cinnamon. Whip until fluffy. When you see cinnamon everywhere, it's done (about 20 seconds). Turn the mixer off. Use a cookie scoop to measure equally and place 1 scoop on the bottom of each muffin pan cup. Scoop out the rest of the mixture into a small bowl and set aside.
4. Combine the ingredients. Use the stand mixer again (don't worry about any leftover cinnamon mixture) to combine the melted butter, flour, sugar, salt, baking powder, milk, and vanilla.
5. To add the flour correctly, use a second measuring cup to spoon flour into the 1-cup measuring cup, flatten off the top, and pour the flour into the mixing bowl. Repeat two more times. In a medium bowl, crack 1 egg. Remove any shell and pour the egg into the mixer. Repeat with the second egg. Mix on medium speed until incorporated, about 20 seconds. The batter will have tiny lumps.
6. Pour the batter into the pan. Scrape the bottom and sides of the mixing bowl with a silicone spatula and stir in any remaining bits of flour. Use an ice cream scoop to measure batter into the cups of the prepared muffin pan, using the spatula to scrape it out completely.
7. Top with the cinnamon mixture. Using a cookie scoop again, drop the cinnamon mixture on top of the cake batter.
8. Bake. Bake for 20 to 22 minutes or until a toothpick inserted into the center of a "roll" comes out clean. Allow to cool for 5 minutes before touching the pan again.
9. Prepare the glaze. While the rolls bake, rinse out the mixer bowl. Add the cream cheese and whip it on high speed until fluffy, about 30 seconds. Stop the mixer and add powdered sugar and milk. Start the mixer on low and beat until smooth, about 30 seconds. Set aside until the rolls are out of the Oster and slightly cooled.
10. Glaze the cinnamon rolls. Flip the pan over onto a cooling rack. When the rolls pop out, drizzle the cream cheese glaze over the bottoms (now the tops). Serve warm or cool.

Cream and Chocolate filled Pies

Prep time: 10 minutes | Cook time: 25 minutes | makes 12 pies

For the pie crusts
1½ cups graham cracker crumbs (10 full graham crackers ground up)
7 tablespoons butter (almost 1 stick), melted
2 tablespoons sugar
1 tablespoon brown sugar
For the filling
3 eggs
4 tablespoons butter (½ stick)
8 ounces (227 g) semisweet chocolate chips (1 bag)
7 ounces (198 g) marshmallow cream (1 jar)
1 chocolate bar, broken into 12 pieces, for garnish

1. Prepare the graham cracker mixture. Place the graham crackers in a sealed plastic bag and crush with a rolling pin, or pulverize them in a food processor. Melt the butter in a medium microwave-safe bowl, cooking 20 seconds at a time until liquefied (about 40 seconds total).
2. Combine the crushed graham crackers with the melted butter, then add the sugar and brown sugar and stir.
3. Make the pie crusts. Fill each cup of the muffin pan with the graham cracker mixture. Use a ½-cup measuring cup to press down on the crumbs. Then press the graham crackers up the sides of the muffin pan with clean fingers, until you have what looks like tiny pie crusts.
4. Preheat the Oster and beat the eggs. Preheat the Oster to 325°F (163°C). In a medium bowl, crack 1 egg. Remove any shell and pour the egg into the stand mixer or mixing bowl. Repeat with the remaining eggs. Beat until they're yellow and fluffy, about 3 minutes.
5. Prepare the chocolate mixture. Rinse out the graham cracker bowl. Using a cutting board and a kid-safe knife cut the butter into 4 pieces and place in the bowl along with the chocolate chips. Microwave for 10 seconds at a time until melted, about 30 seconds total.
6. Combine the ingredients. Add ½ cup of the chocolate mixture to the eggs and whip again for 20 seconds. Add the rest of the chocolate to the eggs and whip for 20 seconds.
7. Fill the pie crusts with chocolate and marshmallow. Use an ice cream scoop to evenly divide the chocolate batter into each of the pie crusts. Use a buttered spoon or ice cream scoop to scoop a small amount of marshmallow cream on top of each pie.
8. Bake. Bake for 20 to 25 minutes, until the filling is fluffy and slightly browned on top. Garnish with a piece of chocolate bar. Serve warm or chilled.

Pistachios Topped Rice Pudding
Prep time: 15 minutes | Cook time: 40 minutes | serves 8

1 cup white basmati rice
2 (13.5-ounce/382 g) cans full-fat coconut milk
½ cup packed light brown sugar
1 teaspoon orange blossom water
1 teaspoon ground cardamom
12 saffron threads, crushed until powdery
¼ teaspoon kosher salt
TOPPING
⅔ cup chopped pistachios
⅔ cup unsweetened coconut flakes
¼ teaspoon ground cardamom
¾ cup canned full-fat coconut milk, stirred until smooth
1½ tablespoons crumbled dried food-grade rose petals, for garnish (optional)

1. Preheat the Oster to 300°F (149°C). In a deep 2-quart round casserole dish, whisk together the basmati rice, coconut milk, brown sugar, orange blossom water, cardamom, saffron, and salt until combined. Place the casserole dish on a baking sheet.
2. Bake the pudding, uncovered, for 30 minutes, then stir and bake for 25 minutes more. Stir the pudding again to dissolve any skin that has formed on top.
3. Bake until the rice is tender and the coconut milk has reduced but the surface of the pudding still looks moist, 10 to 15 minutes more. Remove the pudding from the Oster and let it cool until warm but not hot, about 10 minutes. (The pudding will continue to thicken as it cools.)
4. Meanwhile, make the topping: In a medium skillet, toast the pistachios and coconut flakes over medium-high heat, stirring often, until the mixture is golden and fragrant, about 6 minutes. Transfer to a bowl and stir in the cardamom until combined.
5. To serve, stir the pudding to loosen it, then spoon into small bowls. Drizzle each serving with coconut milk, top with a pinch of the topping, and garnish with dried rose petals (if using). Leftovers can be refrigerated, covered, for up to 5 days and eaten chilled or reheated.

Cinnamon Peach Dessert
Prep time: 10 minutes | Cook time: 40 minutes | serves 6

1 tablespoon butter or nonstick cooking spray, for greasing the pan, plus ¼ cup butter (½ stick), melted
½ cup granulated sugar, plus 1 tablespoon
1 cup flour
2 teaspoons baking powder
½ teaspoon salt
1 teaspoon ground cinnamon
½ cup milk
2 cups frozen peaches, thawed or 4 fresh peaches, sliced
Whipped cream or vanilla ice cream, for serving

1. Preheat the Oster and prepare the pan. Preheat the Oster to 350°F (177°C). Use a paper towel to spread 1 tablespoon of butter over the inside of the baking pan or coat the pan with nonstick cooking spray.
2. Melt the butter. Microwave the ¼ cup butter in a microwave-safe bowl for 20 seconds. Repeat if needed.
3. Mix the batter. Combine the melted butter with ½ cup of sugar, the flour, baking powder, salt, cinnamon, and milk in a large mixing bowl. To add the flour correctly, use a second measuring cup to spoon flour into the 1-cup measuring cup, flatten off the top, and pour the flour into the mixing bowl. Whisk* until smooth.
4. Pour the batter into the pan. Use a silicone spatula to get every bit of batter out of the bowl and into the baking pan.
5. Sprinkle with the fruit and sugar. Add the peaches (but not any extra juice) on top, spreading the slices out evenly. Sprinkle the peaches with the last tablespoon of sugar.
6. Bake. Place the pan in the Oster and bake for 35 to 40 minutes or until the edges of the cobbler are browned.
7. Serve warm or cold. Cobbler is delicious with whipped cream or a scoop of vanilla ice cream.

Sweet Strawberry Pastry

Prep time: 10 minutes | Cook time: 20 minutes | serves 8

2½ cups all-purpose flour, plus 2 tablespoons (if you are using frozen fruit)
¼ cup sugar, plus 1 tablespoon
1 cup butter (2 sticks), cold and cubed
2 teaspoons vanilla extract
¼ cup ice water
2 cups strawberries, sliced
Handful of flour for rolling
1 egg

1. Mix the flour and sugar. Place the flour and sugar in the stand mixer or large mixing bowl and stir until well mixed. To measure the flour correctly, use a second measuring cup to spoon flour into the 1-cup measuring cup, flatten off the top, pour the flour into the mixing bowl, and repeat. Repeat once more with the ½-cup measuring cup.
2. Add the butter. Using a cutting board and a kid-safe knife, slice the sticks of butter into 8 pieces each. Add the butter to the flour mixture and turn on the mixer or use the pastry cutter to blend the butter until you have what looks like white peas.
3. Add the liquid. Pour the vanilla into the mixture and stir with the silicone spatula or wooden spoon. Add the ice water 1 tablespoon at a time and stir. When you are able to make a ball with the dough, stop adding water.
4. Chill the dough. Use clean hands to make a ball with the dough. Cover the ball in plastic wrap and place in the refrigerator for 20 minutes.
5. Prepare the berries. If using fresh strawberries, use a cutting board and a kid-safe knife to slice the tops off and cut each berry in half, lengthwise. If using frozen strawberries, cut the bag open. Add 2 tablespoons of flour to the bag and shake.
6. Roll the dough. After 20 minutes, place a handful of flour on a clean counter or cutting board. Use the rolling pin to flatten the dough into a circle 10 to 12 inches wide (about the length of your arm from your elbow to your wrist.)
7. Assemble the tart. Preheat the Oster to 450°F (232°C). Line a baking sheet with a piece of parchment paper or a silicone baking mat. Roll the dough onto your rolling pin and transfer it to the middle of the baking sheet.
8. Pour the strawberries into the middle. Sprinkle the strawberries with 1 tablespoon of sugar.
9. Fold the edges of the crust up all the way around the tart so 2 inches of the dough rests on top of the berries. It should look like a strawberry pizza with a thick crust.
10. Brush and bake. In a small bowl, crack the egg and remove any shell. Use a fork to whisk it until well mixed. Use a pastry brush to coat the part of the crust that's resting on the berries. Place the baking sheet in the Oster and bake for 20 minutes, until the berries are bubbly and the crust is golden brown.
11. Cool and serve. Allow the tart to cool for at least 10 minutes before serving.

Sweet Bread Roll

Prep time: 10 minutes | Cook time: 50 minutes | serves 8

2¼ teaspoons active dry yeast (1 packet)
2 tablespoons brown sugar
1½ cups warm water (start with ½ cup boiling water, add tap water, alternating until it feels like bath water)
4 cups bread flour, plus more for kneading
2 tablespoons ground cinnamon, plus 1 teaspoon
1 teaspoon salt
½ cup raisins (2 snack size boxes, 1 ounce)
Vegetable or olive oil, for greasing the proofing bowl
1 egg

1. Mix the ingredients. In a stand mixer or large mixing bowl, combine the yeast, brown sugar, warm water, bread flour, cinnamon, salt, and raisins. Stir until the dough starts coming together, about 2 minutes.
2. Knead* the dough. Using a dough hook, knead for 5 minutes on medium speed (you may have to steady the mixer!). Or flip the dough onto a clean counter sprinkled with a handful of flour. Use the heel of your hand to press down, fold the dough in half, and press again over and over for 8 to 10 minutes.
3. Allow the dough to rise. Pour a little oil onto a paper towel and rub the inside of a large bowl until it's well coated. Place the kneaded dough in the bowl. Cover with a clean kitchen towel and set in a warm place (like a sunny window) for 1 hour, until it doubles in size.
4. Boil the water. After about 45 minutes, fill a large pot about half full of water and start bringing it to a boil. Turn the heat down and allow it to simmer.
5. Shape the bagels. When the dough is ready, use a cutting board and a kid-safe knife to slice the dough into 8 wedges, like a pizza. Roll each wedge into a ball. Use your fingers to poke a hole into the center of each one, like a bagel.
6. Cook in hot water. Use a slotted spoon to slide the bagels one by one into the boiling water, boiling no more than four at a time. Cook for 2 to 4 minutes, flip and cook for another 2 to 4 minutes. (The longer you boil the bagels, the chewier they'll be.)
7. Prepare to bake. Preheat the Oster to 425°F (218°C). Place each boiled bagel onto a parchment paper–lined baking sheet (or use a silicone baking mat). Crack the egg into a small bowl and remove any shell.
8. Add 1 tablespoon of water and beat together with a fork until the mixture is yellow. Using a pastry brush, brush each bagel with the egg mixture.
9. Bake the bagels. Put the baking sheet into the Oster and bake for 20 to 25 minutes, until the bagels are golden brown. Remove them from the Oster and allow cooling for at least 20 minutes before serving.

Cheesy Turkey filled Pies
Prep time: 15 minutes | Cook time: 20 minutes | serves 4

For the pie dough
2½ cups all-purpose flour
1 teaspoon granulated sugar
½ teaspoon salt
1 cup butter (2 sticks), chilled
4 tablespoons ice water
Handful of flour, for rolling
1 egg
1 tablespoon water
For the filling
1 cup ground beef or turkey
1 tablespoon taco seasoning
¼ cup water
½ cup cheddar cheese

1. Make the dough. In a large bowl, mix the flour, sugar, and salt with a silicone spatula. Use electric beaters or a pastry cutter to work the butter into the mixture, beating until you have a chunky dough. Gradually add the ice water until you can form a ball.
2. Chill the dough. Wrap the dough in plastic wrap and refrigerate for 20 minutes.
3. Make the taco filling. Cook the ground beef or turkey in a skillet, stirring often, on medium heat until browned, about 10 minutes. Add the taco seasoning and water. Simmer for 5 minutes.
4. Preheat the Oster and prepare the pan. Preheat the Oster to 425°F (218°C). Line a baking sheet with parchment paper or a silicone baking mat.
5. Roll out the dough. Sprinkle a handful of flour onto a clean surface and use a rolling pin to flatten the dough into a large rectangle, about ¼ inch thick. Cut the edges off your dough as needed.
6. Assemble the taco hand pies. Use a pizza cutter to slice the dough into 4 pieces or kid-safe knife. Place one-quarter of the taco meat on each square and top with the cheddar cheese. Fold one half over the top and use a fork to crimp* the edges. Poke your fork into the top of each hand pie to make the shape of an initial.
7. Brush with egg wash. Place the hand pies on the lined baking sheet. Crack the egg into a small bowl and remove any shell. Add 1 tablespoon of water and whisk* with a fork. Use a pastry brush to coat each hand pie with the egg mixture.
8. Bake. Place the baking sheet in the Oster for 15 to 20 minutes, until the edges of the pies are golden brown. Be careful when biting into a hand pie fresh out of the Oster because the filling will be hot!

Cherry Tomato topped Pizza
Prep time: 15 minutes | Cook time: 10 minutes | serves 6

For the pesto
1 cup fresh basil leaves
3 garlic cloves, peeled
3 tablespoons pine nuts
⅓ cup freshly grated Parmesan cheese
½ teaspoon salt
¼ teaspoon freshly ground pepper
⅓ cup olive oil
For the pizza
1 long baguette
1 cup fresh mozzarella cheese, sliced
1 cup cherry tomatoes, sliced in half
Fresh basil leaves, for garnish (optional)

1. Preheat the Oster. Preheat the Oster to 400°F (204°C). Make the pesto. In a food processor, combine the basil, garlic, pine nuts, Parmesan cheese, salt, and pepper.
2. Turn the food processor on low and drizzle the olive oil in through the pour spout until combined. Use a clean spoon to taste the pesto and add more salt or pepper as needed.
3. Slice the bread. Use a bread knife to slice the baguette in half lengthwise (so it looks like a giant sandwich).
4. Add the toppings. Use a silicone spatula to spread a thick layer of pesto on the inside of each piece of bread. Place the bread on the baking sheet, pesto-side up. Lay slices of mozzarella cheese over the top of the pesto.
5. Bake. Bake in the Oster for 8 to 10 minutes, until the mozzarella is melted and bubbly. Top with sliced cherry tomatoes and fresh basil leaves, if you like.

Homemade Simple Bread
Prep time: 5 minutes | Cook time: 50 minutes | makes 1 loaf

3 cups all-purpose flour, plus more for dusting
½ teaspoon instant yeast
2 teaspoons salt
1½ cups warm water (about 110°F, like a warm bath)

1. Mix the dough. In a large bowl, mix the flour, yeast, and salt. To add the flour correctly, use a second measuring cup to spoon flour into the 1-cup measuring cup, flatten off the top, and pour the flour into the mixing bowl.
2. Repeat two more times. Add the warm water and use a silicone spatula to stir until you can't see any more flour. The dough will be sticky and loose.
3. Rest the dough. Cover the bowl with plastic wrap and let it rest at room temperature overnight (at least 12 hours).
4. Place the dough on parchment paper. Put a piece of parchment paper on a clean counter. Sprinkle a handful of flour on top.
5. Flip the bowl over and pour your dough onto the floured parchment paper. Sprinkle another handful of flour on top of the dough. Fold the dough in half two times. Let it rest again, about 30 minutes.
6. Preheat a pot in the Oster. While the dough rests, preheat the Oster to 450°F (232°C). Place a large covered pot in the Oster. Use potholders to remove the pot after the dough have rested. Using the edges of the parchment paper as handles, place the dough and parchment paper in the pot.

Homemade Butter Biscuits
Prep time: 5 minutes | Cook time: 15 minutes | serves 8

1 tablespoon butter or nonstick cooking spray, for greasing the pan, plus ¼ cup butter (½ stick)
2 cups self-rising flour
1 cup milk
¼ cup mayonnaise

1. Preheat the Oster and prepare the pan. Preheat the Oster to 375°F(191°C). Use a paper towel to spread butter in every cup of a muffin pan, or spray with nonstick cooking spray.
2. Mix the ingredients. In the mixing bowl, use a silicone spatula to stir the flour, milk, and mayonnaise until just mixed together. To measure the flour correctly, use a second measuring cup to spoon flour into the 1-cup measuring cup, flatten off the top, pour the flour into a large mixing bowl, and repeat.
3. Bake. Use an ice cream scoop to measure the batter into the prepared muffin pan. Bake for 12 minutes, until golden brown.
4. Brush with melted butter. Microwave the butter in a small bowl for 20 to 30 seconds, until melted. Use a pastry brush to coat each biscuit with butter.

Olive Oil Dressed Tomato salad
Prep time: 10 minutes | Cook time: 10 minutes | serves 4

1 loaf crusty bread, torn into bite-size chunks and left to dry out on a baking sheet for 1 to 2 days
2 tablespoons olive oil, plus extra for soaking, drizzling, and frying
Flake salt, such as Maldon
Freshly ground black pepper
5 large heirloom tomatoes, cut into wedges
1½ cups Sun Gold tomatoes, halved
2 cups fresh basil leaves, rinsed and patted dry
4 chives, finely chopped
2 teaspoons red wine vinegar

1. Preheat the Oster to 425°F (218°C). Toast the bread. Arrange the bread on a baking sheet, and drizzle with olive oil, and season with salt and pepper.
2. Toast the bread in the Oster until golden and crisp on the edges, turning once halfway through as needed, about 8 minutes total.
3. Assemble the salad. Arrange the tomatoes on a serving platter, alternating shapes and colors. Add the basil, and nestle the crispy bread into the mixture, then scatter the chives all around.
4. Make the dressing. In a small bowl, whisk the olive oil and red wine vinegar to combine.
5. Serve. Drizzle the dressing over the salad, saving some for at the table, season with salt and pepper, and dig in. You just made an edible work of art!

Citrusy Anchovies Salad
Prep time: 10 minutes | Cook time: 15 minutes | serves 4

5 anchovies, plus extra for garnish
2 garlic cloves
2 tablespoons Dijon mustard
1 tablespoon freshly squeezed lemon juice
1 tablespoon white wine vinegar or champagne vinegar
1 large egg
¾ cup olive oil, plus additional oil for drizzling
¼ cup Parmigiano-Reggiano cheese, finely grated, plus more for serving
½ loaf crusty bread, 1 to 3 days old, diced or torn into bite-size pieces
2 heads romaine lettuce, root ends trimmed, quartered, and coarsely chopped
Pinch freshly ground black pepper

1. Preheat the Oster to 400°F(204°C). Make the dressing. In a blender, blend the anchovies and garlic until they become a rough paste.
2. Add the mustard, lemon juice, and vinegar, crack in the egg, and blend until the mixture is smooth and creamy. With the blender on, remove the feeder cap and gradually drizzle in the olive oil in a steady stream.
3. Turn the blender off. Add the cheese, and blend again until all ingredients are well combined. Scrape the dressing into a mason jar with a rubber spatula, seal it, and refrigerate for 15 to 30 minutes, or until it thickens.
4. Make the croutons. Meanwhile, on a baking sheet, spread the bread pieces in a single layer and drizzle with olive oil. Bake for 12 minutes, or until golden and crisp at the edges.
5. Assemble the salad. In a large bowl, pour half the dressing over the chopped lettuce, and toss with a large fork and spoon. Add some of your croutons and toss a little more, so that some are coated in the dressing.
6. Serve. Pile the salad into bowls, adding a few more croutons to each serving as you like and one or two anchovies to garnish.
7. Drizzle on additional dressing to taste, grate more cheese on top, and finish with the pepper. The dressing will keep for up to 3 days, sealed in the refrigerator.

Citrusy Brussels sprouts Shallots Roast
Prep time: 10 minutes | Cook time: 30 minutes | serves 4

1½ pounds Brussels sprouts, trimmed and halved
6 shallots, quartered
3 tablespoons olive oil
Sea salt and Freshly ground black pepper, to taste
1 lemon, cut into wedges, for serving

1. Arrange Oster racks and preheat Oster. Place one Oster rack in the top third of the Oster and another in the bottom third, then preheat Oster to 450°F (232°C).
2. Prep the veggie mixture. On two baking sheets, toss the Brussels sprouts and shallots with the olive oil, placing most of the Brussels halves cut-side down. Season with salt and pepper.
3. Roast the vegetables. Swap the pans halfway through, and use tongs to turn the veggies over for even roasting. Cook until caramelized and tender, 25 to 30 minutes.
4. Serve. Transfer the Brussels sprouts and shallots to a serving dish, with lemon wedges to squeeze at the table.

Delicious delicata rings
Prep time: 5 minutes | Cook time: 30 minutes | serves 4

3 delicata squash, halved widthwise
Olive oil, for drizzling
Flake salt, such as Maldon
Freshly ground black pepper, to taste

1. Arrange Oster racks and preheat Oster. Place one Oster rack in the top third of the Oster and another in the bottom third, then preheat Oster to 425°F (218°C).
2. Prepare the squash. Use a pointy teaspoon to scrape the seeds and any stringy bits from each squash half and discard (or save for compost). Slice the squash into ½-inch rings, discarding the stem ends.
3. Prep the squash for roasting. Drizzle 1 to 2 tablespoons of olive oil onto each baking sheet, and spread it around with your fingers to coat the pans. Lay the delicata rings flat in a single layer on each sheet, and lightly drizzle with olive oil. Season with salt and pepper.
4. Roast the squash. Cook for 10 to 15 minutes, until the rings begin to brown on the bottom, then the flip rings to the other side, season again, and swap the pans, returning them to roast for another 10 to 15 minutes, until the squash is tender and deeply golden in spots. Test by seeing if you can pierce them with a fork— if you can, they are ready.
5. Serve warm for a delicious snack or side dish.

Rosemary Herbed Carrots
Prep time: 10 minutes | Cook time: 35 minutes | serves 4

2 tablespoons butter
2 tablespoons honey
Flake salt, such as Maldon
2 to 3 bunches small carrots, scrubbed and greens trimmed, halved lengthwise if thick
2 fresh rosemary sprigs, quills stripped from stems and coarsely chopped
Freshly ground black pepper, to taste

1. Preheat the Oster to 425°F (218°C). Prepare the glaze.
2. In a small saucepan over medium heat, melt the butter. Add the honey, and whisk to dissolve. Season with a pinch of salt, and set aside.
3. Toss the ingredients together. On a baking sheet, drizzle the honey mixture over the carrots, toss to coat, and scatter the chopped rosemary on top. Season with salt and pepper.
4. Roast the carrots. Bake for 30 to 35 minutes, or until the carrots are tender and caramelized in spots, rearranging them for even browning halfway through.
5. Serve. Transfer to a serving platter or plates and eat warm.

Citrusy Cauliflower with Crème Fraîche Sauce
Prep time: 10 minutes | Cook time: 55 minutes | serves 4

FOR THE CAULIFLOWER
1½ cups dry white wine or white wine vinegar
6 cups water
⅓ cup olive oil, plus more for serving
3 tablespoons kosher salt
3 tablespoons freshly squeezed lemon juice
2 tablespoons orange juice
2 tablespoons butter
1 tablespoon crushed red pepper flakes
Pinch black peppercorns
1 bay leaf
1 head cauliflower, stem trimmed
Flake salt, such as Maldon, for serving
FOR THE SAUCE
½ cup crème fraîche
3 tablespoons nonfat Greek yogurt
¼ cup finely shredded Parmigiano-Reggiano
3 teaspoons capers, rinsed and chopped
Freshly ground black pepper

1. Poach the cauliflower. In a Dutch Oster or other heavy-bottomed pot over high heat, bring the wine, water, olive oil, kosher salt, lemon juice, orange juice, butter, red pepper flakes, peppercorns, and bay leaf to a boil.
2. Add the cauliflower, and then reduce the heat to simmer. Turn occasionally, using a pair of serving spoons to submerge each side in the poaching liquid, until a knife easily inserts into center, 15 to 20 minutes.
3. Preheat the Oster to 475°F (246°C). Make the dipping sauce. In a small bowl, mix together the crème fraîche, Greek yogurt, cheese, and capers and season with pepper. Set aside.
4. Roast the cauliflower. Using tongs or the serving spoons, transfer cauliflower to a roasting pan. Roast, rotating the sheet if browning unevenly, until deep golden and crispy in parts, about 35 minutes.
5. Serve. Bring the roasted cauliflower to the table, set on a trivet, and serve directly from the roasting pan with the dipping sauce—and a spoon to dispense it—alongside.

Chapter 12
Casseroles, Frittatas, and Quiches

Asparagus Frittata with Goat Cheese
Prep time: 5 minutes | Cook time: 25 minutes | Serves 2 to 4

1 cup asparagus spears, cut into 1-inch pieces
1 teaspoon vegetable oil
1 tablespoon milk
6 eggs, beaten
2 ounces (57 g) goat cheese, crumbled
1 tablespoon minced chives, optional
Kosher salt and pepper, to taste

1. Preheat the Oster to 400°F (204°C).
2. Add the asparagus spears to a small bowl and drizzle with the vegetable oil. Toss until well coated and transfer to a cake pan.
3. Place the pan in the Oster. Bake for 5 minutes, or until the asparagus become tender and slightly wilted. Remove then pan from the Oster.
4. Stir together the milk and eggs in a medium bowl. Pour the mixture over the asparagus in the pan. Sprinkle with the goat cheese and the chives (if using) over the eggs. Season with a pinch of salt and pepper.
5. Place the pan back to the Oster and bake at 320°F (160°C) for 20 minutes or until the top is lightly golden and the eggs are set.
6. Transfer to a serving dish. Slice and serve.

Asparagus and Grits Casserole
Prep time: 5 minutes | Cook time: 31 minutes | Serves 4

10 fresh asparagus spears, cut into 1-inch pieces
2 cups cooked grits, cooled to room temperature
2 teaspoons Worcestershire sauce
1 egg, beaten
½ teaspoon garlic powder
¼ teaspoon salt
2 slices provolone cheese, crushed
Cooking spray

1. Preheat the Oster to 425°F (218°C). Spritz a baking pan with cooking spray.
2. Set the asparagus in the pan. Spritz the asparagus with cooking spray. Bake for 6 minutes or until lightly browned and crispy.
3. Meanwhile, combine the grits, Worcestershire sauce, egg, garlic powder, and salt in a bowl. Stir to mix well.
4. Pour half of the grits mixture in the pan, then spread with fried asparagus.
5. Spoon half of grits mixture into Oster baking pan and top with asparagus. Spread the cheese over the asparagus and pour the remaining grits over.
6. Place the baking pan in the preheated Oster. Bake for 25 minutes or until the egg is set and lightly browned.
7. Serve immediately.

Shrimp and Cauliflower Casserole
Prep time: 15 minutes | Cook time: 22 minutes | Serves 4

1 pound (454 g) shrimp, cleaned and deveined
2 cups cauliflower, cut into florets
2 green bell pepper, sliced
1 shallot, sliced
2 tablespoons sesame oil
1 cup tomato paste
Cooking spray

1. Preheat the Oster to 360°F (182°C). Spritz a baking pan with cooking spray.
2. Arrange the shrimp and vegetables in the baking pan. Then, drizzle the sesame oil over the vegetables. Pour the tomato paste over the vegetables.
3. Bake for 10 minutes in the preheated Oster. Stir with a large spoon and bake for a further 12 minutes.
4. Serve warm.

Pumpkin-Cauliflower Casserole with Pecans
Prep time: 15 minutes | Cook time: 50 minutes | Serves 6

1 cup chicken broth
2 cups cauliflower florets
1 cup canned pumpkin purée
¼ cup heavy cream
1 teaspoon vanilla extract
2 large eggs, beaten
⅓ cup unsalted butter, melted, plus more for greasing the pan
¼ cup sugar
1 teaspoon fine sea salt
Chopped fresh parsley leaves, for garnish
Topping:
½ cup blanched almond flour
1 cup chopped pecans
⅓ cup unsalted butter, melted
½ cup sugar

1. Preheat the Oster to 350°F (177°C).
2. Pour the chicken broth in a baking pan, then add the cauliflower.
3. Place the baking pan in the Oster. Bake for 20 minutes or until soft.
4. Meanwhile, combine the ingredients for the topping in a large bowl. Stir to mix well.
5. Pat the cauliflower dry with paper towels, then place in a food processor and pulse with pumpkin purée, heavy cream, vanilla extract, eggs, butter, sugar, and salt until smooth.
6. Clean the baking pan and grease with more butter, then pour the purée mixture in the pan. Spread the topping over the mixture.
7. Place the baking pan in the preheated Oster. Bake for 30 minutes or until the topping is lightly browned.
8. Remove the casserole from the Oster and serve with fresh parsley on top.

Parmesan Shrimp Quiche
Prep time: 15 minutes | Cook time: 20 minutes | Serves 2

2 teaspoons vegetable oil
4 large eggs
½ cup half-and-half
4 ounces (113 g) raw shrimp, chopped
1 cup shredded Parmesan or Swiss cheese
¼ cup chopped scallions
1 teaspoon sweet smoked paprika
1 teaspoon herbes de PrOsterce
1 teaspoon black pepper
½ to 1 teaspoon kosher salt

1. Preheat the Oster to 300°F (149°C). Generously grease a round baking pan with 4-inch sides with vegetable oil.
2. In a large bowl, beat together the eggs and half-and-half. Add the shrimp, ¾ cup of the cheese, the scallions, paprika, herbes de PrOsterce, pepper, and salt. Stir with a fork to thoroughly combine. Pour the egg mixture into the prepared pan.
3. Put the pan in the Oster and bake for 20 minutes. After 17 minutes, sprinkle the remaining ¼ cup cheese on top and bake for the remaining 3 minutes, or until the cheese has melted, the eggs are set, and a toothpick inserted into the center comes out clean.
4. Serve the quiche warm.

Prosciutto Casserole with Pepper Jack
Prep time: 5 minutes | Cook time: 10 minutes | Serves 2

1 cup day-old whole grain bread, cubed
3 large eggs, beaten
2 tablespoons water
⅛ teaspoon kosher salt
1 ounce (28 g) prosciutto, roughly chopped
1 ounce (28 g) Pepper Jack cheese, roughly chopped
1 tablespoon chopped fresh chives
Nonstick cooking spray

1. Preheat the Oster to 360°F (182°C).
2. Spray a baking pan with nonstick cooking spray, then place the bread cubes in the pan. Transfer the baking pan to the Oster.
3. In a medium bowl, stir together the beaten eggs and water, then stir in the kosher salt, prosciutto, cheese, and chives.
4. Pour the egg mixture over the bread cubes and bake for 10 minutes, or until the eggs are set and the top is golden brown.
5. Serve warm.

Pork Gratin with Ricotta Cheese
Prep time: 15 minutes | Cook time: 21 minutes | Serves 4

2 tablespoons olive oil
2 pounds (907 g) pork tenderloin, cut into serving-size pieces
1 teaspoon dried marjoram
¼ teaspoon chili powder
1 teaspoon coarse sea salt
½ teaspoon freshly ground black pepper
1 cup Ricotta cheese
1½ cups chicken broth
1 tablespoon mustard
Cooking spray

1. Preheat the Oster to 350°F (177°C). Spritz a baking pan with cooking spray.
2. Heat the olive oil in a nonstick skillet over medium-high heat until shimmering.
3. Add the pork and sauté for 6 minutes or until lightly browned.
4. Transfer the pork to the prepared baking pan and sprinkle with marjoram, chili powder, salt, and ground black pepper.
5. Combine the remaining ingredients in a large bowl. Stir to mix well. Pour the mixture over the pork in the pan.
6. Arrange the pan in the preheated Oster and bake for 15 minutes or until frothy and the cheese melts. Stir the mixture halfway through.
7. Serve immediately.

Parmesan Green Bean Casserole
Prep time: 4 minutes | Cook time: 6 minutes | Serves 4

1 tablespoon melted butter
1 cup green beans
6 ounces (170 g) Cheddar cheese, shredded
7 ounces (198 g) Parmesan cheese, shredded
¼ cup heavy cream
Sea salt, to taste

1. Preheat the Oster to 400°F (204°C). grease a baking pan with the melted butter.
2. Add the green beans, Cheddar, salt, and black pepper to the prepared baking pan. Stir to mix well, then spread the Parmesan and cream on top.
3. Place the baking pan in the preheated Oster. Bake for 6 minutes or until the beans are tender and the cheese melts.
4. Serve immediately.

Tomato, Carrot and Broccoli Quiche
Prep time: 6 minutes | Cook time: 14 minutes | Serves 4

4 eggs
1 teaspoon dried thyme
1 cup whole milk
1 steamed carrots, diced
2 cups steamed broccoli florets
2 medium tomatoes, diced
¼ cup crumbled feta cheese
1 cup grated Cheddar cheese
1 teaspoon chopped parsley
Salt and ground black pepper, to taste
Cooking spray

1. Preheat the Oster to 350°F (177°C). Spritz a baking pan with cooking spray.
2. Whisk together the eggs, thyme, salt, and ground black pepper in a bowl and fold in the milk while mixing.
3. Put the carrots, broccoli, and tomatoes in the prepared baking pan, then spread with feta cheese and ½ cup Cheddar cheese. Pour the egg mixture over, then scatter with remaining Cheddar on top.
4. Put the pan in the preheated Oster. Bake for 14 minutes or until the eggs are set and the quiche is puffed.
5. Remove the quiche from the Oster and top with chopped parsley, then slice to serve.

Mushroom and Beef Casserole
Prep time: 10 minutes | Cook time: 25 minutes | Serves 4

1½ pounds (680 g) beef steak
1 ounce (28 g) dry onion soup mix
2 cups sliced mushrooms
1 (14.5-ounce / 411-g) can cream of mushroom soup
½ cup beef broth
¼ cup red wine
3 garlic cloves, minced
1 whole onion, chopped

1. Preheat the Oster to 360°F (182°C).
2. Put the beef steak in a large bowl, then sprinkle with dry onion soup mix. Toss to coat well.
3. Combine the mushrooms with mushroom soup, beef broth, red wine, garlic, and onion in a large bowl. Stir to mix well.
4. Transfer the beef steak in a baking pan, then pour in the mushroom mixture.
5. Place the pan in the preheated Oster. Bake for 25 minutes or until the mushrooms are soft and the beef is well browned.
6. Remove the baking pan from the Oster and serve immediately.

Swiss Chicken and Ham Casserole
Prep time: 15 minutes | Cook time: 15 minutes | Serves 4 to 6

2 cups diced cooked chicken
1 cup diced ham
¼ teaspoon ground nutmeg
½ cup half-and-half
½ teaspoon ground black pepper
6 slices Swiss cheese
Cooking spray

1. Preheat the Oster to 350°F (177°C). Spritz a baking pan with cooking spray.
2. Combine the chicken, ham, nutmeg, half-and-half, and ground black pepper in a large bowl. Stir to mix well.
3. Pour half of the mixture into the baking pan, then top the mixture with 3 slices of Swiss cheese, then pour in the remaining mixture and top with remaining cheese slices.
4. Arrange the baking pan in the preheated Oster and bake for 15 minutes or until the egg is set and the cheese melts.
5. Serve immediately.

Spinach and Mushroom Frittata
Prep time: 7 minutes | Cook time: 8 minutes | Serves 2

1 cup chopped mushrooms
2 cups spinach, chopped
4 eggs, lightly beaten
3 ounces (85 g) feta cheese, crumbled
2 tablespoons heavy cream
A handful of fresh parsley, chopped
Salt and ground black pepper, to taste
Cooking spray

1. Preheat the Oster to 350°F (177°C). Spritz a baking pan with cooking spray.
2. Whisk together all the ingredients in a large bowl. Stir to mix well.
3. Pour the mixture in the prepared baking pan and place the pan in the preheated Oster.
4. Bake for 8 minutes or until the eggs are set.
5. Serve immediately.

Cheddar Broccoli Casserole
Prep time: 5 minutes | Cook time: 30 minutes | Serves 6

4 cups broccoli florets
¼ cup heavy whipping cream
½ cup sharp Cheddar cheese, shredded
¼ cup ranch dressing
Kosher salt and ground black pepper, to taste

1. Preheat the Oster to 375°F (191°C).
2. Combine all the ingredients in a large bowl. Toss to coat well broccoli well.
3. Pour the mixture into a baking pan, then transfer the pan in the preheated Oster. Bake for 30 minutes or until the broccoli is tender.
4. Remove the baking pan from the Oster and serve immediately.

Broccoli and Chicken Sausage Casserole
Prep time: 10 minutes | Cook time: 20 minutes | Serves 8

10 eggs
1 cup Cheddar cheese, shredded and divided
¾ cup heavy whipping cream
1 (12-ounce / 340-g) package cooked chicken sausage
1 cup broccoli, chopped
2 cloves garlic, minced
½ tablespoon salt
¼ tablespoon ground black pepper
Cooking spray

1. Preheat the Oster to 400°F (204°C). Spritz a baking pan with cooking spray.
2. Whisk the eggs with Cheddar and cream in a large bowl to mix well.
3. Combine the cooked sausage, broccoli, garlic, salt, and ground black pepper in a separate bowl. Stir to mix well.
4. Pour the sausage mixture into the baking pan, then spread the egg mixture over to cover.
5. Place the baking pan in the preheated Oster. Bake for 20 minutes or until the eggs are set and a toothpick inserted in the center comes out clean.
6. Serve immediately.

Feta-Cheddar Vegetable Frittata
Prep time: 15 minutes | Cook time: 21 minutes | Serves 2

4 eggs
¼ cup milk
Sea salt and ground black pepper, to taste
1 zucchini, sliced
½ bunch asparagus, sliced
½ cup mushrooms, sliced
½ cup spinach, shredded
½ cup red onion, sliced
½ tablespoon olive oil
5 tablespoons feta cheese, crumbled
4 tablespoons Cheddar cheese, grated
¼ bunch chives, minced

1. In a bowl, mix the eggs, milk, salt and pepper.
2. Over a medium heat, sauté the vegetables for 6 minutes with the olive oil in a nonstick pan.
3. Put some parchment paper in the base of a baking tin. Pour in the vegetables, followed by the egg mixture. Top with the feta and grated Cheddar.
4. Preheat the Oster to 320°F (160°C).
5. Transfer the baking tin to the Oster and bake for 15 minutes. Remove the frittata from the Oster and leave to cool for 5 minutes.
6. Top with the minced chives and serve.

Feta Chorizo and Potato Frittata
Prep time: 8 minutes | Cook time: 12 minutes | Serves 4

2 tablespoons olive oil
1 chorizo, sliced
4 eggs
½ cup corn
1 large potato, boiled and cubed
1 tablespoon chopped parsley
½ cup feta cheese, crumbled
Salt and ground black pepper, to taste

1. Preheat the Oster to 330°F (166°C).
2. Heat the olive oil in a nonstick skillet over medium heat until shimmering.
3. Add the chorizo and cook for 4 minutes or until golden brown.
4. Whisk the eggs in a bowl, then sprinkle with salt and ground black pepper.
5. Mix the remaining ingredients in the egg mixture, then pour the chorizo and its fat into a baking pan. Pour in the egg mixture.
6. Place the pan in the preheated Oster. Bake for 8 minutes or until the eggs are set.
7. Serve immediately.

Corn Casserole with Bell Pepper
Prep time: 10 minutes | Cook time: 20 minutes | Serves 4

1 cup corn kernels
¼ cup bell pepper, finely chopped
½ cup low-fat milk
1 large egg, beaten
½ cup yellow cornmeal
½ cup all-purpose flour
½ teaspoon baking powder
2 tablespoons melted unsalted butter
1 tablespoon granulated sugar
Pinch of cayenne pepper
¼ teaspoon kosher salt
Cooking spray

1. Preheat the Oster to 330°F (166°C). Spritz a baking pan with cooking spray.
2. Combine all the ingredients in a large bowl. Stir to mix well. Pour the mixture into the baking pan.
3. Place the pan in the preheated Oster. Bake for 20 minutes or until lightly browned and set.
4. Remove the baking pan from the Oster and serve immediately.

Chapter 13
Fast and Easy Everyday Favorites

Buttery Egg and Broccoli Bake
Prep time: 5 minutes | Cook time: 6 minutes | Serves 1

4 egg yolks
¼ cup butter, melted
2 cups coconut flour
Salt and pepper, to taste
2 cups broccoli florets

1. Preheat the Oster to 425°F (218°C).
2. In a bowl, whisk the egg yolks and melted butter together. Throw in the coconut flour, salt and pepper, then stir again to combine well.
3. Dip each broccoli floret into the mixture and place in the baking pan. Bake for 8 minutes in batches if necessary. Take care when removing them from the Oster and serve immediately.

Baked Chicken Wings
Prep time: 5 minutes | Cook time: 41 minutes | Serves 6

2 pounds (907 g) chicken wings, tips removed
⅛ teaspoon salt

1. Preheat the Oster to 425°F (218°C). Season the wings with salt.
2. Working in 2 batches, place half the chicken wings in the baking pan and bake for 18 minutes, or until the skin is browned and cooked through, turning the wings with tongs halfway through cooking.
3. Combine both batches in the Oster and bake for 5 minutes more. Transfer to a large bowl and serve immediately.

Baked Peanuts with Hot Pepper Sauce
Prep time: 5 minutes | Cook time: 6 minutes | Serves 9

3 cups shelled raw peanuts
1 tablespoon hot red pepper sauce
3 tablespoons granulated white sugar

1. Preheat the Oster to 425°F (218°C).
2. Put the peanuts in a large bowl, then drizzle with hot red pepper sauce and sprinkle with sugar. Toss to coat well.
3. Pour the peanuts in the baking pan. Bake for 6 minutes or until the peanuts are crispy and browned.
4. Serve immediately.

Beef Hot Dog with Bacon
Prep time: 5 minutes | Cook time: 10 minutes | Serves 4

4 slices sugar-free bacon
4 beef hot dogs

1. Preheat the Oster to 370°F (188°C).
2. Take a slice of bacon and wrap it around the hot dog, securing it with a toothpick. Repeat with the other pieces of bacon and hot dogs, placing each wrapped dog in the baking pan.
3. Bake for 10 minutes, turning halfway through.
4. Once hot and crispy, the hot dogs are ready to serve.

Cheddar Jalapeño Poppers with Bacon
Prep time: 5 minutes | Cook time: 12 minutes | Serves 6

6 large jalapeños
4 ounces (113 g) ⅓-less-fat cream cheese
¼ cup shredded reduced-fat sharp Cheddar cheese
2 scallions, green tops only, sliced
6 slices center-cut bacon, halved

1. Preheat the Oster to 325°F (163°C).
2. Wearing rubber gloves, halve the jalapeños lengthwise to make 12 pieces. Scoop out the seeds and membranes and discard.
3. In a medium bowl, combine the cream cheese, Cheddar, and scallions. Using a small spoon or spatula, fill the jalapeños with the cream cheese filling. Wrap a bacon strip around each pepper and secure with a toothpick.
4. Working in batches, place the stuffed peppers in a single layer in the baking pan. Bake for about 12 minutes, until the peppers are tender, the bacon is browned and crisp, and the cheese is melted.
5. Serve warm.

Cheese Capicola Sandwich with Mayo
Prep time: 5 minutes | Cook time: 8 minutes | Serves 2

2 tablespoons mayonnaise
4 thick slices sourdough bread
4 thick slices Brie cheese
8 slices hot capicola

1. Preheat the Oster to 350°F (177°C).
2. Spread the mayonnaise on one side of each slice of bread. Place 2 slices of bread in the baking pan, mayonnaise-side down.
3. Place the slices of Brie and capicola on the bread and cover with the remaining two slices of bread, mayonnaise-side up.
4. Bake for 8 minutes, or until the cheese has melted.
5. Serve immediately.

Potato Patties with Colby Cheese
Prep time: 5 minutes | Cook time: 10 minutes | Serves 8

2 pounds (907 g) white potatoes
½ cup finely chopped scallions
½ teaspoon freshly ground black pepper, or more to taste
1 tablespoon fine sea salt
½ teaspoon hot paprika
¼ cup canola oil
1 cup crushed crackers

1. Preheat the Oster to 360°F (182°C).
2. Boil the potatoes until soft. Dry them off and peel them before mashing thoroughly, leaving no lumps.
3. Combine the mashed potatoes with scallions, pepper, salt, paprika, and cheese.
4. Bake the patties for about 10 minutes, in multiple batches if necessary.
5. Serve hot.

Manchego Frico with Cumin Seeds
Prep time: 5 minutes | Cook time: 6 minutes | Serves 2

1 cup shredded aged Manchego cheese
1 teaspoon all-purpose flour
½ teaspoon cumin seeds
¼ teaspoon cracked black pepper

1. Preheat the Oster to 400°F (204°C). Line the baking pan with parchment paper.
2. Combine the cheese and flour in a bowl. Stir to mix well. Spread the mixture in the pan into a 4-inch round.
3. Combine the cumin and black pepper in a small bowl. Stir to mix well. Sprinkle the cumin mixture over the cheese round.
4. Bake for 6 minutes or until the cheese is lightly browned and frothy.
5. Use tongs to transfer the cheese wafer onto a plate and slice to serve.

Cherry Tomato Bake with Basil
Prep time: 5 minutes | Cook time: 4 to 6 minutes | Serves 2

2 cups cherry tomatoes
1 clove garlic, thinly sliced
1 teaspoon olive oil
⅛ teaspoon kosher salt
1 tablespoon freshly chopped basil, for topping
Cooking spray

1. Preheat the Oster to 360°F (182°C). Spritz the Oster baking pan with cooking spray and set aside.
2. In a large bowl, toss together the cherry tomatoes, sliced garlic, olive oil, and kosher salt. Spread the mixture in an even layer in the prepared pan.
3. Bake in the preheated Oster for 4 to 6 minutes, or until the tomatoes become soft and wilted.
4. Transfer to a bowl and rest for 5 minutes. Top with the chopped basil and serve warm.

Halloumi Cheese Bake with Greek Salsa
Prep time: 15 minutes | Cook time: 6 minutes | Serves 4

Salsa:
1 small shallot, finely diced
3 garlic cloves, minced
2 tablespoons fresh lemon juice
2 tablespoons extra-virgin olive oil
1 plum tomato, deseeded and finely diced
2 teaspoons chopped fresh parsley
1 teaspoon snipped fresh dill
1 teaspoon snipped fresh oregano
Cheese:
8 ounces (227 g) Halloumi cheese, sliced into ½-inch-thick pieces
1 tablespoon extra-virgin olive oil

1. Preheat the Oster to 375°F (191°C).
2. For the salsa: Combine the shallot, garlic, lemon juice, olive oil, pepper, and salt in a medium bowl. Add the cucumber, tomato, parsley, dill, and oregano. Toss gently to combine; set aside.
3. For the cheese: Place the cheese slices in a medium bowl. Drizzle with the olive oil. Toss gently to coat. Arrange the cheese in a single layer in the baking pan. Bake for 6 minutes.
4. Divide the cheese among four serving plates. Top with the salsa and serve immediately.

Chile Toast with Mozzarella Cheese
Prep time: 5 minutes | Cook time: 5 minutes | Serves 1

2 tablespoons grated Parmesan cheese
2 tablespoons grated Mozzarella cheese
2 teaspoons salted butter, at room temperature
10 to 15 thin slices serrano chile or jalapeño
2 slices sourdough bread
½ teaspoon black pepper

1. Preheat the Oster to 325°F (163°C).
2. In a small bowl, stir together the Parmesan, Mozzarella, butter, and chiles.
3. Spread half the mixture onto one side of each slice of bread. Sprinkle with the pepper. Place the slices, cheese-side up, in the baking pan. Bake for 5 minutes, or until the cheese has melted and started to brown slightly.
4. Serve immediately.

Cheddar Sausage Balls
Prep time: 5 minutes | Cook time: 18 minutes | Serves 6

12 ounces (340 g) Jimmy Dean's Sausage
6 ounces (170 g) shredded Cheddar cheese
10 Cheddar cubes

1. Preheat the Oster to 400°F (204°C).
2. Mix the shredded cheese and sausage.
3. Divide the mixture into 12 equal parts to be stuffed.
4. Add a cube of cheese to the center of the sausage and roll into balls.
5. Bake for 18 minutes, or until crisp.
6. Serve immediately.

Old Bay Shrimp with Cayenne
Prep time: 7 minutes | Cook time: 12 minutes | Makes 2 cups

½ teaspoon Old Bay Seasoning
1 teaspoon ground cayenne pepper
½ teaspoon paprika
1 tablespoon olive oil
⅛ teaspoon salt
½ pound (227 g) shrimps, peeled and deveined
Juice of half a lemon

1. Preheat the Oster to 425°F (218°C).
2. Combine the Old Bay Seasoning, cayenne pepper, paprika, olive oil, and salt in a large bowl, then add the shrimps and toss to coat well.
3. Put the shrimps in the baking pan. Bake for 12 minutes or until opaque. Flip the shrimps halfway through.
4. Serve the shrimps with lemon juice on top.

Green Beans and Bacon Bake
Prep time: 15 minutes | Cook time: 12 minutes | Serves 4

2 (14.5-ounce / 411-g) cans cut green beans, drained
4 bacon slices, air-fried and diced
¼ cup minced onion
1 tablespoon distilled white vinegar
1 teaspoon freshly squeezed lemon juice
½ teaspoon salt
½ teaspoon freshly ground black pepper
Cooking spray

1. Preheat the Oster to 400°F (204°C).
2. Spritz a baking pan with oil. In the prepared pan, stir together the green beans, bacon, onion, vinegar, lemon juice, salt, and pepper until blended.
3. Bake for 5 minutes. Stir the green beans and bake for 7 minutes more until soft.
4. Serve immediately.

Green Beans Bake with Lemon Pepper
Prep time: 5 minutes | Cook time: 10 minutes | Makes 2 cups

½ teaspoon lemon pepper
2 teaspoons granulated garlic
½ teaspoon salt
1 tablespoon olive oil
2 cups fresh green beans, trimmed and snapped in half

1. Preheat the Oster to 370°F (188°C).
2. Combine the lemon pepper, garlic, salt, and olive oil in a bowl. Stir to mix well.
3. Add the green beans to the bowl of mixture and toss to coat well.
4. Arrange the green beans in the preheated Oster. Bake for 10 minutes or until tender and crispy.
5. Serve immediately.

Chicken Wings with Hot Sauce
Prep time: 5 minutes | Cook time: 30 minutes | Makes 16 wings

16 chicken wings
3 tablespoons hot sauce
Cooking spray

1. Preheat the Oster to 360°F (182°C). Spritz the baking pan with cooking spray.
2. Arrange the chicken wings in the pan. You need to work in batches to avoid overcrowding.
3. Bake for 15 minutes or until well browned. Flip the chicken wings at lease three times during the cooking.
4. Transfer the wings on a plate and serve with hot sauce.

Carrot Chips with Parsley
Prep time: 5 minutes | Cook time: 15 minutes | Makes 3 cups

3 large carrots, peeled and sliced into long and thick chips diagonally
1 tablespoon granulated garlic
1 teaspoon salt
¼ teaspoon ground black pepper
1 tablespoon olive oil
1 tablespoon finely chopped fresh parsley

1. Preheat the Oster to 360°F (182°C).
2. Toss the carrots with garlic, salt, ground black pepper, and olive oil in a large bowl to coat well.
3. Place the carrots in the preheated Oster. Bake for 15 minutes or until the carrot chips are soft. Stir halfway through.
4. Serve the carrot chips with parsley on top.

Okra Chips
Prep time: 5 minutes | Cook time: 16 minutes | Serves 6

2 pounds (907 g) fresh okra pods, cut into 1-inch pieces
2 tablespoons canola oil
1 teaspoon coarse sea salt

1. Preheat the Oster to 425°F (218°C).
2. Stir the oil and salt in a bowl to mix well. Add the okra and toss to coat well.
3. Place the okra in the baking pan. Bake for 18 minutes or until lightly browned. Stir at least three times during the cooking time.
4. Serve immediately.

Shrimp, Sausage and Potato Bake

Prep time: 10 minutes | Cook time: 18 minutes | Serves 2

1 ear corn, husk and silk removed, cut into 2-inch rounds
8 ounces (227 g) red potatoes, unpeeled, cut into 1-inch pieces
2 teaspoons Old Bay Seasoning, divided
2 teaspoons vegetable oil, divided
¼ teaspoon ground black pepper
8 ounces (227 g) large shrimps (about 12 shrimps), deveined
6 ounces (170 g) andouille or chorizo sausage, cut into 1-inch pieces
2 garlic cloves, minced
1 tablespoon chopped fresh parsley

1. Preheat the Oster to 400°F (204°C).
2. Put the corn rounds and potatoes in a large bowl. Sprinkle with 1 teaspoon of Old Bay seasoning and drizzle with vegetable oil. Toss to coat well.
3. Transfer the corn rounds and potatoes on a baking sheet, then put in the preheated Oster.
4. Bake for 12 minutes or until soft and browned.
5. Meanwhile, cut slits into the shrimps but be careful not to cut them through. Combine the shrimps, sausage, remaining Old Bay seasoning, and remaining vegetable oil in the large bowl. Toss to coat well.
6. When the baking of the potatoes and corn rounds is complete, add the shrimps and sausage and bake for 6 more minutes or until the shrimps are opaque.
7. When the baking is finished, serve them on a plate and spread with parsley before serving.

Panko-Chorizo Scotch Eggs

Prep time: 5 minutes | Cook time: 15 to 20 minutes | Makes 4 eggs

1 pound (454 g) Mexican chorizo or other seasoned sausage meat
4 soft-boiled eggs plus 1 raw egg
1 tablespoon water
½ cup all-purpose flour
1 cup panko bread crumbs
Cooking spray

1. Divide the chorizo into 4 equal portions. Flatten each portion into a disc. Place a soft-boiled egg in the center of each disc. Wrap the chorizo around the egg, encasing it completely. Place the encased eggs on a plate and chill for at least 30 minutes.
2. Preheat the Oster to 360°F (182°C).
3. Beat the raw egg with 1 tablespoon of water. Place the flour on a small plate and the panko on a second plate. Working with 1 egg at a time, roll the encased egg in the flour, then dip it in the egg mixture. Dredge the egg in the panko and place on a plate. Repeat with the remaining eggs.
4. Spray the eggs with oil and place in the baking pan. Bake for 10 minutes. Turn and bake for an additional 5 to 10 minutes, or until browned and crisp on all sides.
5. Serve immediately.

Chapter 14
Holiday Specials

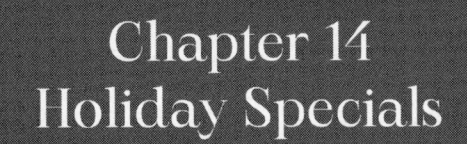

Breaded Olives with Thyme
Prep time: 10 minutes | Cook time: 6 minutes | Serves 4

12 ounces (340 g) pitted black extra-large olives
¼ cup all-purpose flour
1 cup panko bread crumbs
2 teaspoons dried thyme
1 teaspoon red pepper flakes
1 teaspoon smoked paprika
1 egg beaten with 1 tablespoon water
Vegetable oil for spraying

1. Preheat the Oster to 425°F (218°C).
2. Drain the olives and place them on a paper towel-lined plate to dry.
3. Put the flour on a plate. Combine the panko, thyme, red pepper flakes, and paprika on a separate plate. Dip an olive in the flour, shaking off any excess, then coat with egg mixture. Dredge the olive in the panko mixture, pressing to make the crumbs adhere, and place the breaded olive on a platter. Repeat with the remaining olives.
4. Spray the olives with oil and place them in a single layer in the baking pan. Bake for 6 minutes until the breading is browned and crispy. Serve warm

Monkey Bread with Peacans
Prep time: 15 minutes | Cook time: 25 minutes | Serves 6 to 8

1 (16.3-ounce / 462-g) can store-bought refrigerated biscuit dough
¼ cup packed light brown sugar
1 teaspoon ground cinnamon
½ teaspoon freshly grated nutmeg
½ teaspoon ground ginger
½ teaspoon kosher salt
¼ teaspoon ground allspice
⅛ teaspoon ground cloves
4 tablespoons (½ stick) unsalted butter, melted
½ cup powdered sugar
2 teaspoons bourbon
2 tablespoons chopped candied cherries
2 tablespoons chopped pecans

1. Preheat the Oster to 310°F (154°C).
2. Open the can and separate the biscuits, then cut each into quarters. Toss the biscuit quarters in a large bowl with the brown sugar, cinnamon, nutmeg, ginger, salt, allspice, and cloves until evenly coated. Transfer the dough pieces and any sugar left in the bowl to a round cake pan, metal cake pan, or foil pan and drizzle evenly with the melted butter. Put the pan in the Oster and bake until the monkey bread is golden brown and cooked through in the middle, about 25 minutes. Transfer the pan to a wire rack and let cool completely. Unmold from the pan.
3. In a small bowl, whisk the powdered sugar and the bourbon into a smooth glaze. Drizzle the glaze over the cooled monkey bread and, while the glaze is still wet, sprinkle with the cherries and pecans to serve.

Eggnog Bread with Pecans and Fruit
Prep time: 10 minutes | Cook time: 18 minutes | Serves 6 to 8

1 cup flour, plus more for dusting
¼ cup sugar
1 teaspoon baking powder
¼ teaspoon salt
¼ teaspoon nutmeg
½ cup eggnog
1 egg yolk
1 tablespoon plus 1 teaspoon butter, melted
¼ cup pecans
¼ cup chopped candied fruit (cherries, pineapple, or mixed fruits)
Cooking spray

1. Preheat the Oster to 360°F (182°C).
2. In a medium bowl, stir together the flour, sugar, baking powder, salt, and nutmeg.
3. Add eggnog, egg yolk, and butter. Mix well but do not beat.
4. Stir in nuts and fruit.
5. Spray a baking pan with cooking spray and dust with flour.
6. Spread batter into prepared pan and bake for 18 minutes or until top is dark golden brown and bread starts to pull away from sides of pan.
7. Serve immediately.

Maple Vanilla Pecan Tart
Prep time: 2 hours 25 minutes | Cook time: 30 minutes | Serves 8

Tart Crust:
¼ cup firmly packed brown sugar
⅓ cup butter, softened
1 cup all-purpose flour
¼ teaspoon kosher salt
Filling:
¼ cup whole milk
4 tablespoons butter, diced
½ cup packed brown sugar
¼ cup pure maple syrup
1½ cups finely chopped pecans
¼ teaspoon pure vanilla extract
¼ teaspoon sea salt

1. Preheat the Oster to 350°F (177°C). Line a baking pan with aluminum foil, then spritz the pan with cooking spray.
2. Pour the mixture in the prepared baking pan and tilt the pan to coat the bottom evenly.
3. Arrange the pan in the preheated Oster. Bake for 13 minutes or until the crust is golden brown.
4. Meanwhile, pour the milk, butter, sugar, and maple syrup in a saucepan. Stir to mix well. Bring to a simmer, then cook for 1 more minute. Stir constantly.
5. Pour the filling mixture over the golden crust and spread with a spatula to coat the crust evenly.
6. Bake in the Oster for an additional 12 minutes or until the filling mixture is set and frothy.
7. Remove the baking pan from the Oster and sprinkle with salt. Allow to sit for 10 minutes or until cooled.

Asiago Cheese Bread

Prep time: 37 minutes | Cook time: 24 minutes | Makes 12 balls

2 tablespoons butter, plus more for greasing
½ cup milk
1½ cups tapioca flour
½ teaspoon salt
1 large egg
⅔ cup finely grated aged Asiago cheese

1. Put the butter in a saucepan and pour in the milk, heat over medium heat until the liquid boils. Keep stirring.
2. Turn off the heat and mix in the tapioca flour and salt to form a soft dough. Transfer the dough in a large bowl, then wrap the bowl in plastic and let sit for 15 minutes.
3. Break the egg in the bowl of dough and whisk with a hand mixer for 2 minutes or until a sanity dough forms. Fold the cheese in the dough. Cover the bowl in plastic again and let sit for 10 more minutes.
4. Preheat the Oster to 375°F (191°C). Grease a cake pan with butter.
5. Scoop 2 tablespoons of the dough into the cake pan. Repeat with the remaining dough to make dough 12 balls. Keep a little distance between each two balls. You may need to work in batches to avoid overcrowding.
6. Place the cake pan in the preheated Oster.
7. Bake for 12 minutes or until the balls are golden brown and fluffy. Flip the balls halfway through the cooking time.
8. Remove the balls from the Oster and allow to cool for 5 minutes before serving.

Pigs in a Blanket with Sesame Seeds

Prep time: 10 minutes | Cook time: 8 minutes per batch | Makes 16 rolls

1 can refrigerated crescent roll dough
1 small package mini smoked sausages, patted dry
2 tablespoons melted butter
2 teaspoons sesame seeds
1 teaspoon onion powder

1. Preheat the Oster to 330°F (166°C).
2. Place the crescent roll dough on a clean work surface and separate into 8 pieces. Cut each piece in half and you will have 16 triangles.
3. Make the pigs in the blanket: Arrange each sausage on each dough triangle, then roll the sausages up.
4. Brush the pigs with melted butter and place half of the pigs in the blanket in the preheated Oster. Sprinkle with sesame seeds and onion powder.
5. Bake for 8 minutes or until the pigs are fluffy and golden brown. Flip the pigs halfway through.
6. Serve immediately.

Risotto Croquettes with Tomato Sauce

Prep time: 1 hour 40 minutes | Cook time: 1 hour | Serves 6

Risotto Croquettes:
4 tablespoons unsalted butter
1 small yellow onion, minced
1 cup Arborio rice
3½ cups chicken stock
½ cup dry white wine
3 eggs
Zest of 1 lemon
½ cup grated Parmesan cheese
2 ounces (57 g) fresh Mozzarella cheese
¼ cup peas
2 tablespoons water
½ cup all-purpose flour
1½ cups panko bread crumbs
Kosher salt and ground black pepper, to taste
Cooking spray
Tomato Sauce:
2 tablespoons extra-virgin olive oil
4 cloves garlic, minced
¼ teaspoon red pepper flakes
1 (28-ounce / 794-g) can crushed tomatoes
2 teaspoons granulated sugar
Kosher salt and ground black pepper, to taste

1. Melt the butter in a pot over medium heat, then add the onion and salt to taste. Sauté for 5 minutes or until the onion in translucent.
2. Add the rice and stir to coat well. Cook for 3 minutes or until the rice is lightly browned. Pour in the chicken stock and wine.
3. Bring to a boil. Then cook for 20 minutes or until the rice is tender and liquid is almost absorbed.
4. Make the risotto: When the rice is cooked, break the egg into the pot. Add the lemon zest and Parmesan cheese. Sprinkle with salt and ground black pepper. Stir to mix well.
5. Pour the risotto in a baking sheet, then level with a spatula to spread the risotto evenly. Wrap the baking sheet in plastic and refrigerate for 1 hour.
6. Meanwhile, heat the olive oil in a saucepan over medium heat until shimmering.
7. Add the garlic and sprinkle with red pepper flakes. Sauté for a minute or until fragrant.
8. Add the crushed tomatoes and sprinkle with sugar. Stir to mix well. Bring to a boil. Reduce the heat to low and simmer for 15 minutes or until lightly thickened. Sprinkle with salt and pepper to taste. Set aside until ready to serve.
9. Remove the risotto from the refrigerator. Scoop the risotto into twelve 2-inch balls, then flatten the balls with your hands.
10. Arrange a about ½-inch piece of Mozzarella and 5 peas in the center of each flattened ball, then wrap them back into balls.
11. Transfer the balls in a baking sheet lined with parchment paper, then refrigerate for 15 minutes or until firm.
12. Preheat the Oster to 400°F (204°C).
13. Whisk the remaining 2 eggs with 2 tablespoons of water in a bowl. Pour the flour in a second bowl and pour the panko in a third bowl.
14. Dredge the risotto balls in the bowl of flour first, then into the eggs, and then into the panko. Shake the excess off.

Appendix 1 Measurement Conversion Chart

Volume Equivalents (Dry)	
US STANDARD	**METRIC (APPROXIMATE)**
1/8 teaspoon	0.5 mL
1/4 teaspoon	1 mL
1/2 teaspoon	2 mL
3/4 teaspoon	4 mL
1 teaspoon	5 mL
1 tablespoon	15 mL
1/4 cup	59 mL
1/2 cup	118 mL
3/4 cup	177 mL
1 cup	235 mL
2 cups	475 mL
3 cups	700 mL
4 cups	1 L

Weight Equivalents	
US STANDARD	**METRIC (APPROXIMATE)**
1 ounce	28 g
2 ounces	57 g
5 ounces	142 g
10 ounces	284 g
15 ounces	425 g
16 ounces (1 pound)	455 g
1.5 pounds	680 g
2 pounds	907 g

Volume Equivalents (Liquid)		
US STANDARD	**US STANDARD (OUNCES)**	**METRIC (APPROXIMATE)**
2 tablespoons	1 fl.oz.	30 mL
1/4 cup	2 fl.oz.	60 mL
1/2 cup	4 fl.oz.	120 mL
1 cup	8 fl.oz.	240 mL
1 1/2 cup	12 fl.oz.	355 mL
2 cups or 1 pint	16 fl.oz.	475 mL
4 cups or 1 quart	32 fl.oz.	1 L
1 gallon	128 fl.oz.	4 L

Temperatures Equivalents	
FAHRENHEIT(F)	**CELSIUS(C) APPROXIMATE)**
225 °F	107 °C
250 °F	120 ° °C
275 °F	135 °C
300 °F	150 °C
325 °F	160 °C
350 °F	180 °C
375 °F	190 °C
400 °F	205 °C
425 °F	220 °C
450 °F	235 °C
475 °F	245 °C
500 °F	260 °C

Appendix 2 The Dirty Dozen and Clean Fifteen

The Environmental Working Group (EWG) is a nonprofit, nonpartisan organization dedicated to protecting human health and the environment Its mission is to empower people to live healthier lives in a healthier environment. This organization publishes an annual list of the twelve kinds of produce, in sequence, that have the highest amount of pesticide residue-the Dirty Dozen-as well as a list of the fifteen kinds of produce that have the least amount of pesticide residue-the Clean Fifteen.

THE DIRTY DOZEN	
The 2016 Dirty Dozen includes the following produce. These are considered among the year's most important produce to buy organic:	
Strawberries	Spinach
Apples	Tomatoes
Nectarines	Bell peppers
Peaches	Cherry tomatoes
Celery	Cucumbers
Grapes	Kale/collard greens
Cherries	Hot peppers
The Dirty Dozen list contains two additional items kale/collard greens and hot peppers-because they tend to contain trace levels of highly hazardous pesticides.	

THE CLEAN FIFTEEN	
The least critical to buy organically are the Clean Fifteen list. The following are on the 2016 list:	
Avocados	Papayas
Corn	Kiw
Pineapples	Eggplant
Cabbage	Honeydew
Sweet peas	Grapefruit
Onions	Cantaloupe
Asparagus	Cauliflower
Mangos	
Some of the sweet corn sold in the United States are made from genetically engineered (GE) seedstock. Buy organic varieties of these crops to avoid GE produce.	

Appendix 3 Index

A-B

Almond-Coconut Flounder Fillets	51
Almond-Lemon Crusted Fish	52
Almond-Stuffed Dates with Turkey Bacon	72
Apple and Pear Crisp with Walnuts	65
Apple Chips	73
Apple Cinnamon Fritters	64
Asiago Cheese Bread	109
Asparagus and Grits Casserole	98
Asparagus Frittata with Goat Cheese	98
Bacon Whole Grain Tortilla Bar	14
Bacon-Cheese Muffin Sandwiches	6
Baked Bacon-Wrapped Dates	72
Baked Bacon-Wrapped Scallops	54
Baked Chicken Wings	103
Baked Peanuts with Hot Pepper Sauce	103
Balsamic Mango and Beef Skewers	72
Balsamic Ribeye Steaks with Rosemary	36
Basil Egg Frittata	78
BBQ Bacon and Bell Pepper Sandwich	59
BBQ Chicken Breast with Creamy Coleslaw	46
BBQ Sausage with Pineapple and Bell Peppers	36
Beef and Carrot Meatballs	39
Beef and Mushroom Meatloaf	37
Beef and Spaghetti Squash Lasagna	39
Beef Cubes with Cheese Pasta Sauce	72
Beef Hot Dog with Bacon	103
Beef Kofta with Cinnamon	38
Beef Meatloaf with Tomato Sauce	37
Beef Mixture Topped Potato Fries	27
Beef Sloppy Joes	59
Beef Stroganoff with Mushrooms	37
Beef, Kale and Tomato Omelet	36
Blueberry Chocolate Cupcakes	63
Blueberry Muffins	7
Breaded Calamari Rings with Lemon	53
Breaded Fresh Scallops	54
Breaded Olives with Thyme	108
Broccoli and Chicken Sausage Casserole	101
Broccoli, Spinach and Bell Pepper Dip	73
Brown Rice Porridge with Coconut and Dates	7
Brown Sugar-Lemon Applesauce	63
Butter Choco Soufflé	78
Butter Loaf with Dried Currants	78
Buttermilk Biscuits	7
Buttermilk-Marinated Chicken Breast	48
Buttery Egg and Broccoli Bake	103

C

Cajun Cod with Lemon Pepper	54
Candied Cinnamon Apples	69
Carrot Chips with Parsley	105
Carrot, Cherry and Oatmeal Cups	65
Cayenne Mixed Nuts with Sesame Seeds	73
Cayenne Prawns with Cumin	54
Cheddar Baked Eggs	11
Cheddar Broccoli Casserole	100
Cheddar Ham and Tomato Sandwiches	9

Cheddar Ham Hash Brown Cups	10
Cheddar Jalapeño Poppers with Bacon	103
Cheddar Onion Hash Brown Casserole	11
Cheddar Onion Omelet	10
Cheddar Prosciutto and Potato Salad	40
Cheddar Sausage Balls	104
Cheddar Veggie Bacon-Egg Casserole	10
Cheese and Herb mixed Breadsticks	82
Cheese Capicola Sandwich with Mayo	103
Cheese Glazed Sweet Rolls	91
Cheesy Egg Bread Toast	14
Cheesy Garlic Bake	82
Cheesy Salsa Stuffed Mushrooms	73
Cheesy Spinach Pinwheels	21
Cheesy Tomato Skewers with Pasta	27
Cheesy Turkey filled Pies	94
Cherry Tomato Bake with Basil	104
Cherry Tomato topped Pizza	94
Chicken and Bell Pepper Fajitas	43
Chicken and Lettuce Pita Sandwich	60
Chicken Balls in Pasta Sauce	23
Chicken Cordon Bleu with Swiss Cheese	43
Chicken Fingers with Marinara Sauce	31
Chicken Lettuce Tacos with Peanut Sauce	44
Chicken Manchurian with Ketchup Sauce	45
Chicken Nuggets with Almond Crust	44
Chicken Sausage and Tater Tot Casserole	9
Chicken Wings with Hot Sauce	105
Chile Toast with Mozzarella Cheese	104
Chili Kale Chips with Sesame Seeds	74
Chili-Garlic Chicken Tenders	44
Chipotle Flank Steak with Oregano	36
Chocolate Cake with Fresh Blackberries	67
Chocolate Drizzled Cocoa Puffs	76
Chocolate Pie with Pecans	68
Chocolate Pineapple Cake	65
Chocolate Sprinkles Rolled Butter Cookies	29
Cilantro Chicken with Lime	45
Cinnamon Applesauce Oatmeal	15
Cinnamon Nut Mix	75
Cinnamon Oats Granola	79
Cinnamon Peach Dessert	92
Cinnamon Pumpkin Bread	77
Cinnamon S'mores	70
Citrusy Brussels sprouts Shallots Roast	95
Citrusy Cauliflower with Crème Fraîche Sauce	96
Cocoa Butter Brownies	81
Coconut Chia Pudding	68
Coconut Chicken Fingers	28
Coconut Chocolate Cake	68
Coffee Coconut Chocolate Cake	69
Colby Shrimp Sandwich with Mayo	60
Corn Casserole with Bell Pepper	101
Crab and Fish Cakes with Celery	55
Crab Ratatouille with Tomatoes and Eggplant	55
Cream and Chocolate filled Pies	91
Creamy Choco Cookies	79
Crispy Baked Venison	40

Curried Chicken with Orange and Honey	43
Curried Cinnamon Chicken	43
Curried Cranberry and Apple Chicken	44
Custard Dessert with Caramelized Sugar	90

D-E

Delicious Butter Muffins	12
Delicious delicata rings	96
Dijon Mustard Pork Tenderloin	35
Dijon-Lemon Pork Tenderloin	35
Dill Chicken Strips with Italian Dressing	46
Dill-Thyme Beef Steak	35
Double Pepper Zucchini Bake	19
Easy Buttermilk Bread	84
Easy Vanilla Square Cakes	83
Egg in a Hole with Cheddar and Ham	12
Egg- Tomato Cheese Bread	23
Eggnog Bread with Pecans and Fruit	108
Elegant Cheesy Pasta	22
Enticing Blueberry Crumble Pie	84
Enticing Virginia Ham Pizza	17

F-G

Fajita Chicken Strips with Bell Peppers	46
Feta Chorizo and Potato Frittata	101
Feta-Cheddar Vegetable Frittata	101
Garlic Baked Chicken Wings	48
Garlic Cheese Crust	22
Garlic Chicken Thighs with Scallions	47
Garlic Whole Chicken Bake	47
Garlic-Lemon Shrimp	52
Garlic-Paprika Potato Chips	74
Ginger Chicken Thighs with Cilantro	47
Ginger Cinnamon Cookies	67
Ginger Pumpkin Pudding	65
Golden Choux Pastry	76
Golden Crisp Chicken Tortilla	31
Golden Pepper Twists	21
Gouda Egg-Bacon Bread Cups	10
Graham Cracker Chocolate Cheesecake	63
Grandma's Best Ever Chocolate Cake	83
Green Beans and Bacon Bake	105
Green Beans Bake with Lemon Pepper	105

H-I-L

Half-and-half Broccoli Soup	32
Halloumi Cheese Bake with Greek Salsa	104
Halloumi Pepper and Spinach Omelet	12
Havarti Asparagus Strata	11
Havarti Chicken and Ham Burgers	45
Healthy Banana Bread	84
Homemade Butter Biscuits	95
Homemade Cheese Puffs	28
Homemade Coconut Tart	85
Homemade Honeyed Butter Biscuits	24
Homemade Simple Bread	94
Honey-Glazed Cod with Sesame Seeds	51
Honey-Glazed Pears with Walnuts	63
Italian-Style Salmon Patties	52
Lamb Kofta with Mint	38
Lemon Blackberry and Granola Crisp	64
Lemon Poppy Seed Cake	67

Lemon-Caper Salmon Burgers	51
Lemongrass Pork Chops with Fish Sauce	38
Lettuce and Tomato Topped Cheeseburger	29

M-O

Manchego Frico with Cumin Seeds	104
Maple Blueberry Granola Cobbler	8
Maple Milky Toast	13
Maple Vanilla Pecan Tart	108
Mayo Lettuce Pork Burger	32
Meringue Dessert with Whipped Cream	77
Milk Chocolate Cookies	86
Milky Bread and Honeyed Butter	85
Milky Pumpkin Pie	20
Mini Apple Muffins	85
Miso-Sake Marinated Flank Steak	37
Mixed Berry Crisp with Coconut Chips	70
Moms Special Apple Crisp	82
Moms Special Garlic Knots	19
Monkey Bread with Peacans	108
Mozzarella Bruschetta with Basil Pesto	72
Mozzarella Chicken and Cabbage Sandwich	59
Mozzarella Hash Brown Bruschetta	73
Mozzarella Pepperoni Pizza	6
Mushroom and Beef Casserole	100
Mustard-Lemon Sole Fillets	56
Oat Porridge with Chia Seeds	6
Okra Chips	105
Old Bay Salmon Patty Bites	52
Old Bay Shrimp with Cayenne	105
Olive Oil Dressed Tomato salad	95
Orange Almond Cookies	88
Orange Cornmeal Cake	64
Orange Pork Ribs with Garlic	41

P-R

Panko Breaded Chicken Nuggets	48
Panko Breaded Wasabi Spam	40
Panko-Chorizo Scotch Eggs	106
Paprika Deviled Eggs with Dill Pickle	74
Paprika Lamb Chops with Sage	39
Paprika Tilapia with Garlic Aioli	53
Paprika-Mustard Pork Spareribs	72
Parmesan Bacon-Ham Cups	9
Parmesan Cauliflower with Turmeric	74
Parmesan Egg and Sausage Muffins	6
Parmesan Eggplant Hoagies	60
Parmesan Green Bean Casserole	99
Parmesan Ranch Onion Risotto	6
Parmesan Shrimp Quiche	99
Parmesan Sriracha Tuna Patty Sliders	53
Peach Blackberry Cobbler with Oats	68
Pecan Walnut Sweet Pie	20
Pepper Spiced Broccoli Pastry	13
Peppermint Chocolate Cheesecake	69
Pigs in a Blanket with Sesame Seeds	109
Pineapple and Peach Chicken Breasts	45
Pineapple Chicken Thighs with Ginger	48
Pistachios Topped Rice Pudding	92
Pork and Mushroom Rolls with Teriyaki	39
Pork Gratin with Ricotta Cheese	99
Pork Ribs with Honey-Soy Sauce	38

Potato Patties with Colby Cheese	104
Prosciutto Casserole with Pepper Jack	99
Prosciutto-Wrapped Asparagus Spears	74
Pumpkin Apple Turnovers	69
Pumpkin-Cauliflower Casserole with Pecans	98
Raisin Oatmeal Bars	64
Rich Blackberry Cupcake	80
Rich Vanilla Butter Cake	81
Ricotta Phyllo Artichoke Triangles	74
Ricotta Spinach Omelet with Parsley	6
Risotto Croquettes with Tomato Sauce	109
Rosemary Herbed Carrots	96

S-T

Salmon and Carrot Spring Rolls	56
Salmon and Scallion Patties	57
Seed and Nut Muffins with Carrots	8
Shrimp and Artichoke Paella	57
Shrimp and Cauliflower Casserole	98
Shrimp, Sausage and Potato Bake	106
Simple Bread Dessert	87
Smoked Paprika Chicken Wings	46
Smoked Paprika Salmon in White Wine	57
Smoky Beef with Jalapeño Peppers	40
Spanish Mango Pastry	75
Spice-Marinated Chicken Drumsticks	49
Spicy Cake with Whipped Cream	24
Spicy Cheesy Pasta Chicken	25
Spinach and Mushroom Frittata	100
Spinach Scrambled Eggs with Basil	7
Spinach stuffed Chicken Bake	25
Squash Bowls with Meatballs	30
Sugar Dusted Blueberry Tart	30
Sugar Sprinkled Citrus Scones	14
Sweet Almond Butter Cookies	20
Sweet and Citrus Pastry	86
Sweet and Sour Tomato Egg Skillet	16
Sweet and Yummy Milk Pancake	15
Sweet Bread Roll	93
Sweet Butter Cookies	87
Sweet Butter Puffs	75
Sweet Savory Pastry with Figs	90
Sweet Strawberry Pastry	93
Swiss Chicken and Ham Casserole	100
Swiss Greens Sandwich	59
Swordfish Steaks with Jalapeño	56
Taco Pork Chops with Oregano	35
The Best Ever Dark Chocolate Cake	33
The Best French Egg Dish	33
The Best Orange Choco Cake	88
Tilapia Tacos with Mayo	60
Toasted Cereal Fish Mix	25
Tomato Chili Fish Curry	55
Tomato, Carrot and Broccoli Quiche	100
Trout Amandine with Lemon Butter Sauce	53
Tuna Casserole with Peppers	55
Turkey and Pepper Hamburger	61
Turkey Sliders with Chive Mayo	60
Turkey, Cauliflower and Onion Meatloaf	47

V-W-Y

Vanilla Bourbon French Toast	8
Vanilla Butter Biscuits	88
Vanilla Chocolate Brownies	66
Vanilla Chocolate Cookie	66
Vanilla Cinnamon Toasts	8
Vanilla flavored Choco sweets	80
Vanilla flavored Milky Butter Cake	16
Vanilla flavored Peanut Bar	17
Vanilla Peaches with Fresh Blueberries	67
Vanilla Pound Cake	66
Vanilla Soufflé	9
Vanilla-Rum Pineapple Galette	66
White Fish, Carrot and Cabbage Tacos	56
Yellow Cornmeal Pancake	11

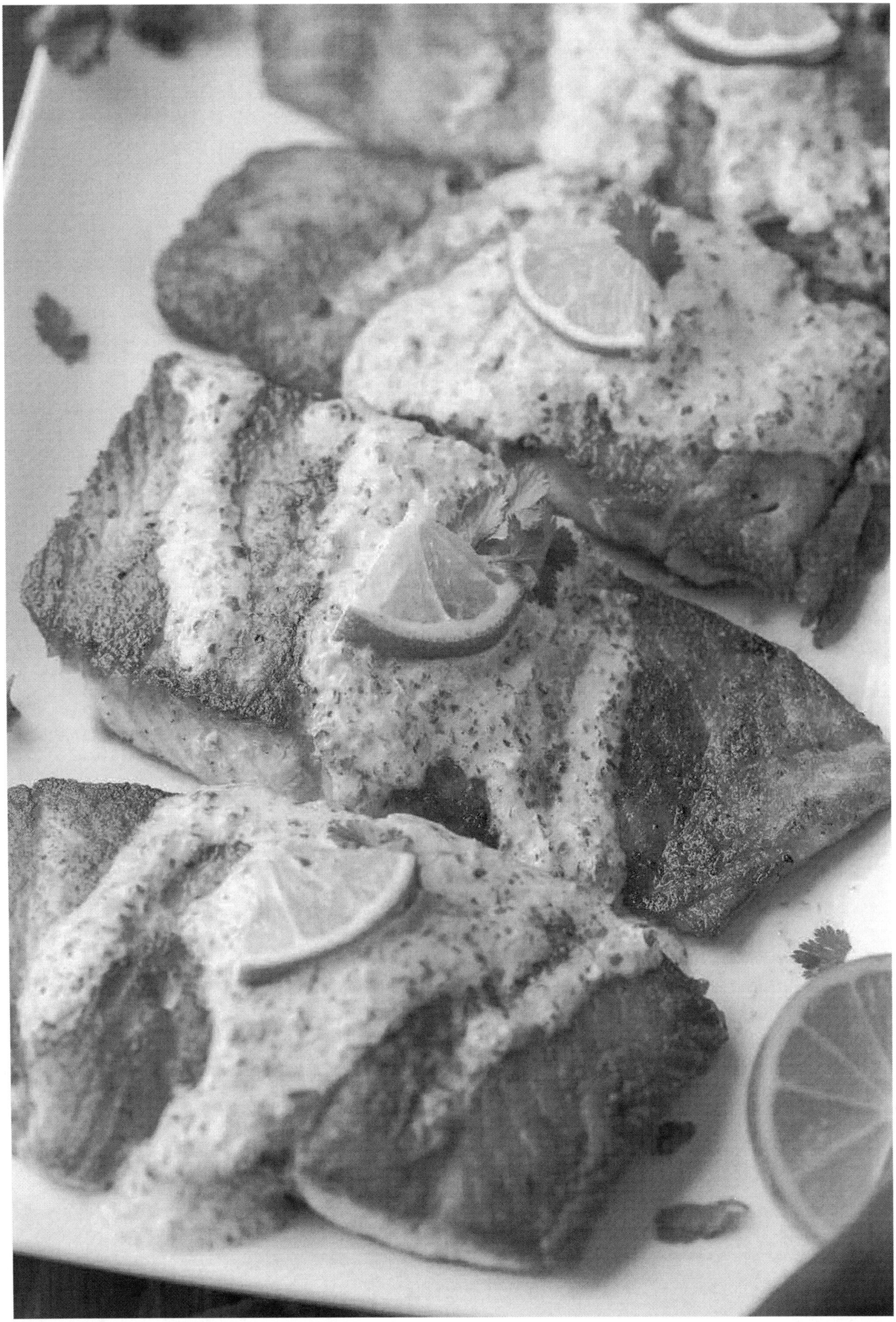

Carol J. Wright

Made in the USA
Middletown, DE
04 February 2022